MODERNIZATION IN SOUTH-EAST ASIA

Modernization in South-East Asia

Edited by
HANS-DIETER EVERS
Professor of Sociology, University of Singapore

Issued under the auspices of the
Institute of Southeast Asian Studies, Singapore

SINGAPORE   KUALA LUMPUR
OXFORD UNIVERSITY PRESS
LONDON   NEW YORK   MELBOURNE

Oxford University Press

OXFORD LONDON GLASGOW NEW YORK
TORONTO MELBOURNE WELLINGTON CAPE TOWN
DELHI BOMBAY CALCUTTA MADRAS KARACHI DACCA
KUALA LUMPUR SINGAPORE JAKARTA HONG KONG TOKYO
NAIROBI DAR ES SALAAM LUSAKA ADDIS ABABA
IBADAN ZARIA ACCRA BEIRUT

◉ *Oxford University Press 1973*
First published 1973
Reprinted 1975

Reprinted lithographically in Singapore by
Dainippon Tien Wah Printing (Pte) Ltd.
Published by Oxford University Press, Bangunan Loke Yew, Kuala Lumpur

For

HARRY J. BENDA,
1919–1972
Former Professor of History,
Yale University and
sometime Director,
Institute of Southeast Asian Studies,
Singapore

Preface

Shortly after the Institute of Southeast Asian Studies came into existence, its first Director, the late Professor Harry J. Benda, entered into correspondence, and later, personal discussion with Professor S. Eisenstadt of the Hebrew University and Professor Hans-Dieter Evers, then his colleague at Yale University, on the subject of modernization in South-East Asia. Out of these conversations grew the idea of holding an international conference on the topic. It took nearly two years of planning before it could be realized. The second Director of the Institute, Professor John D. Legge of Monash University, working closely with a small committee of Singapore academics, gave structure to the original ideas and issued the invitations. It remained for me, the third Director, to see the conference come to life.

This seminar was the Institute's first effort to draw scholars from throughout the world to Singapore for five days of discussion. Using Professor Eisenstadt's paper as the focus, other scholars were asked to develop their own ideas about the several themes he suggested. These papers were circulated in advance of the meeting so that when the participants arrived, all were thoroughly familiar with the ideas and arguments of their counterparts. The meetings therefore, were devoted to discussing and extending the arguments beyond the papers themselves. The participants agreed, after the conference, that it was a challenging and stimulating meeting which had helped them obtain new insights and understanding of the many questions which were raised.

At the invitation of the Institute, Professor Hans-Dieter Evers of the University of Singapore, accepted the responsibility for editing and assembling the papers into a coherent and unified discussion of modernization in Southeast Asia. On behalf of the Institute, I would like to take this opportunity to thank him for transforming the several papers into a study which adds both to the theory of modernization and to the data on the actual process of modernization.

The Institute also would like to take this opportunity to thank the four Foundations which made the conference possible: the Asia Foundation, the Ford Foundation, the Lee Foundation, and the Shaw Foundation.

The facts, interpretations and methods of presentation are those of the authors alone and neither the Institute nor the Foundations noted above are responsible, nor should they be considered as advocating the ideas and interpretations included in this publication.

It is hoped that this volume will stimulate fresh thought and discussions on the subject of modernization in South-East Asia.

Institute of Southeast Asian Studies,   JOSEF SILVERSTEIN
Singapore,
6 June 1972

Contents

Tables

Figure

Introduction:
Modernization and Development

HANS-DIETER EVERS

I

THE papers in this volume are written in a critical spirit of doubt about the validity of previous studies on modernization in developing countries. In the discussions that followed the original presentation of these papers established positions were challenged and new ones defended, but doubt prevailed. The two major categories of structural functionalism in this discussion, traditional versus modern societies, have already been viewed with suspicion for some time, since scholars realised that western ethnocentrism had tended to equate 'modern' with United States society, disregarding other possible models of 'modern societies', like Japan, China, the Soviet Union or the fascist states of Europe. This, as it were, cultural and political superiority complex was only too easily translated into economic imperialism through the attempt of foreign advisers and foreign aid to push development in modernizing societies into the anticipated direction, if necessary by outright intervention, force and war. The most obvious case in South-East Asia is, of course, the American aggression in Indochina.

There is also considerable doubt about modernization as progress in general. Especially the concepts of 'national integration' or 'nation building' suggest a rather mechanical view of complex social, cultural and political processes that just have to be manipulated. In this context it appears that the integrative function of governments is highly overvalued while their oppressive functions are grossly neglected.

There are also grave doubts about the modernizing impact of modern societies. American imperialism and western neo-colonialism can be highly efficient and rationalized systems of retarding social development in non-industrial countries. Similarly the development of local bureaucracies may not turn out to be the embodiments of Weberian rationality fostering modernity but instead paternalistic instruments of oppression, exploitation and corruption. Foreign aid might, under these circumstances, enhance the power of conservative elites who in turn will block progress, and increased higher education may not have the desired impact of stimulating economic and social development but create a proletariat of over-modernized and over-urbanized unemployables.

Several papers are not only written in this spirit of doubt about established theorems but also, more positively, with concern for the internal dynamics of Asian societies, for the importance of cultural patterns and differing social and economic structures, for conflicts, tensions and power struggles, for exploitation and suppression. As all authors have done intensive fieldwork in Asia itself or are members of Asian institutions of higher learning, this concern is only to be expected.

II

Papers written in a spirit of doubt and concern rather than certainty must necessarily be diverse. There are different views and different approaches that go beyond the differences that can be expected between representatives of different academic disciplines: in this volume Anthropology, Economics, History, Political Science and Sociology. In fact the attempt to differentiate and to improve on oversimplifying concepts and theories is evident in all chapters presented here.

The papers can be loosely grouped into four parts, each focusing on a major area in which 'modernization' is said to take place: in the political, economic, social and religious sphere. These spheres are, of course, not clearly separated; the interrelation is frequently stressed and is easily recognizable. The difference of these sections is therefore one of emphasis rather than fundamental substance.

In the headings of the four sections 'modernization' is contrasted with 'development' to indicate the basic stance that both are not the same and therefore not just interchangeable. Contrary to earlier views to which I have alluded above there can be 'modernization without development', as the title of a recent study on Thailand suggests (Jacobs, 1971).

The widest ranging paper in this volume is Eisenstadt's reflection on the influence of traditional and colonial political systems on the development of new social and political orders. During our seminar the original version of this paper served as a keynote address that was intensively debated, attacked, praised and referred to. The chapter in this volume is a heavily revised version of the original paper into which a good number of the discussions have been incorporated.

Eisenstadt, as Dore later on, sets off with a critical note on the 'convergence theory' of development. The earlier simplicistic view on 'traditional' and 'modern' societies as two distinct types is no longer acceptable after the experience of the 1960s. There were cases of 'take off' into self sustained growth but also cases of relapse and breakdown of modernized systems. Grave doubts can therefore be raised as to whether indeed societies converge towards a similar social and political order. The importance of tradition has become more and more apparent.

At this junction one might have to question Professor Eisenstadt what he would regard as a breakdown of modernization. If he still holds the view expressed in an earlier publication on this point (Eisenstadt, 1964), he would have to defend himself against the criticism of Professor Alatas in this volume of subscribing to an older, rather narrow and culturally biased concept of modernization. Alatas points out that Eisenstadt implicitly identifies modernization with the constitutional and democratic form of government based on the Western European model and consequently considers the failures of constitutional democracy in Indonesia, Pakistan, Burma and the Sudan as well as the rise of militarism in modern Japan as 'breakdowns of modernization'. That this view is untenable becomes apparent as soon as we realise that the rise of the People's Republic of China would under these criteria figure as a 'breakdown of modernization'. But perhaps one should not castigate Eisenstadt for past sins but concentrate on the new ideas put forward in his paper.

Modern forces are no longer seen as the sole determinants of emerging modern social and political orders, but just 'impinge' on traditional systems. Because of the powers and importance of tradition the results of this 'impingement' are quite different; that is to say there is not necessarily a convergence of the social and political structures of developing societies. Nevertheless there are, according to Eisenstadt, some common problems in this process: there is a continuing symbolic and cultural differentiation between 'centre and periphery', which is together with limited access to the political centre typical of traditional political systems. Any break-through to modernity is focused on the centre, spreading from there while traditional symbols are replaced by new ones stressing participatory and consensual dimensions. Even dictatorships, while trying to suppress political participation, attempt to create symbols of mass consensus. There is thus development from a traditional socio-political order towards a mass consensual one, containing the propensity to system transformation, that is, social change. This view can be challenged on several counts: though symbols are of great importance, is it enough to discuss modernization in terms of symbols alone without immediate reference to the concurrent economic and social processes? In this respect the absence of economics in Eisenstadt's schemes is especially regrettable. In the example of dictatorships this becomes apparent. The attempt by dictatorial regimes to gloss over blatant oppression with democratic ritual and symbolism, often to pacify possible donors of military aid, is surely less significant than the actual social, economic and political features of the system itself. Oppressive political conditions are, on the other hand, often found in economically fast developing systems. What then is modernization?

Another point of criticism was raised by Professor Wertheim and in some aspects discussed more fully in his paper: why should a breakthrough to modernization start at the centre managed by a central elite? There are examples of effective counter-elites outside an established centre of power, especially in revolutionary situations. As Paul Mus claimed in his study of Vietnam, the modernizing elites were after 1945 scattered in rural areas, whereas a reactionary elite dominated the cities and the political centre (McAlister and Mus, 1970), blocking land reforms and modernization in general. In fact the 'breakthrough' to modernization can often be achieved only by a 'breakdown' and not as Eisenstadt suggests, through differentiation and diversification of structures that are capable of dealing 'in a relatively stable way' with continuous social change.

As a last critical point, the attention of readers might be drawn to the fact that the concept of centre is never clearly defined. It is consequently difficult to detect hypotheses that could be tested and operationalized for empirical research. Professor Eisenstadt discusses in the present version of his paper, however, the first breakthrough to modernity in Europe within the framework of his categories, namely through the development of 'Centres'. According to Eisenstadt, different patterns emerged in Russia, Japan and now in Latin America, Asia and Africa, where centres crystallized into modern patrimonialism, i.e. 'the establishment or continuation of new political and administration central frameworks which have a tendency to maintain the external contents of traditional or of modern symbols without simultaneously maintaining any strong commitments to them'.

Eisenstadt then proceeds to ask how the difference between various types of post-traditional orders can be explained and lists the following variables: the antecedent traditional political and social structures, especially the traditional elites; the impact of modern societies, for example colonial imposition of a new centre against the development of new elites (as discussed in the paper on Group Conflict and Class Formation); and the structure of the international setting (as discussed in the papers by Dr. Goh, Professor Dore and Professor Wertheim). Here the paper ends and it is left to the reader to speculate what types of different socio-political orders have emerged or are likely to emerge in South-East Asia.

A partial answer, at least, is given in the two case studies by Dr. Nawawi and Dr. Agpalo. The two Indonesian provinces of South Sumatra and South Sulawesi and the Philippine province of Occidental Mindoro are used to demonstrate the influence of traditional and colonial political systems on the development (or lack of development) of new social and political orders.

III

Our next section focuses on a problem area that has long been regarded as crucial in any discussion on modernization: economic and technological development. In fact, economic and technological indicators are largely used to measure both modernization and development on the national level with the implicit assumption that societies converge to a similar social structure. It is this implicit or explicit assumption against which Professor Dore's argument is directed. He feels that both the statements of conservative bourgeois social scientists (like Kerr, Marion Levy and others) as well as an earlier Marxist line of argument are equally absurd, namely that the industrially more developed countries show the less developed ones only the image of their own future. Through his own well-known studies on Japan, Dore is led to the conclusion that not only the ways of change are different, but also the outcome. There is no evidence that the convergence theory is true, at least for a long time to come. The most challenging and interesting point in Dore's argument is that he tries to prove his point not by referring to cultural differences between developing and developed countries but by reinterpreting those factors that are normally used to back up the convergence theory: technological and economic factors. Especially the development of international economic systems and the development of communications increase the effectiveness of what Dore calls 'the late development effect'. The early developers in Europe and North America were subjected to quite different constraints than late developers who are again subjected to influences and constraints by their predecessors. From this basic stance Professor Dore develops a number of hypotheses along the following lines: 'The later the development starts, the more likely it is that...'.

The paper of Dr. Goh Keng Swee provides an excellent case study of the problems raised by Professor Dore. After a lengthy discussion of the development of colonial economies in South-East Asia he discusses the dilemma faced by politicians and economic planners after independence. The dilemma was exactly that alluded to by Dore as the 'late development effect'. Trying to develop the manufacturing sector of their economics as the leading sector the South-East Asian leaders 'got into serious trouble before long' precisely because they had overlooked the new constraints to which they were subjected due to the further development of the developed countries or, in other words, due to the fact that they themselves were 'late developers'. The decline of prices of primary export commodities in relation to manufactured goods and deliberate trade discrimination by some developed countries are cited as major factors in the failure of 'import substitution' policies.

But Dr. Goh's paper goes far beyond this point. As the only author in our volume who combines theoretical scholarly accomplishments as an economist with the practical experiences as a Minister of Finance of a South-East Asian nation he proposes practical solutions to the problem of economic development in South-East Asia, providing a strategy for economic planning and for the achievement of a 'breakthrough to modernity' to which Professor Eisenstadt has alluded in his chapter. In this connexion Dr. Goh argues that the breakthrough to modernity for the whole nation will take place in the cities (or in Eisenstadt's terminology the 'centres') 'through the accumulation of wealth and the earning of surplus value on an ever increasing scale by the application of modern science and technology'. Social scientists may, indeed, agree with his suggestion that research efforts should be directed primarily at urban areas, but political leaders in many developing countries might find it hard to accept this advice in view of the fact that usually 70 to 80 per cent of their population live in rural areas, still ridden by poverty and political unrest.

IV

THE third section on modernization and social development is mainly concerned with the impact of changing class and social stratification systems. It is introduced by Professor Wertheim's attack on a bias of most Western scholars, who tend to see the westernized elites of developing countries as the major modernizing force whereas the peasants are regarded as passive, traditional, fatalistic, apathetic and resistant to change.

Though it is true that peasants in most developing countries tend to be slow in accepting innovations and participating in development programmes, the causes have to be sought in the overall social situation rather than in individual character traits of peasants alone. The so-called apathy and inertia of peasants tend to be linked with the general atmosphere of oppression in many parts of the Third World.

Attempts by peasants to improve their lot through their own initiative have often been thwarted by landlords, civil servants and members of modern elites. These modern elites, strengthened by foreign aid and supported by Western powers to buttress their neo-colonial policies, are thus seen by Wertheim as the major obstacles to change. Not the peasants who could support progressive, populist and revolutionary movements but the power elites and their Western allies, namely those who benefit from existing inequalities, provide the major resistance to change.

Wertheim's theme is further developed and substantiated in the editor's own contribution to this volume. This paper was initially stimulated by the observation that nationalist movements aimed at changing the colonial power structure in South-East Asia were originally dominated by new and 'modern' social groups, such as intellectuals, professionals and teachers. After independence the importance of these groups declined and civil servants, military officers and partly business elites started to dominate the political and social scene. Whereas the period just before and after independence meant a period of intense conflict and, in most South-East Asian countries, an overthrow or at least an erosion of the colonial class structure, a new class system emerged or is about to emerge. The new upper class is formed by alliances of former conflicting 'strategic' groups; social access to the new class becomes more difficult and power and wealth become increasingly concentrated. The new upper class, strengthened by sections of the international elite of foreign advisors, diplomats and businessmen, will result in some economic growth but not fundamental social change. 'Modernization' thus produces its own barriers.

Both Professor Wertheim's and the editor's papers contain considerable empirical evidence for the conclusions reached. The arguments are also buttressed by a consistent theoretical framework. Nevertheless they are primarily intended to provide a new critical perspective on long cherished propositions of writers on modernization and social development.

The final chapter in this section remains on much firmer ground. On the basis of intensive fieldwork in one particular country, namely West Malaysia, Dr. Kahar Bador analyses the change of the traditional Malay status system. He comes to the conclusion that the cultural values of the traditional stratification system are still valid and that consequently new groups, such as higher civil servants or members of parliament tend to conform to traditional aristocratic behaviour patterns, though there are only a negligible number of members of the aristocracy among them. Dr. Kahar's paper thus serves as a transition to the next section in which the importance of cultural and religious values for modernization is the major focus of analysis.

V

At the beginning of the fourth section on religion, ideology and modernization Professor Syed Hussein Alatas returns to some of the fundamental questions raised by other authors, especially by Professor Eisenstadt. After a critical evaluation of various concepts of 'modernization' his own definition is advanced: that modernization is, in short, the process by which modern scientific knowledge is introduced, first in the Western civilization, and later diffused to the non-Western world. This is, of course, derived from Max Weber's position and consequently the typically Weberian question is asked whether religion in South-East Asia encourages or hinders modernization.

The case used to discuss this question is West Malaysian society, in which the Chinese dominate the urban economic life whereas the Muslim Malays are concentrated in agriculture and in service occupations. Observers have therefore jumped to the conclusion that religious ethos has been the decisive factor. Alatas in the rest of his paper scrutinizes the religious beliefs of Malays and Chinese and comes to the conclusion that Islam as interpreted in Malaya prior to the expansion of British colonial rule was definitely not hostile to modernization. The decisive factor has been the political and social structure of Malay society at that time, especially the oppression and exploitation of peasants by their rulers and by a 'powerful class of parasites'.

Three additional papers provide further detailed case studies. Roff discusses the bureaucratization of Islamic institutions as a modernization process in the north-eastern Malay state of Kelantan. Tamney analyses the results of his survey in the Philippines, in Singapore and in Indonesia in which he tackles the politically most eminent question whether a strong religious identity hinders the development of an identity with a non-religious nation-state. Jocano discusses millenial and socio-political movements in the Philippines and directs his attention to the 'impingement' (see Eisenstadt's chapter) of traditional values, ideologies and structures on the process of modernization.

The book ends without a concluding chapter for the very simple reason that the state of research on South-East Asia and on problems of modernization in general does not yet allow conclusive statements. In fact to provide a firm conclusion would defeat the major purpose of this book. All chapters are, as pointed out earlier, written in a critical spirit of doubt about previous theories and findings. It is the intention of this book, as it was the intention of the international seminar out of which it grew, to break new ground and to provide new approaches to an increasingly important problem.

PART I
Political Development and Modernization

1 The Influence of Traditional and Colonial Political Systems on the Development of Post-traditional Social and Political Orders

S. N. EISENSTADT

I

THE major premise of this paper is that while we witness today throughout the world a breakdown of traditional socio-political orders, this does not necessarily mean that the development system or order will be patterned according to the initial modern model that developed in Europe, that, in fact, there may arise a great variety of post-traditional orders — and that some such types are developing now in South-East Asia.

These different post-traditional social and political orders may also vary greatly with regard to many crucial aspects of social and political organization, their very conception of modernity or post-traditionality, as well as their attitude to change and their ability to centre formation.

In the following, we shall first briefly analyse the difference between traditional and post-traditional social and political orders. Second, we shall point out some of the basic differences between various post-traditional social orders, and last, some conditions giving rise to them, especially those which may be relevant for the analysis of South-East Asian societies. These last should be seen as tentative hypotheses which can be partially checked against some of the other papers in this volume and may perhaps also be of interest for further research.

This analytical approach presented here stems from a reconsideration of some of the assumptions which have guided the initial studies of modernization and development.

II

The study of the conditions under which modern societies emerge, the differences among them and the condition of their stability and continuity, has been of central interest in the development of modern sociology since its beginning in the late eighteenth and early nineteenth centuries, through the classical period of its founding fathers — de Toqueville, L. V. Stein, Marx, Durkheim, Max Weber and others — and has been revived again in the late forties and fifties of this century.

It was but natural that this concern became transformed in sociological thought into confrontation between modern and non-modern, modern and pre-modern society; and given the conception of modern society as a society oriented towards 'progress' or 'change'. This confrontation tended very often to become defined in terms of modern versus traditional society.

This confrontation of modern versus traditional society in the history of modern social analysis initially took the form of depicting both as more or less completely 'closed' dichotomous types. These types were described in various ways, among the most famous of which were Toennies' distinction between 'Gemeinschaft und Gesellschaft' and Redfield's, more anthropologically oriented, distinction between primitive, folk, and urban societies.

Whatever the methodological and substantive criticism raised against these and similar typologies for decades, they dominated the thinking on this subject for a long period of time and they inspired many researches and investigations. Out of them emerged the picture of traditional and modern societies which prevailed in sociological thought for many years.

In this picture, traditional society was depicted as a static one with but little differentiation of specialization, with a low level of urbanization and of literacy. Modern society, on the other hand, was seen as a society with a very high level of differentiation, literacy and exposure to mass media. In the political realm, traditional society has been depicted as based on a 'traditional' elite ruling by virtue of some Mandate of Heaven, while modern society is based on wide participation of the masses who do not accept any traditional legitimation of the rulers and who hold these rulers accountable in terms of secular values and efficiency. Above all, traditional society has been conceived as bound by the cultural horizons set by its tradition while the modern society is culturally dynamic, oriented to change and innovation.

It is only in the 1940s and 1950s that this view became undermined; and more refined analytical approaches, as well as new *Problemstellungen*, with regard to this whole area, began to develop in the social sciences. True, the conception of modern society in terms of opposition to traditional society and the sharp dichotomization of the two has become even more pronounced with the great upsurge of interest in the breakthrough of non-Western societies into modernity, with the so-called underdeveloped or developing countries, 'New States' and the like, which have emerged since the Second World War. Yet the convergence of this growing interest in underdeveloped societies with the growth of analytical tools in sociology gave rise first of all in the later 1940s and early 1950s, to an analytically more refined and differentiated approach, especially in terms of the study of the two major types of such indices — namely the socio-demographic and the 'structural' which have been mentioned and analysed at least partially above. These new approaches were developed under the impact of the concern with the problem of underdeveloped countries, or New Nations, etc.

Accordingly, instead of concentrating on the distinct characteristics of each of these types of societies, there emerged a growing interest in the *conditions of emergence* of modern societies; instead of taking the emergence of these institutions, of a visible social order, for granted and concentrating on the analytical description of the nature of such an order, the growing concern with the possibility of relatively unsuccessful transition of these societies into modernity gave rise to asking about the *precondition* of such successful 'take-off' into modernity.

Furthermore, given the conception of modern society as a society oriented towards change and having to deal with continuous change, there developed also the search for the conditions of such continued, sustained growth in modern societies.

III

Many researches which took off from the preceding considerations led to or were based on the — usually implicit — assumption that the conditions for sustained growth, for continuous development and modernization in different institutional fields are dependent on, or tantanomous to, continuous extension of these various socio-demographic and/or structural indices of modernization. According to this view, the more a society exhibits or develops the basic characteristics of structural specialization and the higher it is on various indices of social mobilization, the less traditional and the more modern it would be, i.e. by implication the better it would be able to develop continuously, to deal continuously with new problems and social forces and to develop a continuously expanding institutional structure.

In the initial stages of these researches, relatively little analytic distinction between these different *Problemstellungen* was made. Thus, initially, in many of the works which dealt with this problem, the preconditions of emergence of modern societies were very often described in the very same terms which denoted their characteristics (e.g. in terms of universalism, achievement orientation, etc.) — thus in a way neglecting the more specific question about the conditions of emergence of modern societies, of the processes through which they emerge — or fail to emerge — successfully from within the pre-modern societies.

These implicit assumptions about the conditions of continuous modernization became shattered through the experience of the late 1950s and the early 1960s when more and more countries which seemed to have 'taken off' into modernization were tending towards 'breakdown'.

The implicit assumption that existed in many of these studies — namely that the less traditional society is more capable of such sustained growth — has been proved incorrect. The various socio-demographic or structural indices of modernization indicate only the extent to which traditional, self-contained societies or communities became weakened, or disintegrated, the extent to which — to paraphrase the title of Dan Lerner's book—Traditional Society is Passing. But they do not in themselves indicate the extent to which a new, viable, modern society, which is capable of continuous growth, may develop or exactly what kind of a society will develop and what its exact institutional contours will be.

Similarily, it became clear that the mere destruction of traditional forms of life does not necessarily assure the development of such a new, viable, modern society, and that very often the disruption of traditional settings — be they family, community, or even sometimes political settings — tends to lead more to disorganization, delinquency and chaos rather than to the setting up of a viable modern order.

There was a continuously growing awareness of basic historical facts that in many countries modernization has been successfully undertaken under the aegis of traditional symbols — and even traditional elites. In such countries as Japan, or even England, many of their traditional symbols — be they the Emperor, the Japanese crown, the symbols of aristocracy in Britain or the traditional symbols of provincial life in Holland — were retained. In many cases, when the initial impetus to modernization was given under the aegis of anti-traditional elites, there soon followed an attempt, even if in a halting way, to revive some of the traditional symbols.

All these considerations have also contributed to the undermining of the assumption about the assurance of continuity of growth after the 'take-off'. In both the economic and the political spheres it became quite obvious that any assurance of such continuity does not exist. The Argentine in the economic sphere, Burma or Indonesia in the political sphere, are among the most pertinent examples of the possibility of breakdown after some initial — or even sometimes relatively advanced — stages of modernization have been reached.

These examples, however, have also shown that the relation between processes of change which tend to undermine or destroy traditional societies and the development of a viable modern society are not simple. The one does not always necessarily lead to the other. The awareness that a great part of contemporary history in general and of contemporary international relations in particular, is in a way the history of breakdowns or of stagnation of political regimes or economic systems — which have seemingly 'taken-off' into modernity but yet have been unable to continue to fly at all or to attain higher attitudes — and this slowly became accepted as fact.

But the more paradoxical of these processes was that such breakdowns or stagnations did not necessarily lead to the total collapse of these new regimes or to their return to some traditional social and political forms. Such politics and societies certainly differ in many ways from the 'older' (Western) modern ones nor do they necessarily develop into the direction of these 'older' societies. Yet, they are by no means any longer simply traditional societies. Moreover, however stagnating or unstable these regimes are, they evince some capability of reorganization and continuity and they develop various internal and external policies which aim at assuring for themselves the conditions of such continuity.

IV

All these developments have given rise to a series of many critiques of the initial assumptions of studies of modernization — especially of the ways in which the difference between traditional and modern societies was formulated. There are several important themes — all focused around the place of tradition in the studies of modernization.

One such theme was the 'rediscovery' of persistence in modern or modernizing societies of strong traditions, in the sense of some binding ways of behaviour rooted to some degree in the past, in modern societies.

Second, and closely connected with the former theme was the emphasis by many scholars — on how traditional forces or groups, be they castes or tribal units, tend to reorganize in a very effective way, in new modern settings.

Third, and of special importance for our point of view, was the growing recognition that within many of the New States after the initial phases of independence whose politics were yet greatly shaped by modern models of politics, a new phase emerges in which older, traditional models of politics tend to reassert themselves.

V

While, as we shall see later on, all these and similar critical considerations have not necessarily invalidated the distinction between traditional and modern societies and politics, yet they have necessitated the reformulation of this distinction, and have, first of all, shown that while talking about modernity or modernization, we have to distinguish between several aspects of what has been usually designated as 'modernity' or 'modernization'.

They have shown that it is necessary to distinguish, first, between the impingement of forces of modernity and the consequent undermining of the existing traditional settings, second, the 'break-through' to modernity on the structural and cultural levels, and third, the ways in which the new emerging social systems tend to deal with these problems, and their capacity to deal with them.

Let us explicate these distinctions. Given the historical spread of modernity from the seventeenth/eighteenth centuries until today, almost all traditional societies have been, or are being, caught up in the sense that modern forces 'impinge' on them, undermining their existing settings in at least three different ways.

First, they impinge on many of the bases of the various existing traditional institutional spheres — economic, political or community life, or social organization — make various new demands on them, and open new vistas for their members. There obviously exist very great differences among the various modern and modernizing societies with regard to the intensity of this impingement and its specific institutional location.

Second, these forces have a new international system within which difference in strength in modern economic or political terms is a major determinant of relative international standing. Here too, however, great variations exist with regard to the extent of the impingement of these international forces on different traditional societies and of the extent to which they are exposed to it.

These forces of modernity may impinge on different 'traditional' societies by undermining the traditional economic structure and creating more differentiated social and economic frameworks. They may also impinge on many traditional societies in creating the vogue of demand for a growing participation of the citizens in the centre, most clearly manifested in the tendency to establish universal citizenship and suffrage and some semblance of a 'participant' political or social order. These different forces may impinge on various constellations in different historical cases and each of these constellations tends to create different types of breakthrough to modernity and to institutional and cultural problems with which these societies and their new emerging structures have to deal.

But, whatever the details of these differences — some of which we shall yet analyse in greater detail later on — given the unique setting in which modernity has taken place, its spread has given rise to some common characteristics and problems — even though the response to these may indeed vary greatly.

These common problems are derived from the crucial difference between the symbolical and cultural premises of traditionalism, with their structural and cultural limitations, and those which develop with modernity. The most important of these premises in the political field is the continuing symbolic and cultural differentiation between the centre and the periphery; and the concomitant limitation of the access of members of broader groups to the political centre or centres, and on participation within them.

In traditional regimes these premises were closely connected, first, to the fact that the legitimation of the rulers was couched in basically traditional religious terms, and second, to the lack of distinction of the basic political role of the subject societal roles, such as, for instance, membership in local communities; and although it was often embedded in such groups, the citizens or subjects did not exercise any actual direct or symbolic political rights through a system of voting or franchise.

In the cultural sphere, the basic premise of traditionality, common to all 'traditional' societies, however great the differences between them, has been the acceptance of tradition; of the givenness of some past events, order or figure (whether real or symbolic) as the major focus of their collective identity, as the scope and nature of their social and cultural order, as the ultimate legitimizer of change, and as the delineator of the limits of innovation.

The most important structural derivations of these premises were (a) limitation in terms of reference to some past event of the scope, content and degrees of changes and innovations; (b) limitation of access to positions, the incumbents of which are the legitimate interpreters of the scope and the contents of traditions; and (c) limitations of the right to participate in these centres and in forging the legitimate contents and symbols of the social and cultural orders.

Whatever the extent and scope to which the various traditional forms of life in various spheres of society persist, it is then, insofar as such changes in the connotation of tradition on central levels have taken place, that we witness the break-through — which may be gradual or abrupt — to some sort of modern socio-political or cultural order. And insofar as such changes in the connotation of tradition on central levels have not taken place, whatever the extent of structural changes or possible transformation of tradition in different parts of the society, we still have before us some type of traditional order.

Thus, the break-through to modernity is focused both in the change in the contents of the symbols of the centre, in their secularization and in the growing emphasis on values of human dignity and social equality, as well as in the growing possibility of the participation, even if in an intermittent or partial way, of broader groups in the formulation of its central symbols and institutions.

It is such changes in the connotation of tradition and of their major structural implications that provide the impetus to continuous processes of change and to the perception of change as a positive value in itself, and which create the problem of the absorption of change as the major challenge of modernization.

The preceding analysis brings out perhaps the most central characteristics and the problems of modern post-traditional societies — their basic mass-consensual orientation and their predisposition to continuous change.

The consensual or mass aspect of these societies is rooted in the growing impingement or broader strata on the centre, in their demands to partici-pate in the sacred symbols of society and in their formulation, and in the replacement of the traditional symbols by new ones which stress these participatory and social dimensions.

This tendency to broad, mass-consensuality does not, of course, find its fullest institutionalized expression in all types of modern societies. In many regimes in the first stages of modernization it may be weak or inter-mittent, while totalitarian regimes naturally tend to suppress its fullest expression. But even totalitarian regimes attempt to legitimize themselves in terms of such values, and it is impossible to understand their policies and their attempts to create symbols of mass consensus without taking into consideration their assumption of the existence of such consensual ten-dency among its strata and its acknowledgement by the rulers.

VI

The preceding discussion brings out some of the most salient characteris-tics and problems in modern political orders. First, it brings out the fact that it is the break-through from a traditional socio-political order in the direction of a mass consensual one that contains within itself the specific characteristics of social changes to be found in modernity; the propensity to the system-transformation and the persistence of demands for change, protest and transformation. These demands for change could, of course, develop in different directions: they could be reformatory, demanding the improvement of existing institutions, or they could aim at total transforma-tion of a system.

Thus we see modernization evinces two closely connected, yet distinct aspects. There is the development of a social structure with great variety of structural differentiation and diversification, of continuously changing structural forms, activities and problems, and propensities to continuous change and to system transformation. But the mere development of these propensities does not in itself assume the development of an institutional structure which is capable of dealing, in a relatively stable way, with these continuous changes and of assuring concomitantly the maintenance of a civil order.

Thus the crucial problem that modernization creates is that of the ability of the emerging social structure to deal with such continuous changes or, in other words, the problem of sustained development — i.e. the ability to develop an institutional structure which is capable of 'absorbing' continuously changing problems and demands. It is this which constitutes the central change and subsequent problem of modernization. This is the challenge of modernity, of post-traditional social orders.

But if the spread of the forces of modernity creates problems, to some degree common to all modern societies, both its concrete manifestations as well as the responses to it, vary greatly.

All these various orientations to growing participation, to social justice, as well as the various structural aspects of change, are related to the common symbolic and structural cores of modernity mentioned above and derived from them; they vary greatly in their concrete expression or manifestation in different historical situations, giving rise to a very great variety of models of modern social and political order.

VII

One of the weaknesses of the first approaches to modernization has been the assumption that not only some of these problems may be common — but also that the natural direction for answers to these problems lies in the same direction that developed in Europe.

Since the first such break-through from a traditional to a modern social order took place in Europe, and it was here that the problem of defining such order in new terms first became fully articulated, the first definition of the parameters of the modern social order has been closely related to the specific characteristics of the symbolic institutional pattern of modern socio-political order that has developed in the West and constituted, in a sense, part of this pattern or universe.

The major form of this socio-political order — in the post-Counter-Reformation period throughout the eighteenth and nineteenth centuries, and later in the U.S., Australia, Canada, etc. — was the nation-state.

The major characteristics of this type of modern socio-political order have been enumerated as: (a) a high degree of congruence between the cultural and the political identities of the territorial population; (b) a high level of symbolic and effective commitments to the centre and a close relation between these centres and the more primordial dimensions of human existence; and (c) a marked emphasis on politically defined collective goals for all members of the national community.

In greater detail this model assumed that all the major components of centre-formation — i.e. first, the institutionalization, both in symbolic and organizational terms, of the quest for some charismatic ordering of social and cultural experiences, and for some participation in such orders; second, the crystallization of the common societal and cultural collective identity based on common attributes or on participation in common symbolic events; third, the crystallization and articulation of collective goals; fourth, the regulation of intrasocietal and intergroup relations; and fifth, the regulation of internal and external, or power-relations — tend to converge around the political centre of the nation-state.

In many ways many of these characteristics of the European nation-state were derived or transmitted from several parts of their premodern socio-political traditions; that is from Imperial traditions, and from those of city-states and of feudal societies. They combined the strong activist orientation of the city-state, the broad conception of the political order as actively related to the cosmic or cultural order of many Imperial traditions, and the tradition of Great Religions and the pluralistic elements of the feudal traditions.

In the European (especially Western European) traditions these various orientations were rooted in a social structure characterized by a relatively high degree of commitment of various groups and strata to the cultural and political orders and their centres, as well as by a high degree of autonomy in their access to these orders and their respective centres.

It was out of these orientations that some of the specific assumptions about patterns of participation and protest characteristics of the nation-state developed. The most important of these assumptions was that the political forces, the political elites and the more autonomous social forms — the State on the one hand and 'Society' on the other — continuously struggle over their relative importance in the formation and crystallization of the cultural and political centre of the nation-state and in the regulation of access to it; that the various processes of structural change and dis-location — which the periphery was continuously undergoing as a result of processes of modernization — give rise not only to various concrete problems and demands, but also to a growing quest for participation in the broader social and political order; and that this quest for participation of the periphery in such social, political and cultural orders is mostly mani-fested in the search for access to these centres.

This pattern of modern political order was not homogeneous or unitary even in Western Europe. But it was relatively homogeneous, at least in its ideal form, in comparison with the pattern of post-traditional political order that has developed in non - (Western) European societies. These orders have crystallized into a pattern which has evinced several important differences from the 'original' European one — even though the original models of modernity presented to them have indeed mostly been influenced by the pattern.

The difference could have been discerned already from the very begin-ning of the spread of modernization beyond the Empires in Russia or Japan where already new patterns of such orders — which in their turn served as such models with further spread of modernity — have developed.

But these differences can be most clearly seen in the shaping of post-traditional socio-political orders in many of the countries which have not adopted any of these models — especially in the various countries of Latin America, South-East Asia and Africa. In most general terms it can be said that the centres that tended to crystallize in these societies were characterized by what may be called 'modern patrimonialism', i.e. the establishment or continuation of new political and administrative central frameworks which have a tendency to maintain the external contents of traditional or of modern symbols without simultaneously maintaining any strong commitments to them. Such centres tend to display almost exclusive concern for the preservation of the existing weak frameworks of power, thus giving rise to a continuous succession of weak centres.

The major difference between these regimes and seemingly similar regimes that developed frameworks of 'Nation-States' can be seen in many ways — such as in the function of parties, voting and of political participation — all of which tend to develop in all types of modern centres and yet whose significance in the political process greatly differs among them.

Thus, to take just a few illustrations, the function of parties seems to vary greatly among them. The tendency to monolithic — and yet not totalitarian parties, or to single non-totalitarian party regimes in many new states, indicates that many of these parties may seem more as instruments for the forging out of some new common collective identities for the struggle between different contestants of power representing different interests and/or ideological orientations. Such struggle seems to take place more inside such parties than among them.

Concurrently, bureaucracies may seem here often not only as administrative branches of the centre or as small contending groups or cliques within them, but also custodians of whatever common symbols and such centres as may represent whatever civil order they may be able to maintain. Just because of this they may here compete with the parties for the full representation of the centre — a fact which can perhaps to some degree explain the quick succession of a party regime by a military regime — with each regime maintaining some of the organizational framework and activities of the former.

Similarly, voting and suffrage may, in many of these regimes, be only a manifestation of some broad, not fully articulated, orientation to such centre, and neither of total commitment to the regime as in totalitarian regimes, nor as expression of specific concrete interests or ideologies as in many of the pluralistic-constitutional nation-state regimes.

The special characteristics of these regimes can also be seen in the nature — and especially in the outcome — of crises and breakdowns that may occur within them. The general reasons and symptoms of such crises and breakdowns — the rifts and cleavages between different types of elites, between the central and the parochial symbols, between classes and regions, are to a large extent common to all of them.

The specific crises or problems which these regimes face are first, their effectiveness on the new modern international scene; second, the upsurge of unregulated demands of various broader groups, which are very often fostered by these elites, and the concomitant waste of resources. They are confronted with potentially continuous conflicts within the elite and the new centres. The crises and problems that they may develop out of the great intensity of the conflicts between traditionalistic and more modern elites, the new modern ways in which the claims of many of these groups about the nature of the centre itself and the bases of its legitimation, may minimize the possibilities of establishing new, stable and viable centres of any kind.

Similarly the outcomes seem to differ. In societies with strong centres the tendency is more a 'total', dramatic breakdown of the centre — possibly leading to its reconstitution on a new level.

In the patrimonial centres such instability and oscillation tends very often to continue with mobilization, partial economic development and political activity. They may lead to a continuous succession of such patrimonial centres, together with economic regression and growing political apathy.

But within several types of post-traditional regimes, there are many differences. They tend also to vary greatly among themselves, on such dimensions as the scope of political mobilization, the relative predominance of different institutional settings (bureaucracy, military, political parties), the relations between the political and ethnic-national communities, the conception of social hierarchy and organization of social strata, or the degree of relative stability of their respective regimes and collective political boundaries.

Thus, as the papers and discussions in this volume fully attest to, South-East Asian societies evince some specific characteristics, with many differences even among them.

VIII

How can the differences between various types of post-traditional social orders be explained? While, needless to say, there are indeed many factors and conditions which may influence the shaping of these differences, yet it may be worthwhile to point out some conditions which seem to be of special interest, and of great importance.

One such set of conditions is the broad differences in the antecedent traditional political structure and order. As we have seen already above, many differences from the original European pattern can be discerned. For instance, in many of the tribal societies the very existence of a distinct centre or of a status of relatively homogeneous ethnic or national communication could not be taken for granted.

Even in societies, like the Imperial or patrimonial ones, in which there could be no doubt about the existence of a specific centre and State-apparatus, the very inter-relations of the state of the political order with the social order have been envisaged in ways different from those of the Western tradition.

In general, most of these societies did not share the Imperial, city-state and feudal traditions which were specific to the European traditional order. Thus, for instance, in the Imperial Asian societies — as in Russia or Japan — the pluralistic elements were much weaker than in the feudal or city-states. In Russia, for example, there lacked the conception of a relatively autonomous access of the major strata to the political and cultural centres, and the cultural orders were often perceived as subservient to the political one.

Similarly, in Japan, there existed a conception of the close identity between the cosmic and political order and of a very high degree of un-conditional commitment of broader strata to the centre which represented this cosmic-political identity.

In many other societies — in South-East Asia, in Africa, and to some degree in Latin America — the forces of (later) modernity impinged on patrimonial systems where the level of commitment to a socio-political order was much smaller and in which also the active, autonomous relation between the political and the cosmic order was much weaker — even if there existed a closer coalescence between the two.

Their political traditions rarely envisaged the same type of split or dichotomy between State and Society as did the European tradition. Instead, it tended to stress the congruent but often passive relations be-tween the cosmic order on the one hand, and the socio-political order on the other. Unlike the Western tradition, the interrelation between the political and the social orders was not envisaged in terms of an antithesis between two entities of power; rather, it was more often stated in terms of the coalescence of different functions within the same group of organiza-tion, centred around a common focus in the cosmic order.

IX

Another set of conditions which may greatly influence the shaping of the different contour of post-traditional societies is the structure of the his-torical process of impingement of modern forces on the various institu-tions' spheres, i.e. the economic, political, or the sphere of social organiza-tion and stratification of the societies.

It may also take place under different degrees of structural differentia-tion: with broad strata evincing a relatively high level of resistance to change in the new setting, or, conversely, a high level of adaptability to it; with secondary elites and especially with more central elites which may be resistant to change, i.e. 'traditionalistic' in a militant or an erosive way; with elites which are highly adaptable to the new settings, with but a few transformative orientations; or with elites which have transformative capacities, either in a flexible or in a coercive way.

It may take place under different temporal sequences of development in different institutional spheres which may greatly influence both the problems with which these societies were confronted and the responses that they had to develop.

These various structural and temporal differences greatly affect the nature of the concrete problems which arise within these societies, the levels of aspirations and conflicts of various groups as well as some aspects or conditions of the ability of the central elites to deal with these problems, and especially the level of economic, organizational, and educational resources available for the crystallization of new institutional settings.

Each constellation of these processes tends to create the impetus for the break-through to modernity in the socio-political and cultural order and the concomitant impetus to continuous intensive change. But each specific constellation also tends to create different patterns of break-through, different types of institutional and cultural problems with which these societies and their new imerging structures have to deal — as well as the patterns of institutional response to the problem of continuous change — and different degrees and types of ability or lack of ability to deal with the problems and crises specific to each type of modern or modernizing society.

X

Within this context it is important, especially for the study of South-East Asian societies to analyse the specific characteristics of those societies whose major initial experience with modernity was under a colonial regime.

The most important of such common characteristics of these societies was the imposition of an alien centre which is always, to some degree or another, segregated from the other parts of the society, and while it creates various administrative frameworks, it, at the same time, deprives them of legitimate foci of the collective identity.

This situation gave rise, as is well-known, to the development of political mobilization, new elites, and a variety of social and national movements, all of which aimed at the establishment of a new centre which initially was modelled after the European pattern, and which later, greatly diverged from it, creating new types of post-traditional regimes.

But these types of regimes differed not only from those which developed within non-European societies like Japan or China which have maintained their independence, they also differed among themselves. Some of these differences also can be attributed to their different experience under colonial rule.

XI

Of these different experiences, of special importance, seem to be the initial patterns of establishment of central institutional modern frameworks, the relative tempo of modernization and processes of, and the extent of structural flexibility of, strategic groups and elites in the society.

The establishment and continuity of flexible political symbols and central and political and legal frameworks, of common symbols of political-national identification, of organs of political struggle, legislation and administration — is a basic prerequisite for the development of a sense of modern, differentiated political identity and affinity among different groups and strata which are drawn into the context of modern political community.

The non-development of such frameworks may reinforce the closeness of the various modern elites, as manifested by their lack of ability to forge out new, cohesive symbols and by the development of policies which were incapable of forging new interlinking mechanisms in the society and creating cohesive symbols and frameworks, may be of crucial importance in the development and institutionalization of adequate regulative mechanisms which can deal with new emerging problems.

Of special importance in this context has been the establishment and institutionalization — whether formal or informal — of certain rules of the political game such as systems of election or less formal institutional devices of different types which establish some procedural consensus in the society.

Similarly, such successful institutionalization has been usually greatly dependent on, and related to, the development of a relatively flexible and differentiated legal system which, whatever its social or political underpinnings, could assure some basic legal rights to individuals and some protection against the undermining of long-term commitments and activities, and some minimal rights of the citizens.

All such developments greatly facilitate the development of a more cohesive and flexible modern institutional centre which is capable both of promoting and regulating change and which can be responsive to various needs and demands, without succumbing to them so as to become totally ineffective. Last, of great importance here is the structure of the international setting in which the process of modernization takes place, the distribution of political and economic power among the various societies and strata, and the types and processes of dominance and dependence that tend to develop among them.

It is the interaction among these various variables subsumed under the three broad conditions specified above — the different socio-political directions and traditions of these societies in their premodern settings, the nature of the impingement of modernization on them, and the structure of the situation of change, that can, as the various papers in this volume attest to some degree, it seems to us, explain the development patterns of post-traditional socio-political orders, and of change of any one society from one pattern to another.

2 Tradition, Mobilization and Development in Indonesia[1]

MOHD. A. NAWAWI

I

'The most important political distinction among countries concerns not
their form of government but their degree of government.'

THE blunt opening sentence of S. P. Huntington's *Political Order in Changing Societies* quoted above represents an important departure from the
conventional view of political development which Ali Mazrui (1968:
69–83) has recently condemned, with considerable justification, as ethno-
centric. Unfortunately, Huntington's conservative qualms have subtly
forced him to direct his attention away from the extent of authority as such
to the problem of stability which he defines as the positive ratio between
institutionalization and modernization. Political development ceases to
be an absolute change and becomes, instead, a relative state of affairs. The
preoccupation with order leads to the strange suggestion that Ethiopia is
more politically developed than Egypt or Argentina.

To be highly objective, the concept of political development must deal
firmly with the extent of authority or the degree of government itself. Such
conception does not preclude the important notion of political decay, for
surely political authority or a political institution can actually become less
effective absolutely. For example, the army can be defeated or even
destroyed in war and the quality and number of judges and courts can
deteriorate. This view of development highlights the obvious fact that an
institution does not necessarily lose its absolute capacity simply because
it faces more or greater tasks. It also allows for the possibility that tension

[1] I would like to thank the Ford Foundation in Bangkok and the University of
Singapore for making possible my trips to Indonesia in 1970. Drs. Arsjad Pudji of the
Hassanudin State University in Makassar, South Sulawesi, has been especially helpful
with the data. Several colleagues — P. D. Weldon, J. B. Tamney and D. H. Clark in
Singapore and D. S. Gibbons in Penang — have contributed valuable suggestions some
of which have been incorporated in the essay.

and instability may signify the expansion of the capacity of some institutions or the system as a whole.

One way of directly evaluating the capacity of the political system is to measure the quantity of its products and services. Together with de Schweinitz (1970a), we can call these 'political goods'.[1] As de Schweinitz has described them, political goods are characterized first by their being consumed jointly by everyone. Moreover, although everyone must consume them regardless of personal preference, he may not contribute any input for its provision (de Schweinitz, 1970(b): 525). In short, political goods are what the economists call public or government goods — goods and services which only the political authority can provide.

Assuming that these political goods can be satisfactorily measured and aggregated, their extent or amount can give a valuable index to the performance of the government. But such a measure would still be inadequate. Political goods and services may be financed using various resources including windfall from oil wells, foreign aid, loans, and the printing presses. None of these require any marvellous capacity on the part of the government. Indeed, an effective government may, precisely because of its effectiveness, find itself barred from the 'leisure club'. For this reason, governmental capacity must also be measured in terms of its ability to mobilize the internal resources of the country. Primary of these are taxes but they should also include information and human resources.

The joint indices of resource mobilization and provision of political goods define the extent of political development. Unfortunately, both indices present practical problems of measurement.

With regard to the political goods, de Schweinitz has recommended the economists' expedient of valuing them at factor cost, i.e. equating them with governmental expenditures. The main shortcoming of this tactic is the disregard of the important factor of efficiency. Given the low efficiency and the great extent of corruption characteristic of most new nations, the reliance on governmental expenditures would be meaningless. Moreover, some public goods, such as some aspects of defence, are by nature so bulky and concentrated that they do not necessarily require, and thus reflect, a high level of governmental effectiveness. At least, some political goods are better indicators than others of the degree of government. Since government expenditures are not always easily broken into particular programmes or services, reliance on these expenditures to measure governmental capability would be unsatisfactory. A better expedient would be concentration on the major but less concentrated fields of governmental activity such as the public communication systems, public

---

[1]The term 'political good' was coined by J. Roland Pennock (1966). The main problem with Pennock is that he unnecessarily mixes 'political good' with 'politically good'. Similar difficulty confronts C. J. Friedrich's concept of 'intrinsic objective' argued in his 'Political Development and the Objectives of Modern Government' in Braibanti (1969: 107–35). Karl de Schweinitz Jr introduced his formulation in a recent paper (de Schweinitz, 1970a).

health, public education and the judiciary, particularly in the non-urban areas. Careful analyses of activities in these fields would seem to be feasible and the resulting measures of performance would give truer indication of the governmental capacity.

The central problem with measuring resource mobilization is the untenability of relying on the amount collected. Governments which do not have tax provisions are either lucky or hopelessly incompetent, but a government which levies heavier taxes than another is not thereby clearly more capable. An ideal situation would be to have a standard, international index of minimum taxation. Lacking this, we can resort to using either the ratio of actual tax receipts to total liable taxes or the ratio of tax-paying to total taxable citizens.

The aim of this writer has been to apply the concepts of political goods and resource mobilization to measure the political development in Indonesia. Presented here are some very preliminary data obtained from two regions, South Sulawesi and South Sumatra. These data are meant only to demonstrate the very low degree of government in Indonesia. For the present, my purpose is to argue that this low level of political development is to a great extent the reflection of a lack of emphasis on mobilization in the Indonesian traditional notion of government.

II

South Sumatra and South Sulawesi are two of the largest and most important regions in Indonesia. Both are relatively rich in resources and both have played a major role in the past and recent history of the archipelago. South Sulawesi is indeed the most important region in East Indonesia. The two regions differ significantly in their traditional political structures. Being outside Java, they should provide a particularly good indication of the effective extent of the national political system.

Unlike South Sumatra which covers largely riverine lowlands, most of South Sulawesi lies at the foot of a volcanic mountain chain. This physical dissimilarity partially explains the fact that South Sulawesi is about three and one half times as densely populated as South Sumatra. Although it is only slightly more than one half the size of South Sumatra, South Sulawesi has a population of about 5 million compared to about 3 million in South Sumatra. The greater compactness of South Sulawesi has allowed its division into a larger number of districts; it has twenty-three *kabupaten* to South Sumatra's ten.

As the primary means of communication and transportation, roads are vital political goods. In South Sumatra, there are in total 7,551 kilometres of roads, only about half of which are highways designed for regular use by motorized vehicles. Less than 1,000 kilometres of roads, mostly in

Palembang and some of the district capitals, have ever been asphalted (South Sumatra, 1969: 24). Of the 6,829 kilometres of roads in South Sulawesi, less than one-third are state and provincial highways and of these only one-third again have been asphalted (Jasni, 1968: 55).

The provision of public health is more difficult to measure since it cannot be isolated from availability of general medical facilities and services which are not necessarily political. Nevertheless, an indication of the amount of this political good can be provided by the number of government doctors in the rural districts. Of the eight such districts in South Sumatra, one does not have even a single qualified medical doctor, while only two of the others have more than one doctor each, being favoured with two and three doctors respectively.[1] In South Sulawesi only eleven of the twenty-one rural districts enjoy the presence of doctors (Jasni 1968: 54).

Like health services, education is not necessarily or uniquely public. However, since elementary education is generally monopolized by the government, enrolment in the elementary schools may be taken as a reasonable index of governmental activity. In 1968, elementary school pupils in South Sumatra and South Sulawesi numbered 440,000 and 525,000 respectively (Makaliwe, 1969: 34; South Sumatra, 1969: 48). In the case of South Sulawesi, the figure represents about 60 per cent of all elementary school age children (Makaliwe, 1969). Assuming similar age distribution in South Sumatra, the above figure for the region represents about 80 per cent of the total potential elementary school enrolment there.

As the judiciary plays a central role in any political system, the extent to which judicial services are provided constitutes a particularly good measure of the degree of government. A convenient indicator is the number of courts and judges. Since Indonesia employs the district court system, South Sulawesi and South Sumatra are supposed to have 23 and 10 district courts respectively. Up to now, however, one district in each region is still without its own court. In all, there are 121 judges in South Sulawesi compared to 62 in South Sumatra.[2]

The preceding evaluation of the amount of political wealth in South Sumatra and South Sulawesi is only meant to be suggestive. Other types of political goods could have been considered and other aspects of the goods mentioned could have been evaluated. The data are also inadequate in other respects. Since the capacity to mobilize accurate and adequate information is precisely a characteristic of a highly developed political system, the available data have to be treated with more than the customary reserve. More problematic still is the quality of the goods and services. From my own recent tours of the two regions, I would not hesitate to say that the political goods and services in South Sulawesi are generally of higher quality than those in South Sumatra. In South Sulawesi, roads are

[1]Provincial Health Service Headquarters, Palembang.
[2]President, the High Court, Makassar. Also, the High Court, Palembang.

in better repair, school buildings appear to be more well-built and better maintained, and courts seem to be more smoothly functioning.

In a crude way, it can be concluded that South Sulawesi and South Sumatra are providing their populations with few political goods and services. In comparing the two regions, both their population and their size must be taken into account. On *per capita* basis, South Sumatra is providing much more road, public health and educational services than South Sulawesi. The latter region, however, provides a comparable amount of judicial services on this basis. This discrepancy may in part reflect the fact that South Sumatra is relatively more economically well-off than South Sulawesi. Teachers and doctors in this region may be better able to supplement their official salary with outside income. The relatively better provision of judicial services in South Sulawesi may partly reflect the region's greater conservatism. However, *per capita* measurement by itself is inadequate since the same amount of political goods and services would be less effective in a much larger area. A district court or a district clinic is surely less effective in an extensive, though sparsely populated district, than in a more compact one. Taking the size of the two regions into account, South Sulawesi being half as large as South Sumatra clearly provides more political goods and services and is thus more politically developed than the latter.

By far the most important type of resource mobilization is the extraction of material resources. While the government can accomplish this through various means, the only really relevant index of its capacity is the amount collected through taxation, direct taxation in particular. As background to the realities in South Sumatra and South Sulawesi, the following national figures are suggestive. Table 1 dramatically reveals the Indonesian

TABLE 1

REALIZED INDONESIAN CENTRAL GOVERNMENT REVENUES BY DIRECT TAXATION (IN MILLION RUPIAHS)*

Year	Total	All direct taxes	% of total	Direct taxes excluding corporation taxes	% of total
1967	84,899.7	16,815.8	20	6,007.4	7
1968	185,283.4	51,034.0	28	16,033.5	9
1969/70	334,762.0	91,496.0	27	28,096.0	8

*One US dollar was worth Rp. 375.
Source: Theodore M. Smith, 'The political Economy of Regional and Local Finance in Indonesia', unpublished paper, 1970, Table II, p. 7.

government's very great dependence on resources other than those which it can directly mobilize. Since corporation taxes, including taxes on foreign companies, are relatively convenient to collect, the mobilization capacity of the central government is more accurately reflected by the even much smaller receipts from the remaining tax sources.

Directly revealing of the governmental effectiveness at the regional and local levels are the figures in Table 2. Although part of the subsidies from the Central Government originally come from the regions the figures in the table still greatly exaggerate the mobilizational capacity of the government at the local and regional levels. Most of the locally raised revenues, both by the local governments themselves and by the Central Government, do not come from direct taxation.

TABLE 2

ESTIMATED REGIONAL REVENUES IN INDONESIA BY SOURCES

Year	Total (in million Rupiahs)	% raised by regions themselves	% raised by Central Government	% Central Government subsidies
1967	19,209.2	16.8	43.8	39.4
1968	34,808.0	9.8	38.3	51.9
1969/70	63,502.4	7.9	39.5	52.6

Source: T. M. Smith, 'The political Economy of Regional and Local Finance in Indonesia', unpublished paper, 1970, Table I, p. 6.

South Sumatra badly neglects direct taxation of its population as a source of provincial revenue. Being one of the richest provinces in the country, it also does not rely as heavily as most other provinces on subsidies. Of its estimated income of more than three billion Rupiahs for the 1969/70 fiscal year, only 32 per cent comes from the Central Government (Smith, 1970: 18). For the rest, the provincial government seems to rely to a great extent on its shares of the export taxes. At any rate, the provincial government has only in 1970 begun to collect three types of provincial taxes which, by rough estimate, should together bring in about 7 per cent of the region's current revenue.[1]

The mobilizing capacity of the provincial government in South Sulawesi is reflected in Table 3. Since the Central Government subsidies originally come from direct taxation within the region, the percentages in the table somewhat underestimate the level of provincial mobilization. In view of

[1]These taxes are the household tax, tax on motor vehicles and tax on the transfer of motor vehicle ownership. Governor's Office, Palembang, South Sumatra.

the very small proportion of direct taxation receipt in the Central Government total revenue, however, the necessary adjustment would be negligible.

The incomplete data presented above suggest a generally low resource mobilization capability in Indonesia. Although they have increased substantially in the past few years, the amounts of material resources directly mobilized by the Central and provincial governments seem to be very inadequate. Direct mobilization only accounts for less than 10 per cent and 20 per cent of the Central Government and provincial government incomes respectively. Indeed, the provinces are increasingly more dependent upon the Central Government in spite of notable fiscal decentralization in the recent years.

TABLE 3

PROVINCIAL REVENUES, SOUTH SULAWESI (IN MILLION RUPIAHS)

	1967*† (Realized)	% of Total	1968* (Estimate)	% of Total	1969/70** (Estimate)	% of Total
Total Revenues	552.4	100%	1,805.9	100%	2,579.4	100%
Taxes/duties	12.5	2	99.8	5.5	111.6	4.3
IPEDA†	—	0	12.5	0.6	25.0	0.9
Cess	—	0	—	0.0	366.3	14.2
Total Mobilized	12.5	2	112.3	6.1	502.9	19.4
Central Govt. Subsidies	358.0	64.8	935.9	51.8	1,615.5	62

†Contributions for regional development — levied on land and its products — collected for the province and the districts by the Central Government.

Sources: *W. H. Makaliwe, 'An Economic Survey of South Sulawesi', *Bulletin of Indonesian Economic Studies*, V (July, 1969), Table 6, pp. 32–3.

**T. M. Smith, 'The Political Economy of Regional and Local Finance in Indonesia', unpublished paper, 1970, Table III, p. 9.

Comparing South Sumatra and South Sulawesi, it is obvious that the latter region is much more mobilizational than the former. South Sumatra as a whole seems to be very lackadaisical. All the districts in the province are almost completely dependent upon grants from the provincial and

Central Governments. Table 4 illustrates this fact very well since the district chosen is generally regarded as one of the best in South Sumatra; it is also the closest to Palembang, the provincial capital. Although the receipts from mobilization have increased, the total amounts represent miniscule portions of the district's total revenues which mostly come as subsidies from Palembang and Djakarta. This situation is even more disturbing in view of the fact that almost none of the central government and provincial taxes have been collected. Since the development contributions have mostly come from oil pipes passing through the district, most of the people have never paid any taxes. Like the other district governments in the region, the OKI government has largely been absent!

TABLE 4

DISTRICT REVENUES, OGAN KOMERING ILIR (OKI), SOUTH SUMATRA

	1967	1968	1969
Taxes on non-motorized vehicles	72,026	116,129	1,776
Entertainment taxes	13,662	9,225	—
Local retribution	11,311	21,033	927
Market duties	402,484	622,314	683,248
Development levies (IPEDA)	93,250	2,248,236	2,063,673
Local licenses	12,175	12,400	3,550
Rent of fields	—	—	279,152
TOTAL	604,908	2,999,337	3,032,326
Subsidies	na	118,731,940	90,000,000

Source: Governor's Office, Palembang.

In contrast, district governments in South Sulawesi are much more financially independent. In fact, in the case of about one-fourth of the districts, their mobilized revenues have actually been exceeding their expenditures other than the salaries of their officials. Tables 5 and 6 summarize the available data on two of these 'surplus' districts, Bone in the east and Pankep in the west. The percentages demonstrate a very commendable mobilizing capacity. It should be noted, however, that these percentages do not really refer to the full potentials of the districts.

TABLE 5
MOBILIZED DISTRICT REVENUES, PANGKEP, SOUTH SULAWESI
(in thousand Rupiahs)

	1967		1968		1969	
	Actual Receipt	% of Target	Actual Receipt	% of Target	Actual Receipt	% of Target
IREDA[a]	2,212	86	12,718	85	14,013	69
IPEDA	2,860	61	3,708	65	21,467	53
Others	na	na	na	na	15,000[b]	na

[a] Contributions for regional rehabilitation, levied on every adult on the basis
of estimated income.
[b] An estimate by the District Secretary.
Source: District Secretary, Pangkep.

TABLE 6
MOBILIZED DISTRICT REVENUES, BONE, SOUTH SULAWESI
(in thousand Rupiahs)

	1967/68		1968/69		1969/70	
	Actual Receipt	% of Target	Actual Receipt	% of Target	Actual Receipt	% of Target
IREDA	9,346	92	26,948	93	54,486	92
IPEDA	5,608	61	10,880	71	30,515	60
Others	10,846	na	5,946	na	36,078	na

Source: District Secretary, Bone.

With regard to the IPEDA, for example, less than half of the taxable lands
have actually been registered for the purpose. Much of the increase in the
tax receipts has actually resulted simply from more adequate registration.

From the preceding discussion, it is difficult to avoid the conclusion that
both South Sumatra and South Sulawesi, like most of the rest of Indonesia,
have achieved only little political development. Both the amount of
political goods and services and the mobilizing capacity in these two
regions are still depressingly low. These two aspects of development are

integrally related. Being more mobilizational, South Sulawesi is clearly more capable of providing political goods and services than South Sumatra. *The essence of political development is the upward spiraling process of increasing political wealth and intensifying mobilization of the required resources.* While South Sumatra lacks both the will and the capacity to launch this process seriously, South Sulawesi seems to be primarily short of the former.

III

Numerous factors can easily be cited to account for this low level of political development in South Sumatra and South Sulawesi as well as in Indonesia generally. The most important of these is tradition, and many of the other factors can be traced to this basic issue.

There are several interrelated aspects of political tradition in the two regions which have jointly contributed to their lack of dynamism. First is parochialism. In South Sumatra, the largest traditional political unit was the *marga*. In ancient times, this was simply a small genealogical group settled in a village, usually along a river bank. By the time the great trading kingdom of Srivijaya collapsed toward the end of the fourteenth century, some of the *marga* had apparently grown into relatively substantial communities consisting of several villages which had sprouted around the original *marga* seat. To these communities some of the princes of Sriwidjaja might have escaped their enemies.[1] Nevertheless, the point to be emphasized is that these *marga* were never very extensive and were always self-contained. Even now, very few, if any, of the two-hundred odd *marga* in South Sumatra have populations exceeding 50,000 and many of them are still very much isolated. As late as the beginning of the nineteenth century, the *marga* chiefs were almost completely independent of the sultans in Palembang. The latter did claim formal suzerainty over the former but the most they could expect were irregular tributes.[2]

South Sulawesi, too, never really knew centralized authority. It is true that for about fifty years at its height of power, Gowa ruled supreme in South Sulawesi. The actual authority of the Gowa sultans, however, was rather limited for the sultanate did not absorb the other numerous chiefdoms. In any case, since the collapse of Makassar toward the end of the seventeenth century, South Sulawesi had been fragmented into dozens of kingdoms which were highly independent of each other (Lahade, 1966: 33).

[1]This possibility was suggested to me by A. Malik, *ex-Wali Negara* (governor) of South Sumatra during the revolution, who is now fruitfully devoting himself to historical investigations of the region. Much of my understanding of the traditional political system in South Sumatra I owe to him, although he may not agree with some of my own interpretations.
[2]Ex-Resident Raden Hanan, Palembang.

And within these kingdoms, the authority of the kings was largely nominal. As in South Sumatra, the earliest political units in South Sulawesi were the independent genealogical settlements under chiefs called the *matoa* (elders). Quite early in the history of the region, these villages grouped themselves into little federations called *lilik* whose chiefs, according to the legends, were *tomanurung* (the ones who have descended from heaven). These federations eventually expanded by annexing neighbouring villages and some of them finally evolved into kingdoms, the confederations of the earlier groupings. The king was always the chief of the strongest *lilik*. In the course of this evolution, the villages lost their importance but the *lilik* continued to remain more or less independent, each maintaining its own special *aradjang* or 'royal ornaments'. The king, possessing the most powerful *aradjang*, was only a little more than the *primus inter pares*.[1]

The fragmentation of the two regions continued until the beginning of the present century when the Dutch began to exert more than mere hegemony. The second important aspect of the political tradition in South Sumatra and South Sulawesi is the highly personalized nature of the political authority. In both regions, the polity was not separable from the persons of the chiefs and the kings.

The *marga* chiefs in South Sumatra were patriarchs *par excellence*. Although their position was not strictly hereditary they invariably belonged to the 'ruling' family in the principal village of the *marga*. Since their authority was mostly based on kinship, the *pasirah* were far from absolute rulers of their *marga* and their title in fact suggests that they were only leading elders.[2] Nevertheless, the chiefs did exercise considerable authority. The *marga* council was not an independent body and more importantly, there was no separate *marga* treasury. Actually there was no administrative system as such and the *pasirah* relied almost entirely on personal loyalty and obligation. The secondary village chiefs were largely independent and their only ties with the *pasirah* were based on personal loyalty and, in most cases, kinship.

The South Sulawesi kings 'ruled' over larger and more organized territories and therefore were more powerful than the *pasirah*. But the government in South Sulawesi kingdoms was not much less patrimonial and personalized. The relationship between the king and the *lilik* chiefs was more organized in the sense that the chiefs owed the king better defined obligations and that the king could often enforce his will over the lesser lords. Still, there was also no real administrative system and the king's (as well as the chiefs') wealth was not separated from the wealth of the polity. Whether a king was powerful or not depended mostly on his per-

---

[1]This description has been derived from a number of interviews in Makassar. In particular, I would like to thank Pak La Side (a former inspector of schools and presently director of the South Sulawesi Cultural Society) and Pak H. A. Pattopoi, a member of the former royal family of Bone.

[2]According to A. Malik, *pasirah* means one who sums up views expressed in council. Thus he was much like the guide in Sukarno's concept of guided democracy.

sonality. Authority was again based simply on personal loyalty and obligation.

The nature of this personalized patrimonialism is clearly revealed by the way resources were mobilized and used. Unsystematic resource mobilization is the third traditional norm. In the case of the *pasirah* in South Sumatra, the major source of their income was derived from their share of the exploitation of the natural resources of the *marga*, principally the rivers and the forests. The rivers, for example, were auctioned every year and the revenues were divided between the village chiefs and the *pasirah*. The latter of course obtained most of the proceeds from rivers flowing through or nearby his own primary village. The *pasirah* could also expect portions of everything produced by the people in the *marga*, such as grains, vegetable,poultry and cattle, especially during harvest and when the *pasirah* were having celebrations for one reason or another. In addition, tradition provided them with 'voluntary' services from the people. An interesting custom provided that the bachelors, especially in the primary village, served the *pasirah* for a certain length of time during which the chief could presumably assign the young men any tasks he could think of. Finally, the chiefs invariably possessed large farm lands worked in part by voluntary labour. In some cases, this system of resource mobilization was a source of hardship for the people but in general it was rather benign since the parochial environment of the *marga* did not encourage excessive greed. At any rate, although the *adat* or customary law did provide guidelines regarding these obligations and duties, it was flexible and subject to considerable discretion on the part of the *pasirah* and the elders.[1]

Befitting their grander status, the kings of South Sulawesi were much more affluent. Like the South Sumatran *parisah*, the *lilik* chiefs derived large incomes from the exploitation of the natural resources of their areas and from the share of the fruits of labour of their people. They also benefitted from the various 'voluntary' services. Unlike the *marga*, each *lilik* furthermore possessed large pieces of choice farmlands which were completely worked by the populace. These were apart from the personal holdings of the chiefs. As the lords of the biggest *lilik* in their kingdoms, the kings were thus assured of considerable revenues. In addition, they received from the other *lilik* grandees yearly tributes which oftentimes included slaves. Substantial income also came from the extensive royal lands and fields. Finally, the kings received port and other retributions. All in all, the South Sulawesi 'feudal' kings generally lived in some splendour. A member of the former royal family of Bone can recall playing as a child with basketfuls of gold coins![2] Again, the significant fact is that this mobilization was not very systematic. It is true that the *adat* was even

---

[1]The preceding description has been derived from family recollections and interviews, particularly with *ex-Pasirah* Daud of Sekaju and *ex-Resident* Hanan in Palembang.

[2]This recollection was made to me by H. Andi Pattopoi. Much of the information in this paragraph was gained during my interview with him.

more well developed and elaborate here in South Sulawesi than in South Sumatra. In general, the mobilization was also harsher to the extent that those of the common people who could not meet the prescribed obligations could be reduced to slavery. Nonetheless, a great deal of flexibility, or at least arbitrariness, prevailed in the absence of any formal administrative system.

The manner in which the mobilized resources in the two regions were utilized constitutes the fourth important aspect of their political tradition. Instead of being used to create and enlarge political wealth, these resources were spent almost entirely for conspicuous consumption. In fact, the *marga*, the *lilik* and the kingdoms provided very little political goods. The administrative structure was non-existent and the judicial system was undeveloped. *Adat* and religious courts did exist in both regions but they were mainly *ad hoc* in nature and their jurisdictions were highly circumscribed. Moreover, the *pasirah*, the chieftains and the kings were invariably judges themselves. Public health and education were of course not known while what roads existed were built and maintained by 'voluntary' labour mobilized by the village heads. In South Sumatra *marga* even organized police and military forces were non-existent since being small and relatively isolated from each other the *marga* never really indulged in significant warfare. Law and order were adequately maintained by irregular, voluntary militia. In South Sulawesi, at least some of the kingdoms did maintain regular standing armies. The kings also enjoyed the feudal right to demand military aid from the *lilik* chiefs. The fact remains, however, that these forces were personal servants of the kings. Furthermore, ever since the establishment of Dutch hegemony toward the end of the seventeenth century, local wars among the kingdoms had been less frequent and less decisive. Hence their military establishments had also slowly decayed.

In summary, it must be said that up to the beginning of the present century, South Sumatra and South Sulawesi had attained only minimal political development. Their resources were not effectively and systematically mobilized and their political wealth was almost non-existent. This political poverty went hand in hand with personalized authority which was in turn encouraged and maintained by parochialism resulting from the continued political fragmentation of the two regions. From this perspective, the real complaint against the Dutch is not that they came and subjugated but that they were not dominant enough. It took the Dutch more than 200 years after they had established their hegemony in the archipelago to make their authority actually felt in the regions outside Java. When they finally turned to actual government of the outer regions at the beginning of the present century, their efforts were too little and too late.

Following the dissolution of the Palembang sultanate in 1823, South Sumatra finally came under the direct control of the Dutch. The sultan was replaced in Palembang by a *Resident* representing the Governor-General. In due course, the region was divided into three major areas each under an assistant *Resident*. At the bottom were the controllers who were in charge of districts comprising several *marga*. Throughout the nineteenth century, this set-up was mainly on paper since the assistant *Residents* and the controllers were not given specific administrative duties other than general supervision of their territories. It was only after the passage of the Decentralization Act of 1903 that the administrative system took on firmer shape. The controllers were provided with administrative staffs and in 1907 their areas were broken into smaller *marga* groupings each under an Indonesian official called *demang*. Five years later, the sub-district heads were designated assistant *demang* while the *demang* was the chief administrative and liaison officer in the office of the controller. It was not until about 1912, then, that the *marga* were brought, for the first time, into the wider context of the region.[1]

After they finally and thoroughly subjugated the South Sulawesi kingdoms in 1905, the Dutch superimposed the same administrative structure as was introduced in South Sumatra. The region was divided into territories which in turn were subdivided into areas under the controllers which, in most cases, coincided with the existing realms. The one departure is that there were two further administrative levels below the controller. In 1908 several *lilik* were federated into a district and each *lilik* was transformed into a sub-district. Although the heads of these minor divisions were still selected from the local grandees, they were assisted by the official representatives of the controller, the *demang* and the assistant *demang*.

The Dutch did introduce important changes in the two regions which were aimed at making the political authority less personalized. The controller was the pivotal power figure. With the assistance of the salaried *demang* and assistant *demang* he exercised considerable control over the *pasirah*, the *lilik* chieftains and the king. Through the special Local Government Ordinance of 1919, the *marga* were formally transformed from genealogical groupings into territorial and legal units designated as 'adat communities'. Although they were not reduced to salaried officials, the *pasirah* were no longer 'natural' patriarchs; from then on they were elected, albeit for life, by popular election. Actually, the title *pasirah* itself was made honorary. The general title of *marga* chief was *depati*, a term which had formerly referred to the principal lieutenant of the *pasirah*. A *depati* could become a *pasirah* only by the decision of the *Resident*, presumably on the basis of outstanding and loyal service. All the village chiefs, including that of the principal village, also came to depend formally on the popular vote. In addition to introducing the principle of election, the Dutch also formalized and strengthened the *marga* council by giving it legislative authority and making its membership elective. The *depati* or

[1]Information regarding colonial administration in South Sumatra has been obtained principally from interviews in Palembang with *ex-Residents* Hanan and Razak, both of whom joined the colonial administrative system at its beginning and have successfully risen through its ranks to become the highest civil administrators after independence. *ex-Pasirah* Daud of Sekaju Marga has also provided valuable recollections.

pasirah remained the chairman of the council but he no longer completely dominated it. In addition to all these changes was the requirement that all the decisions of the *pasirah* and the *marga* council had to be approved by the controller and/or the assistant *Resident*.

In South Sulawesi, a more indirect colonial rule prevailed.[1] Formally, the kings remained supreme with regard to the internal affairs of their kingdoms. In actuality, the controller did not limit himself to giving advice. The abolition of the *lilik* and its transformation into a sub-district, plus the introduction of the districts, seriously undermined the authority of the kings. The king himself could no longer rule in a completely autocratic manner since he had to heed the advice of an executive council whose members were elected by the district heads on the suggestion and with the approval of the controller. Moreover, all the decisions of the king and the executive council had to be approved by the controller who also had to be informed of all important issues in the kingdom.

The impersonalization of authority entailed more systematic resource mobilization. First of all, the Dutch created formal treasuries. The greater part of the former income of the *pasirah*, particularly the revenues derived from the exploitation of the natural resources, now went into the *marga* treasury. In addition, the controller was directly in charge of a 'government treasury' which handled revenues primarily from the income tax which replaced the former tributes in kind and which had become the specific source of income for the district. All forms of 'voluntary' labour except for the building and maintenance of roads were discouraged by making them payable in money. Even the latter was later changed to road tax. Similar systematization was also introduced in South Sulawesi. There each *wanua* (district) maintained its own treasury separate from the treasury of the kingdom which was in turn distinct from the government treasury under the controller. Tributes and voluntary labour were also discouraged and to a large extent replaced by taxes such as the income tax and the poll tax.

These changes by no means reduced the chiefs and the kings to poverty. They still received their ample share of the revenues and the custom of tribute-giving persisted among the populace. Above all, they still possessed their extensive land holdings. The changes nevertheless amounted to important innovations. The creation of formal treasuries made it possible to prevent the conspicuous consumption of the resources and thus made these available for the creation and accumulation of political wealth. The introduction of taxation permitted more systematic mobilization and easier accounting. From the point of view of the populace, the changes generally meant a heavier burden; the system of mobilization lost much of its flexibility and the absolute amount of resources mobilized also generally increased. It is important to note that both in South Sumatra and in South

---

[1]The following description and much of my knowledge about colonial administration in South Sulawesi I owe to Pak La Side and *ex-Resident* Andi Tjatjo in Makassar.

Sulawesi most of the districts were self-sufficient if not actually positively contributory to the colonial treasury.

The greater amount of mobilized resources was necessitated first by the introduction of the administrative system. Money had to be spent now on the salaries of field administrative officials. A regularized police force and the introduction of a formal court system also meant new expenditures. In addition, resources were needed to introduce political goods such as public health, formal education, agricultural service, better roads, and the postal-telephone-telegraphic system. Unfortunately these remained very rudimentary until independence. For example, in both regions the Dutch had actually managed to introduce only a few trappings of the formal court system. Professional judges were unknown and the chiefs, with the assistance and supervision of the colonial officials, still dominated the proceedings. Modern elementary education was not even introduced in the regions before 1920.

In sum, although the changes introduced by the Dutch were significant innovations they were too little and too late. In both South Sumatra and South Sulawesi, relatively effective colonial administration lasted less than thirty years. By the end of the Dutch colonial period, political development in the two regions was both rudimentary and fragile. The Japanese occupation, the revolution and the early years of independence certainly did not give it added vigour; they actually smothered it. In South Sumatra where the traditional political leadership was especially fragmented and weak, the turbulent post-colonial period has created a real authority vacuum. As Governor Asnawi recently remarked, 'the administrative corps and the administrative system [in South Sumatra] has, ever since the Japanese occupation ..., been in the state of continuous decay, both with regard to their functions and duties as well as in terms of their authority ...' (Mangkualam, 1969: 12). Thanks to the continuing vitality of its comparatively larger traditional nobility, South Sulawesi has escaped a similar extent of political decay.

Tradition has bequeathed not only political poverty. An even more important legacy is a set of political attitudes. The revolution contributed to the destruction of the rudimentary political infrastructures developed by the Dutch and brought about antipathy toward the colonial innovations. The struggle for independence thus led to the revival of the traditional ideas of government. As we have seen, the chief characteristic of the traditional system in South Sulawesi and South Sumatra was its lack of mobilizational dynamism. The revolutionary leaders clearly rejected the necessity of political mobilization and in celebrating liberation they actually emphasized only the flexibility and 'democratic' aspects of the traditional political system. Resource mobilization was successfully dismissed as both colonial and feudalistic. This underlying ideology explains why most present-day officials, administrators and politicians seem to be unable to bring themselves to make serious effort at employing and improving the mobilizational capacity of the government. The writer repeatedly observed that revenues do not come in simply because no serious attempt has been made to collect them.

Another inherited value which shows obvious vitality is personalism. In both South Sumatra and South Sulawesi personal leadership remains the dominant political style. This is clearly reflected by the fact that a few dynamic leaders and administrators have far surpassed the general level of effectiveness. A more common manifestation is unwillingness of government officials to provide truthfully even the most innocuous information. There is clearly a prevalent attitude that government is the private business of the officials concerned. In the absence of effective administrative control the growth of which it surely inhibits, this attitude also finds expression in the 'privatization' of public funds.

IV

The chapter has urged the definition of political development in terms of actual performance of the political system in mobilizing resources and providing political goods and services. Judged from this perspective, the level of political development in Indonesia, as revealed by the conditions in South Sumatra and South Sulawesi, is still very low. For example, the average *per capita* resource mobilization by direct taxation in these two regions is only about one US dollar a year. It is the argument of this chapter that this political underdevelopment reflects above all their political traditions. The personal-patrimonial governments which existed in these regions before the actual introduction of the colonial administration did not leave much political wealth. Most of what the Dutch introduced during the short period of effective colonial control did not survive the Japanese occupation, the revolution and the early years of independence. Unfortunately, the very attitudes and values which made the traditional government undynamic have actually been revived. Personalism and a lackadaisical attitude toward resource mobilization and the provision of political goods and services are preventing more rapid political development in both South Sumatra and South Sulawesi as well as the rest of Indonesia generally.

3 Political Modernization in the Philippines: The Politics and the Political Elite of Occidental Mindoro

REMIGIO E. AGPALO

I

IN this chapter the politics and the political elite of Occidental Mindoro are described and characterized and related to the study of modernization, especially political modernization. Occidental Mindoro's modernization, as shown in the development of the province's politics and political elite, is, or ought to be, interesting and illuminating in this respect.

First, Occidental Mindoro's political modernization can shed light on the problems of the Philippines, for even if Occidental Mindoro is not typical of the Philippines as a whole, nevertheless it may be regarded as more representative of the country than most other provinces. The economy of Occidental Mindoro, like that of the nation, is predominantly agricultural and underdeveloped; and most of its communities are rural. At the same time, like the nation, Occidental Mindoro has some manufacturing, industrial, and commercial enterprises in a separate urbanized core area. In terms of population, Occidental Mindoro, like the Philippines, is not inhabited by only one linguistic-ethnic group; it has Tagalogs, Ilocanos, Visayans, Pampangos, Bicolanos, Muslims, and others. The percentage of distribution is not congruent with that in the entire country, but as the 1960 census figures show, it is more representative of the nation than Bulacan or Batangas, Ilocos Norte or La Union, Samar or Iloilo, Albay or Camarines Sur, and Sulu or Lanao. Also, as in the nation, two political parties — the Nacionalista Party and the Liberal Party — are dominant in the province; and both parties at the provincial level exhibit the same fissiparous and factional characteristics of the national parties. Furthermore, the values of the people of Occidental Mindoro appear to be the same as those of lowland Filipinos in general; and the formal structure of the provincial and municipal governments of Occidental Mindoro is the same as in all other provinces.

Second, Occidental Mindoro has several features found in most of the developing countries of Asia, Africa, and Latin America. These include, among others, a polity with a politics of patronage and clientage; an economy that is predominantly agricultural and extractive; a society with under-developed transportation and communications technology, as well as publics, groups, and political parties; and a culture based upon personalistic, particularistic, and parochial orientations.

And third, in spite of the province's shortcomings, Occidental Mindoro has made some significant progress in modernization in general and political modernization in particular. The factors responsible for these, once identified and analysed, will provide insights into the complexities of the problem of social and political change not only in the Philippines but also in other developing countries.

But before describing and characterizing the politics and the political elite of Occidental Mindoro and relating them to political modernization, some clarificatory remarks regarding some of the key terms in this paper must be made. The concepts which need to be clarified are political elite, modernization, and political modernization.

I shall distinguish *political elite* from *ruling power elite* and *counter-elite*. The political elite, as used here, refers to the persons who were successful in the competition or struggle for elective governmental posts.[1] As such, they are persons who hold formal elective positions in the provincial government. The ruling power elite, on the other hand, is a well-knit, united, and homogeneous power group which has the heaviest *weight*, the broadest *scope*, and the largest *domain* of power. In this connection, I shall adopt Lasswell's and Kaplan's usage of weight, scope, and domain of power. They said: 'The weight of power is the degree of participation in the making of decisions; its scope consists of the values whose shaping and enjoyment are controlled; and the domain of power consists of the persons over whom power is exercised.' (Lasswell and Kaplan, 1950: 77).

The counter-elite is a group or an aggregation of individuals attempting to dislodge the political elite from the government in order to control and run it themselves.

Modernization and political modernization have been discussed and analysed quite extensively since the 1950s and, therefore, we do not lack scholarly information on these concepts.

Modernization, according to Rustow, is a process which 'comprises many specific changes', denoting 'rapidly widening control over nature through closer co-operation among men'. It includes 'all the more specific changes such as industrialization, rationalization, secularization, and bureaucratization' (Rustow, 1967: 5-8). To Black, it is 'the process by which historically evolved institutions are adapted to the rapidly chang-

---

[1]Frey's (1965) and Singer's (1964) usage of political elite is essentially similar to the one adopted here.

ing functions that reflect the unprecedented increase in man's knowledge, permitting control over his environment' (Black, 1966: 7). This process, he continues, is too complex to be reduced to simple terms; it involves revolutionary changes in general aspects — intellectual, political, economic, social, and psychological. Eisenstadt also regards modernization as a process entailing 'continual changes in all major spheres of society'. (Eisenstadt, 1966: 20). In an earlier work, he pointed out that modernization implied

not only the development of ... various indices of social mobilization and of growing structural differentiation, but also the development of a social, economic or political system which not only generates continuous change, but unlike many other types of social or political systems, is also capable of absorbing changes beyond its own institutional premises (Eisenstadt, 1963: 5).

Apter, however, defines it simply as 'the process leading to the state of modernity', which 'begins when man tries to solve the allocation problem' (Apter, 1965: 9–13). 'To be modern', Apter puts it in other words, 'means to see life as alternatives, preferences, and choices' (Apter, 1965: 9–13). Shils, however, says that 'among the elites of the new states, "modern" means dynamic, concerned with people, democratic and equalitarian, scientific, economically advanced, sovereign and influential' (Shils, 1966: 7).

In spite of the various definitions of modernization — and they are still proliferating — a consensus has developed in at least two points. First, as one student has put it, modernization implies 'transformation, i.e. a deep, fundamental, and continuing change in all systems by which man organizes his life' (Bill, 1970: 19). Second, the most important spheres of social life where such transformation occurs are the psychological, the intellectual, the demographic, the social, the economic, and the political.

Huntington has summarized the transformation involved in these levels as follows:

At the psychological level, modernization involves a fundamental shift in values, attitudes, and expectations. Traditional man expected continuity in nature and society and did not believe in the capacity of man to change or control either. Modern man, in contrast, accepts the possibility of change and believes in its desirability.... At the intellectual level, modernization involves the tremendous expansion of man's knowledge about his environment and the diffusion of this knowledge throughout society through increased literacy, mass communications, and education. Demographically, modernization means changes in the patterns of life, a marked increase in health and life expectancy, increased occupational, vertical, and geographical mobility, and in particular, the rapid growth of urban population as contrasted with rural. Socially, modernization tends to supplement the family and other primary groups having diffuse roles with consciously organized secondary associations having much more specific functions.... Economically, there is a diversification of activity as a few simple occupations give way to many complex ones; the level of occupational skills rises significantly; the ratio of capital to labour increases; subsistence agriculture gives way to market agriculture; and agriculture itself declines in significance compared to commercial, industrial, and other nonagricultural activities (Huntington, 1968: 32–33).

Political modernization sometimes is distinguished from political development, as is done by Huntington; but usually the two are taken to be synonymous terms. Pye and Organski, as well as Almond and Powell, for instance, use the two terms more or less interchangeably.

To Organski, political development involves four stages: '(1) the politics of primitive unification, (2) the politics of industrialization, (3) the politics of national welfare, and (4) the politics of abundance' (Organski, 1965: 7). Pye, after noting ten definitions of political development, eventually views this as a syndrome with three dimensions — equality of the participants of the political process, the capacity of the political system, and the differentiation and specialization of its structures (Pye, 1966: Ch. II). Almond and Powell analyse political development, however, in terms of successful responses to four types of problems or challenges — state building, nation building, participation, and distribution (Almond and Powell, 1966 : 34–37).

Huntington's distinction between political modernization and political development revolves around the idea of political decay or breakdown. To this author, 'political modernization involves the rationalization of authority, the differentiation of structures, and the expansion of political participation' (Huntington, 1968: 93); and this may or may not result in political decay or breakdown. If the political organizations and procedures of the political system become institutionalized, then political development results.[1] If they do not, then political decay follows.

In this paper, we adopt Huntington's definition of political modernization. He elaborated his conception as follows:

First, political modernization involves the rationalization of authority, the replacement of a large number of traditional, religious, familial, and ethnic political authorities by a single secular, national political authority.... It means national integration and the centralization or accumulation of power in recognized national lawmaking institutions.

Secondly, political modernization involves the differentiation of new political functions and the development of specialized structures to perform those functions. Areas of particular competence — legal, military, administrative, scientific — become separated from the political realm, and autonomous, specialized, but subordinate organs arise to discharge those tasks. Administrative hierarchy become more elaborate, more complex, more disciplined. Office and power are distributed more by achievement and less by ascription.

Thirdly, political modernization involves increased participation in politics by social groups throughout society.... The citizens become directly involved in and affected by governmental affairs (Huntington, 1968: 34–35).

[1]Huntington (1965: 393) defines political development as 'the institutionalization of political organizations and procedures'.

II

Let us now turn to Occidental Mindoro and its politics. The fifty-first province of the Philippines, it emerged as a legally constituted political sub-division of the country only in 1950 by virtue of R.A. No. 505.[1] According to this law, Occidental Mindoro shall comprise of 'the municipalities of Abra de Ilog, Looc, Lubang, Mamburao, Paluan, Sablayan, San Jose, and Santa Cruz'.[2] When the province was launched in 1950, therefore, it was composed of only eight municipalities. In June 1966, a ninth municipality, Calintaan,[3] was created; and in April, 1969, two other municipalities, Magsaysay[4] and Rizal,[5] were added to the province. Today, therefore, Occidental Mindoro is composed of eleven municipalities.

The province has a total land area of about 5,880 square kilometres (Census, 1960). However, most parts of the province are mountainous. The coastal plain extending from Mamburao to San Jose and some small valleys or stretches of flat land surrounding the mouths of some rivers account for practically all the arable land of the province; and these constitute only about 5 per cent of the total land area.

The population of Occidental Mindoro in 1903 was only 13,223; and its 1960 population of about 84,000 is almost double that for 1948. Today there are about 145,000 inhabitants.[6] This spectacular increase is due not only to natural causes but also to a large influx of immigrants from other islands, mainly Ilocanos from densely populated areas in north-western Luzon. Tagalogs still predominate but Ilocanos now run as a strong second, and the Visayans as a significant third. The aboriginal Mangyans had dwindled to less than a thousand by 1960.

The politics of Occidental Mindoro is not a politics of violence. Neither is it a politics of charisma, nor of ideology, nor discussion. Instead, it is a politics of *pandanggo sa ilaw*,[7] characterized by heavy reliance upon manipulation of the people by the political elite and counter-elite through the leverage primarily of patronage, with strong accent on manoeuvring for occupation of strategic positions which affect or control the allocation of

[1]This Act was approved on 13 June 1950.   [2]R.A. No. 505, Sec. 1.
[3]R.A. No. 4732, approved on 18 June 1966.
[4]R.A. No. 5459, approved on 3 April 1969.
[5]R.A. No. 5460, approved on 3 April 1969.
[6]Preliminary data on the 1970 population census of Occidental Mindoro, Local Office of the Bureau of the Census and Statistics, at Mamburao, Occidental Mindoro.
[7]This characterization of the politics of Occidental Mindoro was originally written in the author's 'Pandanggo Sa Ilaw: The Politics of Occidental Mindoro', *Philippines Social Sciences and Humanities Review*, XXVII (December 1963), pp. 445–88 and *Philippine Journal of Public Administration*, 8 (April 1964), pp. 83–111. A shorter and edited version of this article was published by the Ohio University Center for International Studies, Southeast Asia Program, 1969, Athens, Ohio. The author's final and detailed account of this type of politics appears in his book, *The Political Elite and the People: A Study of Politics in Occidental Mindoro*. (Manila: College of Public Administration, University of the Philippines, 1972).

patronage by all participants of the political process — the political elite, the counter-elite and the people.

This type of politics has been termed *pandanggo-sa-ilaw* politics by the writer because it has several elements analogous to the 'oil lamp dance', or *pandanggo sa ilaw*, a favourite Filipino folk dance. In this dance male and female dancers move along rhythmically while they balance and manipulate lighted glass oil lamps on their heads and on the backs of their hands. Agile of hands and nimble of feet, *pandanggo* dancers do not trip nor do they drop their glass oil lamps. Analogous to the *pandanggo* dancers are the political elite and counter-elite; to the *pandanggo* audience, the people; and to the *pandanggo* glass oil lamps, the power and status of the political elite. Corresponding to the stage where the *pandanggo* is danced is the political arena — Occidental Mindoro. The movements of the political elite and the counter-elite can be compared to those of the *pandanggo* dancers; these consist in skilful manipulation and manoeuvring. The behaviour of the people can be compared to that of the *pandanggo-sa-ilaw* audience; it consists of interacting and reacting to the principal participants. In the *pandanggo sa ilaw*, those who are close to the principal participants are enthusiastic clappers and applauders; they share some of the light that emanates from the glass oil lamps of the *pandanggo* dancers. On the other hand, those who are far from the *pandanggo* dancers are not enthusiastic; they hardly get any ray of light. In *pandanggo-sa-ilaw* politics, those who are close to the political elite are also enthusiastic and militant 'rah-rah' men who share some of the power and the status of the political elite. On the other hand, those who are far from the political elite hardly get a share of power and status emanating from the power holders.

To show the operation of *pandanggo-sa-ilaw* politics in Occidental Mindoro in the public sector, let us look briefly at two aspects: the appointment of judges and the choice surrounding the site of a major building.

An analysis of the careers of the eight judges who served Occidental Mindoro in 1965 shows that the determining factor in their appointment is personalistic and partisan politics.[1] The top political elite, in this case the Congressman and the Governor in particular, recommend to the President for the judgeship someone they know well and approve of, either because he is a consanguineal relative, a former employee, a party leader, or a consanguineal relative of a party leader (See Table 7).

Our second case is the choice of the location of the provincial Capitol, an issue which confronted the administrations of Governors Federico Castillo (Nacionalista, 1952–5), Mariano Tajonera (Nacionalista, 1956–9), and Arsenio Villaroza (Liberal, 1960–71).[2]

[1] The data were gathered from the files of the Department of Justice and from personal interviews of the judges.

[2] The data are based upon personal interviews conducted in 1962 and 1963 with former Governor Federico Castillo and Cipriano Liboro, former Judge Ildefonso Bleza, ex-Congressman Jesus Abeleda, and Governor Arsenio Villaroza, as well as ocular inspection of the Provincial Capitol and the Capitol site in 1965.

During the administration of Governor Castillo, the Provincial Board was prevailed upon by the Governor to select a site at the *hacienda* of the late Mr. Jaime Rosales, who donated ten hectares to the provincial government. At that time, Governor Castillo was living in the house of his good

TABLE 7

APPOINTMENT OF JUDGES IN OCCIDENTAL MINDORO

Justice of the Peace	*Affiliation*	*President who Made Appointment*
1. Ildefonso Bleza (Mamburao)	Nacionalista leader and provincial campaign manager.	Ramon Magsaysay (Nacionalista)
2. Rizalino Cusi (Santa Cruz)	Brother of local Nacionalista chairman.	Carlos Garcia (Nacionalista)
3. Teodoro Malabanan (Lubang)	Former Nacionalista mayor; political leader.	Carlos Garcia (Nacionalista)
4. Leandro Reyes (San Jose)	Office Assistant of Liberal Congressman.	Elpidio Quirino (Liberal)
5. Alfredo Tejada (Abra de Ilog)	Liberal leader and campaign manager of Congressman.	Diosdado Macapagal (Liberal)
6. Carlos Tria (Sablayan)	Liberal member[1]	Carlos Garcia (Nacionalista)
7. Bernardo Villar (Paluan)	Nephew of Nacionalista Governor	Carlos Garcia (Nacionalista)
8. Marciano Virola (Looc)	Son of provincial Liberal leader; secretary to Liberal Congressman.	Diosdado Macapagal (Liberal)

[1]This is one appointment which does not seem to fit the pattern. However, Liberal Governor Villaroza who recommended the appointment had received budgetary aid of P50,000 from President Garcia for supporting him indirectly in the 1961 election by not campaigning for the Liberal Party candidate, Diosdado Macapagal.

friend, Vicente Rosales, a son of Mr. Jaime Rosales. However, with the change of administration after Governor Tajonera took office, his new Provincial Board chose another site located on the property of Don Emilio Aguinaldo, whose heir and representative also donated land and received the Governor's support. Another change occurred after a new administration took office in 1960. Several Liberal Party members — one of whom is a relative of the Governor — offered to donate land. The area ultimately selected as the proper site was the one offered by the Governor's party colleagues. Since the construction of the Capitol was begun in 1963 and finished in 1965, it can be presumed that the provincial capitol site can no longer be manipulated by the political elite.

Our third case deals with the Barahan Home Economics Building and School Fence.[1] The records show that the contract to build the structure was awarded for P8,500 to Narciso Barales, but the actual construction was carried out under the suprvision of Honorio Mercene. Both men used to be Nacionalistas but later joined and campaigned for the Liberal Party, which won in Barrio Barahan in 1959. Equally interesting is why the home economics building was built in Barahan, a barrio of Santa Cruz, and not at the *poblacion* (heart of the municipality).

The *poblacion* and its public buildings represent the dignity and personality of Santa Cruz. A permanent home economics building had been urgently needed for a long time. The old home economics department was located off-campus in a rented house. Petitions by school officials and the local Parent-Teachers Association requesting the Liberal Congressman to support a new building were, however, ignored. The reason was simple; Santa Cruz was being punished for its Nacionalista leanings while Barahan was rewarded for its strong Liberal turnout.

So far we have been looking at public decisions to illustrate *pandanggo-sa-ilaw* politics. Let us now observe some of the political actors. Our first example is Salvador Domocmat, a barrio lieutenant of Batong-buhay, Sablayan.[2] Domocmat used to be a Nacionalista inspector but switched his party affiliation in 1962. He was an Ilocano immigrant who had arrived from Ilocos Sur in search of land in 1955. In Batong-buhay the jungle was thick and savage. He cleared it with brawn and sweat. Then he planted crops. At first the harvest was fair and he still had some money which he brought along from Ilocos Sur. But then the worms came, followed by rats. The family had to dig wild roots for food. Then came the rains, the floods, and malaria. Some migrant families became discouraged and returned. Domocmat stayed because he still believed that he could overcome the problems of the new barrio. But the people needed

[1]The data were gathered from the records in the Bureau of Public Works, Mamburao Occidental Mindoro, and from personal interviews with Mr. Honorio Mercene, Mr Narciso Barales, Mr. Florante Tria, and Mrs. Lourdes San Augustin Cordero in 1962.

[2]Based upon personal interviews with Mr. Salvador Domocmat in 1962 at the *pob lacion* of Sablayan and in 1963 at his home in Batong-buhay.

help in their struggle — feeder roads, an annex to the school, a radio, agricultural equipment, medical service, and the like.

Naturally, they had to turn to the town or provincial officials who could act directly on their needs or could represent them to the national officials. But practically all officials were Liberals. Domocmat's decision to join the Liberal Party was explained by him as follows:

I am almost alone here. I have enough of struggling. I have fought hordes of worms and rats. I cannot now afford to fight the municipal and provincial political elite. I shall be slaughtered. The barrio may not get the feeder road and other things it needs. I have to survive first in Sablayan.

Numerous other illustrations of *pandanggo-sa-ilaw* politics can be given, but let us conclude the case studies with an account of the politics of ex-Congressman Felipe Abeleda which, no matter how brief, is bound to highlight the nature of the politics of Occidental Mindoro.

Felipe Abeleda received his Bachelor of Laws degree from the University of the Philippines in 1931.[1] He was first elected Representative of Occidental Mindoro in 1953 and had served in Congress continuously since that time until 1965. In other words, he won the congressional elections three consecutive times — in 1953, in 1957, and in 1961. While he had spectacular successes at the polls, as a legislator he did not have a brilliant or outstanding record.

'Privileged speeches' are means by which legislators can express the problems and needs of their constituents or inform and educate the public about significant issues. The records of the House of Representatives show that 735 such speeches were made in the period 1954–62 (Pareja, 1963a: 18 and 60). However, during this nine-year period, the Congressman had delivered neither any privileged speech nor his maiden address.

The number of times that members of the House of Representatives participated in floor deliberations had been tabulated for the years 1958–61. Congressman Abeleda's name was not found among the first ten under debates, explanations of votes, interpellations, motions, privileged speeches, questions of privilege, speeches for or against bills, and sponsorship speeches on bills. His name only appeared among the first ten under amendments of which he introduced 45 (Pareja, 1963b: 34 and 36).

The Congressman's record falls below average in regard to bills.[2] Of the 29,685 bills introduced from 1954 to 1965, only 171 were sponsored by Congressman Abeleda; and of this number 106 had been introduced in co-operation with other legislators. Of the 65 bills which can be credited to the Congressman exclusively, 42 were constituency bills. They dealt

[1]House of Representatives, *Official Directory: 1958–1961* (Manila, 1958), pp. 237–39.

[2]The data were gathered by Mr. Jose Endriga, Researcher of the Community Development Research Council; Mrs. Rosario Mendoza-Cortes, Instructor in the U.P. Preparatory High School; and Misses Maria Ligaya Abeleda and Julieta L. Pequet, graduate students working for their M.A. Degree at the University of the Philippines from the *Congressional Record* of the House of Representatives.

with franchises to certain individuals (13), changing of names (4), establishing schools (8), creating barrios or municipalities (3), establishing agencies in the province (6), appropriating money for a road (1), changing a provincial road to a national road (2), protecting the *tamaraw*, a rare animal from extinction (1), and miscellaneous bills (4). Abeleda's attendance record in Congress (82.39 per cent for the period 1954–65), however, is good.

Congressman Abeleda was mentioned as one of the ten outstanding Congressmen in 1963 as evaluated by the *Philippines Free Press*. He received this honour primarily for his fairness in dealing with the investigation of a Congressman's alleged misuse of a 'privileged speech' before the House of Representatives. Abeleda at that time was the chairman of the committee charged to investigate the case.

On the basis of the above information, the Congressman's success at the polls is obviously not based on his legislative record. Victory had been achieved due to his ability to grant or withhold patronage, as well as to exploit the personalistic and particularistic needs and orientations of the people. In some municipalities he was a generous road-builder, legal counsellor, recommendation-maker, job-giver, and guardian angel; in others, he could be harsh by refusing to release funds for school buildings and other projects. He had won the loyalty of his sub-leaders and followers by taking care of them whenever needed and extended his family through consanguineal, affinal, and *compadrazgo* relationships. He had multiplied his Party followers through patronage at the Bureau of Public Works and the Emergency Employment Administration. His lieutenants had devised an ingenious system whereby labourers were placed on public works projects on a rotating basis. Numerous persons were thus helped to a job and developed *utang na loob* (debt of gratitude) to Abeleda and the Liberal Party.

Abeleda's strategists also had devised methods of dividing the Nacionalista Party and the immigrant population. Ilocano and Visayan subleaders were recruited and supported as official candidates of the Liberal Party by channelling most of the public works funds their way and by supporting them in their area during the campaign period. Abeleda made extensive use of his consaguineal relatives in other areas; he endorsed their candidacy or asked them to campaign for him.

Aside from these methods, the Congressman won political support through his warm personality. He had a nice smile, a hand-shake for almost everyone, and his house was open to any person who needed his personal services.

In short, all chains were used to bind the voters and minor leaders of Occidental Mindoro to the Congressman's leadership — *utang na loob*, love and friendship, fear of deprivation of desired goods or services, the party system, and consanguineal, affinal, and *compadrazgo* relationships.

What are the factors which shape, affect, and invigorate the *pandanggo-sa-ilaw* politics of Occidental Mindoro? The four most important factors are (1) the motivations of the participants of the political process; (2) the traditional cultural values of the people and the political elite; (3) the wide gap between the political elite and the people; and (4) the infrastructural and governmental characteristics of the province.

With regard to the motivations of the participants in the political process, they vary between the political elite and the counter-elite on the one hand and the people on the other. The political elite and the counter-elite are motivated by power and status; the people, by particularistic desiderata.[1] The problem for all the political participants, therefore, is how to get their respective desiderata. In order that the political elite or the counter-elite can get their power and status, they must maintain themselves in occupation and control of the government or oust those who control the governmental fort so that they can occupy and control it themselves. In order to succeed in this objective, they must get the support of the majority, or in some cases the plurality, of the people. The political elite and the counter-elite know that the people are moved by particularistic desiderata; so, they manipulate the people to support their leadership by providing patronage to the people. The people also know that those who can provide patronage are those occupying and controlling the governmental fort; so the people also attempt to manipulate the political elite and the counter-elite by making use of their votes for leverage. Besides resorting to the techniques of manipulation, the political elite, the counter-elite, and the people also make use of the method of manoeuvre for the occupation of strategic positions. In the case of the political elite and the counter-elite, the strategic position they manoeuvre to occupy is the government because it is the principal source of patronage. As for the people, they seek to manoeuvre to get close or be attached to the political group which can provide patronage or is believed to be powerful enough to win control of the governmental fort.

As regards the traditional cultural values of the people and the political elite, the most significant appear to be organic hierarchy, co-operation and sociability, *utang na loob* (debt of gratitude), familism, pragmatism, and cautionism. The first value prescribes that the society and the polity must be accepted as an organic body of unequal but interdependent parts, each part with assigned roles. The second value prescribes that a person must be co-operative and sociable. The third calls upon a person who had received any favour to recognize his debt of gratitude and reciprocate with loyal support or with return favour. The fourth asks the consanguineal, affinal, and ritual members of the extended family to promote the family interest and to give each other mutual help and support. The fifth prescribes that one must bend with the wind of facts in accordance with

[1]For details and supporting data, on this and the following paragraphs, see the author's book, *The Political Elite and the People*.

common sense. And the sixth urges deliberation and caution in actions regarding new ideas or things.

These values definitely support the pattern of *pandanggo-sa-ilaw* politics. The personalistic or paternalistic orientations in the values of organic hierarchy, co-operation and sociability, *utang na loob*, and familism strengthen the roots of patronage, the means which provides leverage to *pandanggo-sa-ilaw* politics. The value of pragmatism can legitimize the techniques of manipulating people and manoeuvring for occupation of or linkage to strategic political positions in order to advance individualistic or selfish interests, even if such actions will result in the fissiparousness and irresponsibility of political parties, the weakness or paralysis of national or more inclusive efforts, and slow progress of the economy, the polity, and the society. And the value of cautionism discourages the development of modern non-*pandanggo-sa-ilaw* style of politics, such as a politics of discussion or significant popular participation.

Concerning the wide gap between the political elite and the people, this is obvious from the following facts. (1) The people are predominantly young, more than one-half under twenty years; but the political elite tend to be much older, generally in their forties and fifties. (2) The people are almost evenly divided into males and females; but the political elite are almost all males. (3) The people are poorly educated, the main bulk reaching only the elementary grades or getting no schooling at all; but the political elite tend to be well-educated, every one reaching or graduating from college, especially in the case of the Congressman, the Governor, and the Vice-Governor. (4) The people tend not to be members of civic, political, economic, or other social organizations (other than the family); but the political elite tend to be members of organizations. (5) The people are economically poor, as revealed in various indices — radio ownership, dwelling unit, income, occupation, and land-holding. The political elite, on the other hand, tend to be economically independent or prosperous. (6) The people do not occupy and control the strategic positions in the government, but the members of the political elite do.

Because the political elite are very much superior to the people in proportion to their relative numbers in terms of maturity, masculinity, education, power based on organizations, economic resources, and access to government patronage, the former are provided the means or encouraged to manipulate the latter to advance the former's interests. When this is related to the political elite's motivations for power and status, then the sufficient condition for manipulation and manoeuvring is definitely met.

Finally, with regard to the infrastructural and governmental characteristics of the province, these also support its *pandanggo-sa-ilaw* politics.

In Occidental Mindoro, there are hardly any vigorous or significant socio-political infrastructures, such as political parties, interest groups and politics-oriented publics. Likewise, physical infrastructures, such as roads, bridges, wharves, piers, and airports, are inadequate and poorly developed. Considering the poor state of education of the people, we can easily see that these infrastructural conditions of Occidental Mindoro reduce the people into isolated and fragmented numerous communities. The people, therefore, do not constitute a province-wide community, except during province-wide or national elections. Thus, they do not easily become aware of what policies the political elite had or had not formulated and adopted. Mobilization of ideas and people is hampered or even paralysed. Therefore, the political elite can make use of manipulation and manoeuvring without significant countervailing opposition.

At the governmental level, Occidental Mindoro is part of a centralized national political system. The province, like all other provinces, has no taxing authority. Its sources of income or budget credits are various allotments and contributions from the national or municipal governments. Furthermore, most of its significant official actions, such as appointments, financial allocations, purchases, public works, and the like, are made and carried out with active control or supervision of the national government. Thus, the political elite of Occidental Mindoro are vulnerable to and have become victims of the manipulation by the national government. Their appointments are turned down, if they do not comply with various requirements, some legal and others political. Their pork-barrel funds are not released, if certain political considerations are not met. Their requests for budgetary aid are taken care of, but they must pay some kind of *quid pro quo*. And so on. After having been manipulated by national officials and agencies, they learn the techniques of manipulation well. They also learn how to manoeuvre to get better or the best results from the national government. They, in turn, manipulate the national officials, making use of their numerous and significant resources in their political bailiwicks — their big families, their army of clients, their wealth, their leadership of local parties, and the like. When finally, they have to use their powers in the province, they also apply the manipulative and manoeuvring skills which they learned while dealing with national officials upon the people whom they are required by law to serve.

III

Who are the political elite who were recruited from the people to serve Occidental Mindoro? Do they constitute a ruling power elite? What are their accomplishments thus far? What are their failings? From 1952 to 1970, what is the nature of the circulation of the political elite?

Since we have already touched upon the age, sex, educational, associational, and economic attributes of the political elite in the preceding section, insofar as their profile is concerned at this juncture we shall limit our discussion to their affiliation in terms of family, party, and region.[1]

The Congressmen who served Occidental Mindoro from 1951 to 1970 were Jesus Abeleda, Felipe Abeleda, and Pedro Medalla. Their family, party, and regional affiliation, by terms in Congress, is presented in Table 8.

TABLE 8

SOCIO-POLITICAL AFFILIATION OF CONGRESSMEN, BY TERM IN CONGRESS

Congressman	Term	Family	Party	Region
Jesus Abeleda	1952–53	Abeleda	Nacionalista	I
Felipe Abeleda	1954–57	Abeleda	Liberal	I
Felipe Abeleda	1958–61	Abeleda	Liberal	I
Felipe Abeleda	1962–65	Abeleda	Liberal	I
Pedro Medalla	1966–69	Medalla	Nacionalista	II
Pedro Medalla	1970–73	Medalla	Nacionalista	II

With regard to the Governors who served the province during the same period, they were Federico Castillo, Mariano Tajonera, and Arsenio Villaroza. Their family, party, and regional affiliation, by term of office, is presented in Table 9.

[1]Occidental Mindoro may be divided into three regions — Region I, composed of Looc, Lubang, and Paluan; Region II, of Abra de Ilog, Mamburao, and Santa Cruz; and Region III, of Calintaan, Magsaysay, Rizal, Sablayan, and San Jose. Region I is inhabited by early immigrants of the latter part of the nineteenth and the early part of the twentieth centuries, mainly Tagalogs from Cavite and Batangas; Region II, principally by early Ilocano immigrants from Zambales, who came during the latter part of the nineteenth century and the Tagalogs from Region I, Cavite, and Batangas, who arrived in the early part of the twentieth century; and Region III, to some extent by early Visayan immigrants, who came in the latter part of the nineteenth century and the early part of the twentieth century, and principally by very recent immigrants from Luzon and other islands, who came since the 1950s, the bulk of whom are Ilocanos. Each of the three regions also exhibits characteristic physical features — Region I is hilly, with little arable agricultural land; Region III, with big rivers and vast agricultural lands; and Region II, with some big rivers and wide agricultural lands. In terms of homogeneity and heterogeneity, Region I has a homogeneous population, with almost 100 per cent Tagalogs; Region III, a heterogeneous population, composed mainly of Ilocanos, Tagalogs, and Visayans; and Region II, a somewhat heterogeneous population, principally of Tagalogs and Ilocanos.

TABLE 9
SOCIO-POLITICAL AFFILIATION OF GOVERNORS, BY TERM OF OFFICE

Governor	Term	Family	Party	Region
Federico Castillo	1952–55	Abeleda Protege	Nacionalista	III
Mariano Tajonera	1956–59	Abeleda Relative	Nacionalista	I
Arsenio Villaroza	1960–63	Abeleda Relative	Liberal	I
Arsenio Villaroza	1964–67	Abeleda Relative	Liberal	I
Arsenio Villaroza	1968–71	Abeleda Relative	Liberal	I

As regards the Vice-Governors who had served Occidental Mindoro, there are only two thus far — Catalino Punzalan and Felix Gabriel, Sr. Their family, party, and regional affiliation, by term of office, is found in Table 10.

TABLE 10
SOCIO-POLITICAL AFFILIATION OF VICE-GOVERNORS, BY TERM OF OFFICE

Vice-Governor	Term	Family	Party	Region
Catalino Punzalan	1960–63	Abeleda Leader	Liberal	III
Felix Gabriel, Sr.	1964–67	Abeleda Leader	Liberal	III
Felix Gabriel, Sr.	1968–71	Abeleda Leader	Liberal	III

Finally, concerning members of the Provincial Board, the following persons had served the province from 1952 to 1970: Emilio Villamar, Agaton Cosuco, Cosme Tria, Francisco Liboro, Potenciano Abeleda, Loreta Urieta, and Julia Ovalles. Their family, party, and regional affiliation, by term of office, is shown in Table 11.

TABLE 11

SOCIO-POLITICAL AFFILIATION OF MEMBERS OF THE PROVINCIAL BOARD,
BY TERM OF OFFICE

Board Member	Term	Family	Party	Region
Emilio Villamar	1952–55	Villamar	Nacionalista	I & III
Agaton Cosuco	1952–55	Affinal Abeleda	Liberal	II
Francisco Liboro	1956–59	Liboro	Nacionalista	I & II
Cosme Tria	1956–59	Tria	Nacionalista	I & III
Potenciano Abeleda	1960–63	Abeleda	Liberal	I
Loreto Urieta	1960–63	Urieta	Liberal	III
Emilio Villamar	1964–67	Villamar	Liberal	I & III
Francisco Liboro	1964–67	Liboro	Nacionalista	I & II
Julia Ovalles	1968–71	Ovalles	Nacionalista	III
Emilio Villamar	1968–71	Villamar	Nacionalista (Independent)	I & III

From the data presented in the tables in this section, what generalizations can we make as regards the circulation of the political elite from
1952 to 1970?

First, regarding their family-affiliation circulation, insofar as the
principal members of the political elite are concerned — the Congressman
and the Governor — there has been hardly a circulation, for the offices of
the Congressman and the Governor have been dominated by the Abeledas.
The Abeledas constitute the biggest family in Occidental Mindoro, with
numerous members in practically all towns of the province. It is also a
historic family, for it produced the general of the revolutionary forces of
Mindoro in the latter part of the Philippine Revolution, a governor of
Mindoro in 1919–1926, one of the two delegates to the Philippine Constitutional Convention in 1934–5, and the first Congressman of Occidental
Mindoro, elected in 1951. However, in 1965, a non-Abeleda had crashed
into this Abeleda-dominated domain with the election of Medalla as

Congressman. Considering that the governorship and the vice-governorship have been continuously occupied by relatives, proteges, or leaders of the Abeledas, we will have to reiterate our first generalization.

Second, Region I is the favoured recruiting ground for the principal political elites, although Region II and Region III indicate that in the future either region has a very good chance of becoming the recruiting ground for such officials. In any case, one Congressman and some members of the Provincial Board already had been recruited from Region II; and Region III has been the consistent recruiting place for vice-governors. Region III also had produced one governor and several members of the Provincial Board.

Third, circulation of the political elite in terms of party affiliation has tended to be a regular occurrence.

At this point, we may now consider whether the members of the political elite constitute a ruling power elite. The case studies presented in the preceding section and the data in this section show that they do.

First, they are a well-knit, homogeneous, and united power group primarily for the following facts: (1) they are few; (2) they are professional politicians; (3) the principal members are recruited from the same family; (4) the sub-leadership is co-opted by the principal members of the political elite; and (5) they are recruited from the same socio-economic stratum.[1]

Second, their weight of power, their domain of power, and the scope of their power are significantly heavy, or broad, or wide. In any case, they are indeed powerful. They can transfer the capitol site to any place they want to, usually to lands of their party colleagues or friends. They can cause the appointment, as well as removal, of local judges and other national officials assigned in the province. They can succeed in transferring national civil service officials from the province to another place. They head the local political party, and they co-opt its sub-leaders. They can extend various kinds of service — legal, medical, baptismal, funeral, etc. — to political supporters. They can use the people's money as allowances, to be spent for travel, confidential agents, and others. They designate the men who make recommendations at the Bureau of Public Works and the Bureau of Public Highways. They cause the release or freezing of the funds appropriated for public works and the public highways. They are the social VIP's and political notables in the municipalities and the province. They assist in crowning *fiesta* queens, and they usually are met by public officials and numerous private individuals at the airport when they arrive from Manila. They pass particularistic resolutions or public acts; they neglect many of their official duties; and still usually they can get away with their poor public performance.

Regarding this last point, the legislative record of ex-Congressman Felipe Abeleda from 1954 to 1965 may be considered as partial evidence.

[1] If municipal and barrio political elites are included in the analysis, a qualified form of ruling powder elite is found (Agpalo, 1972, p.165).

The poor public performance of the Governors and the members of the Provincial Board from 1952 to 1970 as regards the most important problems of the province provide also further substantiation.

Consider, for instance, how the provincial political elite tackled the basic problems of the province as identified by the first elected Governor in 1953. According to this official, the basic problems of the province were the construction of a Capitol, the establishment of a public high school, the building of a provincial hospital, the construction of a provincial road system, electioneering appointive national officials, local autonomy, and lack of civic consciousness of the people (Castillo, 1953). As shown in the case study on the provincial capitol site, it was like a football which was kicked around by each provincial administration. It was not until 1965 that the building was finally completed. With regard to the provincial high school, it was not built until 1965 also. The provincial hospital was built a little faster, but it did not start operation until 1963. As for the roads, up to 1971 the province-wide road system is incomplete. Concerning electioneering national officials, the provincial political elite abet in their electioneering activities by asking them to join the election campaign actively, threatening them of being transferred to another place if they did not campaign. With regard to local autonomy, the political elite nip its growth by adopting mendicant resolutions addressed to national officials or agencies. And concerning the lack of civic consciousness of citizens, the members of the political elite have not been imaginative or resourceful enough to devise effective and institutionalized ways and means to awaken the bulk of the people from their political and civic apathy.

IV

Considering that *pandanggo-sa-ilaw* politics is regnant in the province, that there is hardly any significant circulation of the principal political elite, and that the political elite are not vigorously active or simply conscientious in carrying on their official functions, shall we then conclude that Occidental Mindoro has not been awakened by modernization from her deep slumber in traditional lifeways?

The impression that modernization, especially political modernization, has not made any significant advance in Occidental Mindoro is the result of a structural analysis of a short period — 1950–1970 — without considering developments in various aspects of society and the dynamic trends in the province. These developments are examined in this section.

Starting with the intellectual aspect of modernization, the literacy percentage of the province in 1903 was only 18.3 per cent (Census, 1903, Vol.

II: 529, 621). In 1960 this was raised to 76.9 per cent (Census, 1960). Considering that several countries of Africa, Asia, and Latin America had literacy rates below 40 per cent during roughly the same period (Russett *et al.*, 1964: 223–4) — for instance, Nicaragua, 38.4 per cent; Bolivia, 32.1 per cent; Ghana, 22.5 per cent; Egypt, 19.9 per cent; India, 19.3 per cent; Indonesia, 17.5 per cent; Pakistan, 13 per cent; Nigeria, 10 per cent; Afghanistan, 2.5 per cent; Ethiopia, 2.5 per cent — we must conclude that Occidental Mindoro had been modernized quite significantly at the intellectual level by 1960.

Besides, high schools increased significantly after World War II. Before the war there was only one high school in the province — the Stella Maris School at Lubang founded in 1923. Between 1945 and 1965 seven high schools, one of them public, were established in Occidental Mindoro.[1] By the school year 1970–71, eleven other public high schools also had been opened.[2]

Furthermore, the transportation and communications system in the province improved significantly after the war, especially after 1950. As late as 1951–2, there were only 52.60 kilometres of national roads in the entire province. By 1961–2, these were lengthened to 161.41 kilometres, and by 1970–1, to 275.39 kilometres.[3] Mamburao, San Jose, and Lubang were connected to Manila by air through the Philippine Air Lines and Filipinas Orient Airways; and the shipping lines connecting Lubang (at Tilik) and San Jose (at Caminawit) to Manila were further developed. Abra de Ilog, Santa Cruz, and Paluan by 1965 were connected to Mamburao by macadamized road; and Looc was connected to Lubang by the same type of road. Although only 5 per cent of the people had radios in 1960, radio ownership increased extensively with the transistorized radio revolution during the latter half of the 1960s.

At the demographic level, the health of the people improved due to better educational attainment of the people and the services provided by increasing numbers of municipal doctors and rural health units. A provincial hospital was established in Mamburao in 1963, and puericulture

[1] These were West Mindoro Academy, 1945; Paluan Academy, 1947; Divine Word College (High School Department), 1951; St. Joseph's School, 1951; Holy Family Academy, 1957; San Sebastian Academy, 1957; and Occidental Mindoro High School (the provincial public high school), 1965.

[2] These were San Jose National High School, Magsaysay Municipal High School, Calintaan Municipal High School, San Jose North High School, Buenavista Barrio High School, Barahan Barrio High School, Sta. Cruz Municipal High School, Looc Municipal High School, Tilik Barrio High School, Cabra Barrio High School, and Iling Barrio High School.

[3] The data were provided by the Office of the District Engineer, Mamburao, Occidental Mindoro.

centres were established in all towns. By 1970, even family planning centres were established at Mamburao and San Jose. As transportation improved, greater and greater numbers of people migrated to Occidental Mindoro; and within Occidental Mindoro, from one town to another. Three towns — Mamburao, Sablayan, and San Jose — owing to the influx of numerous immigrants, rapidly became more urbanized, as indicated by their relatively low percentage of farm population in 1960 — Mamburao, 37.7 per cent; San Jose, 50.5 per cent; and Sablayan, 54.6 per cent (Census, 1960). In fact, one barrio of Sablayan and two barrios in San Jose had grown so tremendously in population that they were created as new municipalities in 1966 and 1969.

At the social level, there was some development too. Most of the towns, which did not have priests before the war, were assigned permanent priests. Thereafter, religious organizations were established by the priests in their respective parishes. Mamburao, San Jose, and Sablayan organized tennis and basketball clubs, and in all towns Parent-Teachers Associations were likewise organized. In San Jose, a Rotary Club was also established, and labour unions mobilized more and more members at San Jose and Lubang. However, province-wide economic interest groups or promotional groups did not develop. But in Mamburao, a local chapter of the national Philippine Government Employees Association was established in 1964.

Considering the advances made in literacy, the establishment of high schools, the progress in the transportation and communications system, the influx of various and ambitious immigrants from Luzon and the Visayas, and the establishment of various local associations, one can infer that there were a significant number of people in Occidental Mindoro who believed in the desirability of change by 1970. In any case, when the election of delegates to the constitutional convention was held in November 1971, there were as many as nineteen persons who filed their candidacies. The province was entitled to two seats in the convention. The candidates came from all regions of the province. Everyone of them called for far-reaching reforms not only of the existing form of government but also of the social and cultural values and the economic institutions of the nation. In other words, at the psychological level, there was advance, too, in modernization.

At the economic level, significant progress in modernization was also made. The largest salt industry in the Philippines was established at San Jose. Several new businesses, such as rural banks, electric plants, restaurants, lodging houses, tricycle and jeep transportation business, piggeries, and the like, were established in San Jose and Mamburao. In San Jose movie houses were also installed. Public markets and more retail stores were established in all towns. As the economy progressed, Occidental

Mindoro moved up from the lowest class of province — seventh class — in 1951 to third class in 1969.[1]

Finally, at the political level modernization also advanced significantly. Structural differentiation has occurred continuously since 1950 as the province was compelled progressively by demographic, legal, and other forces to render various services to the people. At the barrio level, the most important structures which had emerged were the barrio council, the barrio captain, and various local units of national agencies, such as the Presidential Assistant on Community Development. At the municipal level, some of the most important structures which appeared were municipal party chapters, government employees' association, constabulary units, and the like. At the provincial level, various governmental agencies dealing with law-enforcement, collection of taxes, assessment of property, elections, education, public works and public highways, and the like, also emerged. Rationalization of authority, as expressed in centralization and integration of the province to the national government, likewise developed, for the local or provincial officials or units of national agencies or offices geared the province to the national governmental machinery as they carried out their various functions in Occidental Mindoro. The provincial political elite likewise articulated the province to the national government.

With regard to popular participation in public affairs, significant progress in this aspect was effected primarily through periodic elections and the work of political parties. From 1950 to 1970 eleven elections had been held regularly in Occidental Mindoro. Two of these elections were special; one was held to elect the first officials of the province in 1951 and the second in 1970 to elect the two delegates of Occidental Mindoro to the 1971 constitutional convention. In these elections great numbers of people were mobilized to participate in public affairs, and these are plain upon examination of Table 12, showing the numbers of registered voters, as well as registered voters who actually voted, in the elections from 1951 to 1965. It is also interesting to note that the average voting percentage

[1]The information was provided by the Office of the Provincial Treasurer, Mamburao Occidental Mindoro. Provinces are classified by income, in accordance with the following schedule:

Classification of Provinces by Average Annual Income*

Class	Average Annual Income	
1st	1,500,000 and above	
2nd	1,000,000 but less than	1,500,000
3rd	700,000 but less than	1,000,000
4th	500,000 but less than	700,000
5th	300,000 but less than	500,000
6th	150,000 but less than	300,000
7th	less than P150,000	

*Average annual income for the last five years. A reclassification of localities may be ordered by the President every year, but a longer period usually elapses before this is done. Source: Ocampo, 1966: 129.

during this period was 81.92 per cent, indicating high voting turnout. Furthermore, it must be noted that the electors of Occidental Mindoro during this period constituted nearly all of the adult population of the province. Considering that only about 1.5 per cent of the people participated in the elections of 1907,[1] the state of political participation and mobilization in Occidental Mindoro in the 1950s and the 1960s was indeed impressive.

TABLE 12

THE VOTERS OF OCCIDENTAL MINDORO, 1951–1965

Election Year	Registered Voters	Voters Who Actually Voted	Percentage of Voting
1951	14,351	13,623	94.92
1953	17,458	14,774	84.62
1955	21,228	17,327	81.62
1957	23,408	18,269	78.04
1959	29,378	23,996	81.67
1961	31,406	23,977	76.35
1963	36,684	29,460	80.31
1965	38,707	30,124	77.83

Source: Commission on Elections. *Reports to the President and the Congress,* 1951, 1953, 1955, 1957, 1959, 1961, 1963 and 1965.

At this juncture, we may now look at modernization in Occidental. Mindoro, with special emphasis on political modernization, by considering the dynamic political trends in the province. By examining and evaluating these trends, we shall not only make up for the deficiency which resulted from the static, structural analysis of Occidental Mindoro in Section II and the short-period, time-series analysis in Section III but also be able to make a reasoned estimate of the prospects of the political modernization of the province.

Five significant political trends are now sufficiently clear in Occidental Mindoro. First, a new social force embodied in Big Money based on commerce and industry is arising in the province, challenging the traditional social force embodied in Big Family based on agriculture or historic name. Second, relatively large and old immigrant families in various towns of the province are now flexing their political biceps, seeking more participation in provincial politics. Third, barrio power is awakening, seeking

[1]This percentage was the figure for the voting turnout of the voters of Mindoro in 1907, but it is assumed that what held true for the whole province of Mindoro must also be the same for the western part of the province, which became Occidental Mindoro in 1950. See Macario Z. Landicho, *The Mindoro Yearbook* (Manila: Yearbook Publishers, 1952), p. 72.

to have more participation in public affairs. Fourth, the *tao*, the common man, is becoming more prepared for political mobilization and participation. And fifth, the political formula of liberal democracy is continuously becoming more legitimized in the province.

The first political trend started with the coming of vigorous and ambitious immigrants to Occidental Mindoro after the province was born in 1950. Joining the massive waves of immigrant farmers, several extremely wealthy and modernization-oriented businessmen came to establish new businesses or industries. Among these were Francisco Gomez, a colonel in the Philippine Army, with a college degree in agriculture from the University of the Philippines, who came to San Jose in 1951, serving as vice-president of the Philippine Milling Company in that town; Jose Maxino, a major in the Philippine Army, former Deputy Chief of Police of Manila in 1949–1952, who migrated to San Jose in 1955, becoming the manager of the Mina de Oro Rural Bank; Ricardo Quintos, son of a Manila businesswoman and a Judge Advocate General of the Armed Forces of the Philippines, studying veterinary science at the University of the Philippines and later commerce at San Beda, who came to Mamburao in 1959, buying an *hacienda*, operating an electric plant, and establishing a modern, high-finance-type of poultry and livestock industry; and Pedro Medalla, a lieutenant-colonel in the Philippine Army, with degrees in business administration and law, who came to Mamburao in the latter 1950s, buying agricultural lands and establishing a rural bank.

These new men soon entered the political ring. Gomez ran for the congressional seat in 1957 and Maxino for the same office in 1961 against Felipe Abeleda. Both were defeated. Quintos ran for the gubernatorial post in 1967 against Arsenio Villaroza. He, too, was defeated. But it was significant that they ran for the positions of the political elite. Medalla ran for the gubernatorial position against Arsenio Villaroza in 1963; and he was, likewise, defeated. However, when he ran against Felipe Abeleda for the congressional post in 1965, Medalla won. Medalla was also re-elected in 1969. Quintos also ran for a post in the constitutional convention in 1970, and this time he won. The victories of Medalla in 1965 and 1969, and of Quintos in 1970 definitely established the trend of Big Money replacing Big Family. However, the social force of Big Family is still very vigorous.

The second political trend is partially reflected in Table 11, listing the names of successful members of the Provincial Board. Included in that list are Cosuco, Urieta, and Villamar. They came from old immigrant and relatively large families. This trend, however, is better reflected in the attempts by several people similar to the Cosucos, the Urietas, and the Villamars in circumstances to participate in provincial politics either as becoming candidates for provincial seats, or acting as campaign managers or civic leaders. These persons are now flexing their political biceps because after three or four generations in the province since the arrival of their pioneering ancestors, several have climbed the ladder of social mobility from the socio-economic stratum of the *tao* to the middle stratum; or from the middle stratum to the rich. Their principal vehicle of social mobility is the school.

The third trend — barrio power is awakening, seeking to have more participation in public affairs — started with the Magsaysay Administration (1954–1957). During Magsaysay's term of office, the barrio was invigorated through the establishment of the Presidential Assistant on Community Development and the enactment of R.A. No. 1408, providing for the election of barrio councils.[1] In subsequent administrations this law was improved and strengthened by the passage of other barrio autonomy laws, particularly R.A. No. 3509, otherwise known as 'The Revised Barrio Charter'.[2] Awakened barrio power, however, is also given more life by the establishment of barrio schools, the construction of more roads, especially barrio feeder roads, among others we have already discussed earlier in connexion with the modernization of Occidental Mindoro.

The fourth trend — the rise of the *tao* — subsumes the third trend. Its beginning may be traced to the Philippine Revolution of 1896–1901 when the *tao* assumed a significant political role by attempting to re-structure the existing political system through the arbitrament of arms. When the Revolution collapsed, the *tao* continued to become vigorous as the laws, during the American regime, the Commonwealth period, and the Republic, provided for the popular election of more and more public officials and the enfranchisement of greater and greater numbers of people. The rise of percentage of voters from 1.5 per cent in 1907 to almost 100 per cent of the adult population by the 1960s is merely one of the indices of the rise of the *tao*. Another index, of course, is the rise of literacy from 18.3 per cent in 1903 to 76.9 per cent in 1960. No doubt the schools have played a very significant role in the rise of the common man in Occidental Mindoro.

The last significant political trend — the growing legitimation of the political formula of liberal democracy — has roots in the Reform Movement and the Philippine Revolution of the latter part of the nineteenth century. The germinal seed of this political formula was the belief-system developed by the men of ideas — the cultural elites — of the Reform Movement, especially Jose Rizal, Marcelo H. del Pilar, and Graciano Lopez Jaena, and crystallized in the Malolos Constitution of 1899 and the political ideas of Apolinario Mabini.[3] The principal elements of this

[1] This law was approved on 9 September, 1955. Its full text is found in *Philippine Law Journal*, XXX (September, 1955), pp. 632–4.

[2] R.A. No. 3509 was approved on 22 June 1963. Its full text is found in Jose N. Nolledo, *The Constitution of the Philippines Annotated* (Manila: National Book Store, 1966), Appendix G. pp. 115–30.

[3] For a full analysis, see Cesar A. Majul, *The Political and Constitutional Ideas of the Philippine Revolution* (Quezon City: University of the Philippines Press, 1967). For an analysis of Jose Rizal's contribution, see Remigio E. Agpalo, 'Jose Rizal: Filipino National Hero and His Ideas of Political Modernization', *Solidarity*, IV (December 1969), pp. 1–14.

political formula are (1) a republican system of government; (2) a system of government limited by a bill of rights and designed to promote individual freedoms and social justice; (3) a system of government based on separation of powers of the executive, the legislature and the judiciary; and (4) a system of government based on the principle of separation of Church and State. This political formula was reinforced and provided with viable institutional foundations and structures by the McKinley's Instructions of 1900, the Philippine Bill of 1902, the Jones Law of 1916, and the Philippine Constitution of 1935. Through legislative elaboration, executive implementation and amplification, judicial interpretation, public education, and the participation of the people in its political processes since 1900, it has become more legitimized in the Philippines.

In Occidental Mindoro, this political formula has become more legitimized as a result of governmental and popular participation in the political institutions it established and the political processes it provided. The elections, public education, and governmental service are the three most important agencies of its legitimization.

Considering these significant political trends, what can we say, then, regarding the prospects of the political elite and the future of *pandanggo-sa-ilaw* politics of Occidental Mindoro?

The pattern of recruiting the principal members of the political elite from big historic families and Region I will definitely be broken. The most probable and logical challengers of the big historic families and Region I during the initial phase of the circulation of the political elite will be the new immigrant big businessmen, as well as elites of old and relatively large families, although the new immigrant big businessmen will have a better fighting chance. The challengers will attempt to gain control of the positions of the political elite by mobilizing support mainly from the rapidly increasing population of Region II and Region III. The election of Medalla in 1965 and 1969 as Congressman and Quintos in 1970 as delegate to the constitutional convention, in fact, is the first significant indication of the circulation of the political elite from Big Family to Big Money.

During the first phase of the circulation of the political elite from Big Family to Big Money, initially the *pandanggo-sa-ilaw* politics of the province will remain entrenched. The challengers will exploit the political culture of the people based on particularistic and personalistic values to gain control of the government fort; and after they have won, they will continue exploiting the same political culture to maintain themselves in power. But, because the elites based on Big Money are also 'new men' oriented towards modernization, eventually during the latter part of this phase, when the province has already been modernized, one may expect that the *pandanggo-sa-ilaw* politics of Occidental Mindoro will have weakened or even expired. The principal reason for this is the fact that modernization will usher in universalistic values which will emasculate or even destroy the particularistic and personalistic values giving life to *pandanggo-sa-ilaw* politics.

The next phase of circulation of the political elite could be characterized by ideological political elites, bringing about a politics of ideology. The ideology that might emerge may be fanatical socialism, utopian or otherwise; or communism or fascism; or some type of messianic ideology. This type of politics could naturally develop in Occidental Mindoro, if, after the province has undergone modernization in the various sectors of society, the gap between the people and the plutocratic political elite remains extremely wide.

Assuming that a politics of ideology does not develop after the triumph of modernization in various sectors of society, while the gap between the people and the plutocratic political elite remains wide, one may expect a politics of violence to replace the politics of the political elite based on Big Money. There will be riots, rebellions, and widespread criminality.

The politics of ideology and the politics of violence are not necessarily unrelated. The former may result in the latter, and vice versa. In a political system where the regnant spirit is ideology, the political actors struggling for political power, who are armed with closed and intransigent belief-systems, regard each other as enemies, for each one regards his group as right and good and the others not belonging to his group as wrong and evil. This condition of enmity, therefore, leads to a politics of violence. On the other hand, in a political system characterized by violence, even if at first ideologies have not developed, eventually the belief-systems of the conflicting political actors become transformed into ideologies. Thus the politics of violence can develop into a politics of ideology.

The politics of ideology or the politics of violence, however, is not likely to follow the politics of political elites based on Big Money. More probable to follow this phase is the full flowering and fruition of democratic politics, where the political elite are sprung from the people from any town, region, family, or any sector of the province, as long as they are well-qualified and meritorious to serve as political elite; the political elite are responsive and responsible to the people; and the people are able to control the political elite. This type of politics is based on Big Numbers of people. This kind of politics is more likely to follow the politics of the political elite based on Big Money because it is the system which is being ushered in by the remaining political trends of the politics of the province — awakening barrio power, rise of the *tao*, and legitimization of the political formula of liberal democracy. This type of politics is also a more probable development because the political culture of the province based on organic hierarchy, co-operation and sociability, *utang na loob*, familism, pragmatism, and cautionism, as it clashes with the forces of modernization, makes the politics of democracy the natural and logical resultant of the earlier phase of political change. In other words, mature democratic politics is the synthesis of the peculiar blend of Occidental

Mindoro traditional political culture and the particular constellation of the province's modern political trends.

'The sleep has lasted for centuries, but one day the thunderbolt struck, and in striking infused life' (Rizal, 1912: 393). These eloquent words, first published in 1887 and written by Rizal about his countrymen and the 1872 execution of Mariano Gomez, Jose Burgos, and Jacinto Zamora, were originally applied to the political apathy of Filipinos and the political force or event which jolted them from their political slumber in the latter part of the nineteenth century. Today, they apply to the *pandanggo-sa-ilaw* politics and domination of political life by a big historic family and Region I of Occidental Mindoro. For in the province today, there are several thunderbolts striking and infusing new life in the poverty-stricken, politically emasculated, and poorly educated people, preparing them for modern politics and mature democracy.

PART II
Economic Development and Modernization

4 The Late Development Effect
RONALD P. DORE

I

No-ONE nowadays would lightly admit to believing in any unilineal theory
of social and economic evolution. And yet people are still moved to write
whole books denouncing the abuse of the 'metaphor of developmentalism
with its hoary concepts and premises of immanence, continuity, direction-
ality, necessity and uniformitarianism,' (Nisbet, 1969: 303). Preachers at
least deserve the benefit of the assumption that the sins they inveigh against
are reasonably tempting sins. And it is true, I think, that the simplicity
and attractiveness of the unilineal assumption is such that, despite our
intellectual convictions, we all too easily slip into it.

After all, some of the changes associated with the transformation of the
world's societies in the last two or three centuries *are* unilineal and in some
sense universal. *All* societies which move from a state in which 75 per cent
of the population are farmers to a state in which 10 per cent are farmers
pass through a point in time when precisely 42 per cent — or for that
matter 42.7 per cent — of the population are farmers. There are enough
of these single-scale parametric changes associated with growth —
urbanization, *per capita* consumption of energy or newsprint, capital/
labour ratios, primary school enrolments, patient/doctor ratios and so on
— to cause to spring for ever in the development student's heart the
eternal hope that somehow (a) all these quantifiable indicators can be
made to correlate, and (b) all the non-parametric dimensions of change —
in the technology in which capital is embodied, in the quality of medical
care or primary education, in the structure of politics and class relations —
can somehow be brought into relation with them to produce a roughly
coherent picture of the processes by which, and the stages through which,
societies — *all* societies — develop.

It would indeed be nice if one could put history into such neat order.
One would then be able to say: Ghana's scores on development indicators

a, b, c, d, ... n are such and such: this puts her, according to our scientifi-
cally established integrated scoring system, roughly where England stood
in 1890. Consequently one can expect that in the next ten years ... — and
we could read off our predictions from the history books. 'The industrially
more developed country shows the less developed only the image of its
own future.'

Of course it is absurd. It has steadily proved more absurd as the history
of the last century has unfolded. As Trotsky pointed out, qualifying the
dictum of Marx just quoted, 'England in her day revealed the future of
France, considerably less of Germany, but not in the least of Russia and
not of India' (Trotsky, 1932, vol. 3: 369).

In a sense, though, Trotsky tried to rescue the theory. The law of
combined development by which he sought to resolve the paradox that the
socialist revolution came to the most backward European capitalist state,
recognizes the uniqueness of each country's historical situation. But the
uniqueness consists in different temporal combinations of events which are
themselves part of an ordained sequence in different sectors of society —
the combination in the Russia of 1917, for example, of 'a peasant war —
that is a movement characteristic of the dawn of bourgeois development —
and a proletarian insurrection, the movement signalising its decline'
(Trotsky, 1932, vol. 1: 70).

There is a second way of preserving the essence of the unilineal theory,
best summed up in the Buddhist phrase about people reaching the mountain top by different paths, but all seeing the same moon when they get
there. In this category come all the theories that derive their origin from
Henry Maine and Toennies, and more particularly from Weber's ideas about
the growth of rationality as the factor common to capitalism, bureaucracy
and the other changes in society commonly subsumed under the term 'modernization'. A quite sophisticated modern example of the 'many roads to
modernity' thesis is the book by four American authors, *Industrialism and
Industrial Man* (Kerr, Dunlop, Harbinson and Myers, 1962). They boldly
specify five different kinds of paths that can lead to the modern industrial
state, classified according to the pattern of leadership — the dynastic elite,
the middle class, the revolutionary intellectual, and so on. But the end
point is still the same kind of society, and the different roads are all detours,
some a little to the west-nor'-west, some veering a little south, in the same
westerly direction — away from poverty and towards affluence, away from
industrial conflict towards a web of rule, away from group orientation
towards individualism and legal contract, away from diffuseness of social
roles towards contractual specificity, away from arbitrary authority
towards bureaucracy, and so on.

I don't believe it. In the very long run, the convergence theory may be
true. In the long run, technology may make morons, and the same kind
of morons, of us all. But not for a long time yet. (And even then more
probably as a result of conquest or cultural diffusion than from any work-

ing out of the law that superstructures are determined by infrastructures). My reasons for thinking so are intimately connected with the fact that one cannot read off reasonable predictions about the next ten years in Venezuela or India, say, by looking at what happened in America or Japan in the 1870s or the 1920s.

I am led to these reflections by the fact that I have spent the best part of my life studying the history of Japan over the last century. Everybody knows that the Japanese are different; that Japanese industrial society has features found in no other industrial society. (And, ironically enough for the assumptions of technological determinism underlying the convergence thesis, one could make out a good argument for the case that Japan is *more* different in the social organization of industry — at the epicentre of the shock waves that technological changes send through society — than in the social organization of politics.) But why is Japan different? The most common answer is that the cultural base was different. That is to say that the present difference between Japan and, say, England, is simply a modified form of the difference between Japan in 1800 and England in 1800.

This is part of, but not necessarily the whole answer. These differences are also due to the fact that (to use Kuznets' concept and the necessarily arbitrary dates which Kuznets (1966: 64–65) takes as cutting points) the modern economic growth which got Britain to a level of $1,500 *per capita* income by 1969 started around 1780, while the modern economic growth which got Japan to a level of $1,350 *per capita* in that year started around 1880. My propositions are three-fold:

1. The constraints operating in late-starting development are sufficiently different from those operating on the early developers of Europe and North America for the character of the development process to be greatly altered.

2. That these differences in the process persist in differences in the structure of society well on into very advanced stages of industrialization.

3. That the 'late development effect' is in some respects systematic; i.e. it is possible to suggest generalizations of the form: 'the later the start of the late-starting developer, the more likely it is that....'

II

The main purpose of this chapter is to illustrate the third proposition, but it might be worthwhile to prolong this introduction in order to elaborate the first proposition by briefly listing some of the many ways in which the constraints on the late-starter are different from the constraints on the early starters. Some of these differences are such as to facilitate the *rate* of growth, some are such as to retard it. They are all such as to alter its pattern.

1. First, there is the vast difference in economic opportunities. The world no longer contains many cottage industries to be displaced by the cheap textiles and consumer goods of pioneer industrializers. When the early starters were starting it was they who dominated the world financial and trading system, such as it was. The late-starters have to operate under the domination of those who started earlier. The late-starters cannot seize and exploit colonies. Many of them have had to build a base for economic growth on the export of primary products, and structure their economies accordingly. And so on.

Those who speak of underdevelopment as being 'created' by the developed countries and deny any possibilities even of national autonomy to the less developed countries, as subordinate units in an integrated international system of domination,[1] are mistaken in seeing this as the *only* relevant aspect of late development. But it is certainly an important one.

2. Secondly, there is the technological gap; the later the start, the more sophisticated the technology available for manufacturing or the modernization of agriculture. This has enormous advantages. It is much better *not* to have to invent the steam engine all over again, nor to have to repeat the whole process of trial and error which led from Indian corn to the hybrid maize of Iowa. On the other hand, as we all know nowadays, the blessing is mixed. The latest techniques are not always the most appropriate given relative factor endowments, or given policy needs to maximize employment. The more sophisticated the technology, the more the developing countries are at the mercy of those in the rich countries who control it, and that control may be exercised to the detriment of the economic welfare of most or even of all groups of the poor country's population, as well as constraining their independence and affronting their self-respect.

3. 'Self-respect' suggests an important aspect of another bundle of differences — those which spring from the fact that the early starters 'modernized' (intransitive verb) and late starters 'are modernized' — a 'transitive' process implying deliberate intent. In the early starters the economy changed and politics were dragged along — suffrages were gradually extended, monarchies and aristocracies were gradually cut down to size. From this historical experience Marx could generalize about the infrastructure determining the superstructure. But for late-starters, and not only in Mao's China, 'politics are in command'. Britain had no model of modernity to emulate: late-starters do, and the political will to catch up, to raise the nation's status in the international pecking order of nations, contributes a good deal of the driving force of development. Some of the advantages of this are clear. In Gerschenkron's (1962) illustration of the late development effect, comparing Britain, France, Germany and Russia

[1]See, e.g. Frank, 1967 on Latin America.

in the nineteenth century, the later the start was made, the more centralized and generally the more efficient became the modes of investment in industry — from joint stock companies to investment banks, to the state.

Again, there are attendant disadvantages over and above those disadvantages which attend centralization of decision-making in any country, rich or poor — the fact that mistakes tend to be big mistakes, for example. To start with, when the will to develop stems from the political will to raise the nation's status in the world community, there are constant temptations to wasteful short-cuts — expenditure on glittering airports, on armies, on white-elephant steel mills, or on capturing the leadership of organizations of African or Asian unity. Secondly, when the process of development involves conscious imitation of foreign models, the need to compensate for the demeaning status of pupil by finding some source of national pride can take some pretty counter-productive turns — witness the 'Japanism' of Japan in the 1930s, or the ideology of Jan Sangh (Matossian, 1958).

4. The fourth respect in which the constraints on the late-developer differ from those on the early developer concerns, as distinct from the 'technological gap', what one might call the different socio-technical mix — something akin to what Trotsky had in mind when he spoke of uneven or combined development. Certain advanced technologies, being relatively cheap, find widespread use at very low levels of *per capita* income in late-starters, whereas they were unknown in the early careers of the early starters. Medical and communications techniques are obvious examples. Again, the blessings are mixed. Levels of ill-health and work-capacity *need* not be as low in, say, modern Algeria as they were in early nineteenth century Britain, and probably are not. On the other hand, the fall in death rates produces the population problem. So, too, with communications. Cheaper internal communications aid economic growth. But cheaper international tele-communications and air travel also affect the multi-national corporation. The same processes as have altered diplomacy and turned ambassadors into messenger boys and spade-workers for flying foreign ministers have altered the role of the foreign subsidiary. The British-owned railway in the nineteenth-century Argentine was a part of the Argentine economy with all but major strategic decisions being taken in the Argentine, even though some of the decision-takers were resident aliens. IBM Buenos Aires in 1970 may have few Americans in its management, but still remains under day-to-day control from New York. New means of communications also alter political patterns by increasing the mobilization power both of government and its opponents. Marx once pointed out that without the railways there would have been no development of a working class movement, and probably not even a working class consciousness. It is doubtful if even Mao could have unified China without the radio, and certain that Cuba's style of communism would have been rather different without television.

5. Some things move across frontiers even more quickly than cheap technologies — ideas, expectations, aspirations. The demonstration effect is well-known. Those who see economic growth as coming primarily from individual strivings for higher consumption levels would take it to be a good thing.[1] Those who see it as the mechanism whereby the traditionally assumed connexion between profits and savings is destroyed, import composition patterns are distorted towards emphasis on luxury consumption goods, and income distribution made more unequal, may have doubts. And, of course, it is not only ideas about the appropriate living standards of respectable middle-class persons which are diffused from the rich to the poor countries. The latter also take over the latest conventional wisdom of the developing countries concerning the ends of life and the aims of economic policy. The concern for the environment — the new form of self-indulgence of the rich-country middle-classes — already finds echoes in the poorer countries. When Professor Galbraith says that growth doesn't matter we can nod agreement, but when the same doctrines take hold among the politicians and planners of the poor countries, comfortably enjoying salaries twenty or thirty times their country's *per capita* income, it is altogether a different matter. It is possible to argue in America that the plight of the poor could immediately be solved by redistribution. In India it is not. And it is a bold, or a thoughtless, man who would argue it even in England.[2]

Among the most pervasive and rapidly diffused ideas are political ideas — ideas about the rights of man or about the proper role of the state. Japan — or at least Japanese political leaders — was 'lucky' to start economic growth at a time when the state was still generally seen in the rest of the world as at best a night-watchman mechanism for regulating the market, if not as a transcendent Hegelian object of loyalty which had an unreciprocated right to exact sacrifices from its citizens. Today, the notion developed in the rich countries that a major function of the state is to guarantee a minimum level of welfare to its citizens has found worldwide diffusion. Not such a bad thing, perhaps. But it does make survival difficult for governments which cannot begin to meet these expectations, and it makes capital investment difficult for governments which give welfare high priority.

Simultaneously, the same changes in world public opinion circumscribe the power which a government can command. Internal opposition movements *can* be treated in the same way as the demonstrators at Peterloo were treated. And they often still are. But governments incur a good deal more odium in the process and there are now physical places like the

---

[1]One writer (Foster, 1966) suggests that reinforcement of the demonstration effect is, via this mechanism, the only real contribution which the diffusion of primary education makes to economic growth. P. Foster, 'The vocational school fallacy in development planning', in C. A. Anderson and M. S. Bowman, *Education and economic development*, 1966.

[2]See, e.g. Crosland, 1971.

United Nations where the odium can crystallize into formal resolutions and occasionally, even, into sanctions. And the prospect of odium, within limits, *does* restrain. Modern protest movements draw a sense of righteousness and confidence from world public opinion; they can even hope for arms and medical supplies. Compare the help Biafra got with the help the Armenians got in 1896 — for all the eloquent speeches of Gladstone to the citizens of Liverpool.

In short — and this is one of the generalizable features of the late development effect referred to above — *the later development starts, the greater the demands made on government, the less its chance of being accepted 'because it's there' and the greater its dependence either on active consensus or active coercion* — both for better and for worse.

6. None of the above observations are very original, but my final category of aspects of the late development effect — the transfer of social technology — has received less attention. To be sure one can find plenty of humourous reflections of a condescending kind concerning the transplant of Westminster-type mace-and-wig parliaments to tropical African countries. But there is much less discussion of the more important matter of the transfer from the early starters where they were invented of the rules of committee procedure or of the routines of bureaucratic administration. At the oldest of Japan's modern universities, founded in the 1870s, the only original building which is still preserved as a historical monument is the Speech House, built by the founder for the students to get practice in Western techniques of public debate. (The Chinese cultural tradition had its Socrates in plenty, from Confucius on, but no Demosthenes.) Whatever one might feel about the relative advantages of rule by committee and of despotism, it has to be admitted that if what are nowadays fashionably called participative values are going to be diffused anyway, then it is better that there should go with them the techniques which help participation actually to result in decisions which are accepted as legitimate.

The two forms of social techniques whose diffusion I propose to examine a little more closely are, first, the use of higher education for purposes of occupational selection; secondly, employment practices and trade union organization.

III

One particular contrast between Britain and Japan will provide as good a starting point as any other for this discussion. In a sample of leading business men drawn from a Japanese *Who's Who* of 1955, 83 per cent were graduates of universities[1] (Asō, 1960: 158-9). A sample study of British managers in 1958 found that 21 per cent were university graduates.

[1] Even in 1910 the figure had been 15 per cent.

Among a sub-sample of 200 top managers in top firms, the proportion was 24 per cent (Clements, 1958: 184).

The explanation of this difference will lead to another general proposition about the late-development effect. One can, at the risk of a certain degree of over-schematization, divide the history of occupational training and social placement in Britain into three phases: the phase of apprenticeship and selection by job performance; the phase of apprenticeship and selection by job performance plus mid-career qualification, and the phase of pre-career qualification. The first civil engineers of the eighteenth century gradually distinguished themselves from the artisans, the clockmakers and millwrights who were their professional predecessors, by virtue of the fact that they were better artisans, that they could intellectualize and generalize their skills, extend them by invention, adapt them and enlarge them in new engineering projects. They were 'men trained in millwrights' shops' who 'were borne up by the force of their practical skill and constructive genius into the highest rank of skilled and scientific engineering'.[1] The next step was for those who had become recognized, and who recognized each other, as engineers to form societies such as the Institution of Civil Engineers, founded in 1818 with the object of 'facilitating the acquirement of knowledge necessary in the civil engineering profession and for promoting mechanical philosophy' (Carr-Saunders and Wilson, 1933: 157), i.e. for the primary purpose of exchanging information and ideas, but for the secondary purpose of safeguarding the title of engineer, of certifying competence. In the case of some of the professional organizations created around this time the second purpose seems to have been the primary one. Twenty years after its foundation the Pharmaceutical Society explained in its journal that it 'was designed as a means of raising the qualifications of pharmaceutical chemists and placing between them and unqualified persons a line of demarcation' (Carr-Saunders and Wilson, 1933: 133) — to protect the conscientious apothecary from the stigma earned by the drug-peddling quacks. Training in all the professions except the Church was still by apprenticeship, but qualification became formalized; it became a matter of admission to a professional society — recognition by one's peers.

As the body of knowledge utilized by the professions became more sophisticated and more systematized, embryonic patterns of pre-career qualification began to emerge. Engineering became a university subject in London and Glasgow around 1840. But although university study provided a short cut to qualification as an engineer, it did not take one all the way — further apprenticeship and job performance certified by one's peers was still necessary for Institution membership.

A parallel result of this systematization of knowledge was a change in the professional societies' criteria for membership. The Northcote-

[1]Quoted in A. M. Carr-Saunders and P. A. Wilson, *The Professions*, 1933, from S. Smiles, *Lives of the Engineers*, 1861, vol. I, p. 312.

Trevelyan reforms of civil service entry had a general effect in increasing the importance attached to formally examined book knowledge as a test of competence. The engineers resisted formal examinations until 1894, and they still insisted on evidence of job performance, but the process of mid-career qualification changed in character; it required evening study and the mastery of general principles.

In this century the trend in the professions in Britain has gradually been towards a complete transition to the pattern of pre-career qualification by university study. The transition took place early in medicine. In engineering, still, in a recent survey, only 22 per cent of a sample of full members of the Institution of Mechanical Engineers were found to have a university degree — the rest got there by apprenticeship, part-time study and mid-career qualification (Gerstl and Hutton, 1966: 42). But under the most recent reforms of the Council of Engineering Institutions it will in future be very difficult to achieve the status of engineer unless one has graduated in one's early twenties from a university or technical college. Accountancy and architecture are still in a transitional phase. In management, pre-career qualification is only just beginning.

The reason for this transition does not lie simply in the advance of knowledge and the increasing complexity of the body of theory which has to be mastered. It lies also in increasing affluence. From the point of view of the individual aspiring to a professional position, it is obviously better to achieve qualified status at the age of twenty-two after a reasonably enjoyable period in a university than to get there in one's mid-thirties by the painful process of learning on the job, combined with evening study. And as the level of living rises and more people can afford to choose the pre-career qualification route (perhaps aided, in the name of equality of educational opportunity, by state subsidy) the supply of those who have the motivation and the native ability to get there by the other route dwindles. This point is to be stressed in view of the argument that follows. Pre-career qualification is not necessarily *the most efficient* means of career selection from the point of view of maximizing the use of talent. A sufficient explanation of the change to pre-career qualification can be given in terms of individual preferences and the increasing availability of the means to exercise those preferences.

Japan, by contrast, jumped straight into the phase of pre-career qualification almost from the beginning of its period of industrialization. The reason is fairly clear. To stick to engineering as an example although medicine or accountancy or law would do equally well, engineering was already, in the Western countries which provided models for Japan's modernizing efforts, a systematized body of knowledge taught in universities at the time when Japan began industrialization. It was imported into Japan as such, as something new, entirely discontinuous with traditional artisan techniques. It might, to be sure, have been possible to establish from scratch the kind of apprenticeship system which had evolved without design in the early industrializers. There were, after all, foreign engineers — some 355 in the peak year, 1878 (UNESCO 1966: 134) — working in Japan to be apprenticed to. But Japan was in too much of a hurry. Systematic training was necessary to accelerate the learning process, and the Western university provided the model — specifically, the Zurich College of Technology; the 25-year-old leader among the band of chiefly Scottish engineers imported to staff the Tokyo Engineering College in 1873 preferred the later Swiss model to the by then outdated Scottish model in which he had been reared.[1]

Once the pattern of pre-career university training was established in such professions as engineering and medicine it was hard to break. Japan's engineering associations, the equivalent of the British Institutions, were, and remain today, dominated by university professors, not, as in Britain, by practising engineers. And just as the influence of practising engineers in the British Institutions probably helped to preserve patterns of mid-career qualification, the university-dominated Japanese associations naturally reinforced the pre-career pattern. It spread rapidly to other professions, aided by the fact that universities selected students by stiffly competitive entrance examinations which hence provided the best available national test of native ability plus effort. Altogether irrespective of what a man did with his four years in university, the fact that he got there at all was considered evidence of his potential. By the early decades of this century it had become almost impossible to enter the management ranks of the big companies or to become a journalist with a national newspaper without a degree. Because the university became in this way the only route into professional occupations, the demand for university education so far exceeded the supply from the state institutions that in the early decades of this century large numbers of private free enterprise universities were founded. That is one of the reasons why some 30 per cent of the men of each age group enter university in Japan today, compared with less than 10 per cent in Britain.

In the countries which are even later starters than Japan the dominance of the pre-career qualification pattern is even more marked. The university degree becomes the indispensible ticket of entry into the professions right from the start. This is only partly to be explained by the exigencies of the situation — the fact that apprenticeship is not a viable alternative because there is no one to be apprenticed to. It is also the result of the *unthinking diffusion to the developing countries of the social institutions which in the developed countries are the recent product of a high level of affluence.* Once the pattern has been established it is rarely called in question — not only because the manpower planning advisers from the developed countries help to reinforce it, but also for the same reasons as in Japan — because

---

[1]He describes his experiences — and outlines his claims to have improved considerably on the Zurich model — in Henry Dyer, *Dai Nippon, the Britain of the East. A study in national evolution*, London, 1904.

the professional associations begun by university graduates are unwilling to countenance other forms of qualification. But in countries such as India where the groundwork is already laid and where patterns of apprenticeship and mid-career qualification might theoretically be feasible, it is not by any means obvious that the pre-career qualification pattern is the better one, and this for several reasons.

First, the pre-career training is not necessarily relevant to the occupation for which it qualifies. There are complaints enough in Britain about the irrelevance of much engineering training, for instance, to the actual work of engineers. A great deal still has to be learned on the job and some things have to be unlearned.

Second, in some professions the escalation of qualifications in the developed countries is more the result of attempts to raise the status of the profession and the salaries of those who profess it, than of attempts to match training to the requirements of jobs. And yet it is the current developed-country standards of qualifications which are transferred to developing countries. Do countries which have difficulty in importing enough books to maintain a small number of good libraries really need a steady supply of librarians with a post-graduate qualification in librarianship?

Thirdly, the pre-career qualification system probably produces more wastage and a less good fit between aptitude and occupation. The protracted business of apprenticeship and mid-career qualification at least ensures that those who complete the course have chosen their occupation in full knowledge of what it offers and what it demands, and their motivation is likely to be high. Pre-career qualifiers often stumble into occupation as the result of a toss-up choice of university faculty at the age of eighteen. They may give up when they leave university and discover what it's really all about, or they may not give up and remain ritualistic and inefficient practitioners of a profession they have never in any real sense chosen.

Fourthly, the pre-career qualification pattern carries the danger of enhancing the element of ritualism in education itself. In the early starters the present system of higher education traces its tradition continuously back to pre-industrial periods when schools and universities had a clear class (or more accurately 'status-group') character. They were then not primarily mechanisms of social placement and social mobility since occupation was for the most part hereditarily ascribed. Their function was to make the gentry into better gentry and merchants into better — morally and intellectually better — merchants. Today, when university education has become a means of social selection and a university degree a near-guarantee of a doubling of lifetime earnings, the older traditional definition of schooling as being concerned with education — with intellectual curiosity, human enrichment and the like — still survives in many of the practices of universities and in the self-conceptions of their teachers. These 'useful fictions' operate to modify and push into the background of consciousness the instrumental qualification-earning purposes of the students. They help to stimulate an interest in ideas and knowledge for their own sake and not merely for their usefulness in passing examinations. In many late-starting countries, however, particularly those where the first schools ever were started by colonial authorities to qualify for posts in the lower ranks of colonial administrations, the universities' instrumental, qualification-granting role has been predominant from the very beginning, both in fact and in the perceptions and motivations of students, with nothing but a weak transplant of the aristocratic university traditions of the metropolitan countries to counteract it. The complaints of rote-learning are too common for the point to need elaboration. If, with the development of apprenticeship alternatives, universities could be relieved of part of their social sieve function, if they were to concentrate on the education, perhaps a little later in life, of those whose career was already determined by other means of selection, there would be a better chance of changing the social definition of universities and making them educational rather than qualification-granting institutions — with considerable advantage to the society's reserves of creativity and intellectual initiative.

Fifthly, in countries where the salaried middle class is becoming consolidated and, in a situation of great income inequality, increasingly pre-empting the opportunities for higher education for their own children, the absence of alternative channels of mobility through apprenticeship prevents the optimum use of the nation's best talents. Pre-career qualification in the early starters did at least come after a substantial move towards equality of educational opportunity.

Sixthly, the pre-career qualifiers, with qualifications modelled on those of the rich countries, are more likely to emigrate.

From all of these considerations one might hazard, by way of summary, the following general preposition: *the later the start of the late-starter, the more exclusively is it likely to adopt pre-career qualification patterns of occupational selection and the more inappropriate they are likely to be for the promotion of development.*

IV

Again I begin with a contrast between Britain and Japan. Britain has something which can reasonably be called a labour market. There is considerable job mobility. Individuals are likely, in the course of their life, to enter the market several times to gain employment at a wage or salary which is supposed to approximate to the going price for the skills and experience they can offer. In so far as the market is regulated by collective bargaining, this is done largely on a national or regional scale, setting the minimum price for different kinds of skills — so much for a fitter, so much for a plumber, so much for a labourer. The unions and employers' federations which make these bargains are national in scope. The unions restrict their membership to those in a certain range of skill grades.

In the large-firm sector of Japanese industry, however, the situation is different. The really active labour market is the market for school and university leavers who do not yet have specific occupational skills. Workers are hired for their presumed trainability, as judged by their educational record. Job mobility is low and a high proportion of those who enter the big firms at the start of their career stay in the same firm for the rest of their working life and never enter the labour market again. Wages, within certain broad grades, are determined by seniority, assessments of merit and family responsibilities. Manual workers can expect to more than double their wages in the course of their working life, even if they continue doing the same job. There is no going rate for particular skills, and men of the same seniority doing the same job in different firms may receive very different wages. Wage scales are bargained over between the management of particular enterprises and unions which represent workers of all grades from labourer to junior executive in that enterprise and are exclusive to that enterprise. There are hardly any national or regional agreements.

There are several associated differences. The enterprise in Japan does more than in Britain, and the state less, to provide social security. In Japan, training is more often at the expense of the firm which can expect to keep its workers and get its money back, whereas in Britain, where skills, as it were, belong to the individual who sells them in the market, they are a cost to individuals or to the state.

Again, the historical reasons for this difference are complex. The nature of the Japanese system may owe something to cultural traditions of group loyalty. But it is possible to see a rationale in these differences which follows from the different historical circumstances of early starter and later starter development.

Early industrial England was a country of small workshops with manufacturers in the same trade clustering in particular localities, constantly taking on and laying off labour from the same pool of skilled men. There was something like a real labour market in which a going rate for a particular skill was established. There was little variation between different firms in the wages paid to men of the same skill, and a steady pattern of differentials running consistently across firms.

Techniques developed slowly. The skills required by modern industry grew gradually out of the traditional artisan techniques of the millwright and clockmaker. Employers could find the skills they needed on offer in the market. The manufacturer with a new invention may have had to do a little topping up of the skills of the men he hired, but by and large traditional patterns of apprenticeship were quite adequate to maintain the supply of skilled labour.

And when trade unions were formed they were quite naturally combinations of men in the same trade who sold their skills in the same local market, and who were concerned pre-eminently with one thing — maintaining the market price of their particular skill. Their natural bargaining partners were employers' federations.

The early history of Japanese industry was somewhat similar in the early years, but as industrialization got going with a swing in the first two decades of this century, the pattern changed: there appeared the typical features of what might be called the late-starter industrialization syndrome: viz.:

The enterprises are large *ab initio*.

They take a bureaucratic management form from the beginning, being spawned by already bureaucratic merchants and banking concerns. This also implies a certain amount of forward planning and predictable labour requirements.

The technology used is that of the contemporary advanced early starters, and the amount of capital used per worker is much greater than in the early industrialization period of the early starters.

The new big firm probably has few, if any, competitors using the same type of labour skills in the vicinity: it may even be situated in a wholly rural area.

It is easy to see why, in such circumstances, no real market for skilled labour develops. The discontinuous leap in technology of the late-starter means that traditional artisans skills and apprenticeship systems are inadequate to supply skills to the new factory — even in 19th century Japan with a higher level of traditional artisan skills than any of today's developing countries. The employer must do his own training. Having invested in training, he does not want to lose his skilled men. Hence the motive for offering them long-service increments, tied housing and other welfare benefits conditional on continued service. Since the firm has a great deal of capital locked up in its plant, it can less easily afford idle machines than the early starters' early entrepreneurs with simpler machines. It is consequently more concerned about absenteeism and high turnover and has an incentive to stabilize even its less skilled workers by the same measures. And its labour costs being a smaller proportion of total costs than for the early starters' early entrepreneurs, it can more easily afford the increases in labour costs required by these measures. These policies, together with the smallness of the number of employers competing for these high technology skills anyway, reduces labour turnover. There never really develops a labour market in any true sense, or any real concept of a going price for a particular skill.

Consequently, when unions develop (as, since the foundation of the ILO, they are almost certain to develop in some form or other) since there is no concept of a market price for turner skills which all turners should combine to raise, the turner in factory A does not have much in common with the turner in factory B. Instead he finds his natural allies among the electricians and labourers of factory A — particularly in the common dual economy situation in which factory A, heavily capitalized and making handsome profits, could, if forced by a sufficiently determined enterprise union, pay double the wage of Factory B, a small inefficient workshop with second-hand machines.

One can see how the whole pattern of seniority increments, low turnover, lifetime employment, enterprise unions and high enterprise welfare costs can develop. It becomes even more understandable if one adds in the further circumstances that:

(a) In late starters centralized and standardized primary education is typically well established before industrialization starts so that employers recruiting in the virgin school-leaver market can get from school records reasonably good estimates of applicants' presumptive trainability.

(b) From peasant agriculture the main immigration flow is of young surplus sons with schooling.

(c) Given the population situation of late-starters the flow exceeds demand,

(d) and consequently employers can 'cream off' the applicants using school records and other tests, and having got the cream have every reason for keeping it.

(e) Again because of the population situation the as yet ununionized applicants can be had for very low wages, so that seniority increments which raise the wage to a level that supports a family are feasible without bankrupting the employer.

(f) Again because of the employment situation and the scarcity of jobs the unions themselves show a keen interest in job security.

If the late-starter syndrome has appeared in Japan, why should it not appear elsewhere? The answer, I think, is that in many countries it has emerged. To take a random example, Colombian trade unions are typically enterprise unions.[1] In other, particularly ex-colonial, countries, something more like the British pattern has developed, and partly because, once again, of the unthinking diffusion of the social technology of the early starters — because expatriate firms are locked into their preconceptions that the only way to pay wages is on a rate-for-the-job basis, because trade unions have been organized by men who saw the only proper form of organization as one which unites workers in similar trades, and because governments have offered to provide training institutions to produce the skills which otherwise employers would have had to produce themselves.

The whole subject is complex. There are plenty of signs that the industrial relations system of England — the product of the small workshop period of British industrialism — is itself accommodating to the emergence of the mammoth corporation by moving in the Japanese

[1]See M. Urrutia, *The development of the Colombian labour movement*, 1969, 151–6.

direction. It may be that there are virtues in *trying* to preserve the market-oriented patterns of nineteenth-century Britain in modern Nigeria: it can be argued that they do foster a spirit of individualism and independence in the individual worker: or alternatively that they promote class consciousness in a way necessary for the healthy development of society.

The situation is complex, but being only at the beginning of my research into these matters I am prepared to offer the following final 'late development effect' proposition as a hypothesis: *the later the start of the late-starter the less appropriate the employment institutions of the contemporary advanced countries are likely to be to its situation, but this does not necessarily mean that they are less likely to be copied.*

'And so what?', citizens of developing countries are entitled to ask. What exactly are you suggesting? In detail, I admit, my prescriptions are not entirely clear. Apropos of education my tentative message is: don't be conned into adopting wholesale the social institutions characteristic of the affluent present of the advanced countries. Look at the possibilities of going *back* to the institutions of the early starters' early period, of trying to *repeat* their history with some modifications. Apropos of employment relations, on the other hand, my message is: don't be conned into adopting wholesale the social institutions which are, in the early starter, only a hangover from the particular circumstances of their early industrial history — a history which you are *not* likely to reproduce in other respects.

What the two points have in common is this: the transfer of social technology, like the transfer of material technology, should not be based on the automatic assumption that the early starters in their present phase provide a model of how things should be done. Every horse which they offer as a gift needs to have its teeth examined. And some of them will be found to be, given the needs of late-starters, non-starters.

5 Economic Development and Modernization in South-East Asia

GOH KENG SWEE

IT is but fitting that the theme selected for this volume is 'Modernization in South-East Asia'. The subject is one that is exercising the minds of many people, in academia, in Government and among leaders in many walks of public life. The subject of modernization is rightly drawing increasing attention, not only in South-East Asia, not only in the less developed countries of the world, but also in the modern states. For the difficulties experienced in this field in the contemporary political scene appear intractable. And many people have expressed the fear that as a consequence, the growing disparity of wealth between rich and poor nations, between the modern states and those aspiring to be modern, may reach critical and explosive dimensions in the course of this century.

I will not try to define the term 'modernization' and 'modernity'. The subject is one which straddles several disciplines of learning and it is unlikely that any definition will secure general acceptance. It is more likely to give rise to sterile controversy. I shall take the robust position that modernization is like the elephant, difficult to define but easy to recognize when one sees the beast.

Probably three disciplines of learning are most intimately concerned with the subject — economics, political science and sociology. My experience with the subject is that of a practitioner in Singapore. My specialization is economics and it is from this standpoint that I will discuss the modernization process. In so doing, I do not decry the importance of other disciplines. Indeed, it would be clear from what I shall say, that it is not possible to understand the modernization process purely in terms of economic principles. Furthermore, it is dangerous to execute an economic development plan which has reference only to economic variables, important though these are.

Economists do not have a special theory of modernization. The process itself is subsumed under the general principles of economic development. In practice, however, in the field of applied economics, a vast literature has proliferated on economic development of the third world countries.

There is now clear recognition among economists that economic growth involves more than economic variables. Gunnar Myrdal's monumental *Asian Drama* makes the most thorough and explicit study of non-economic factors which have a bearing on economic growth. However, Myrdal's plea for a new set of economic principles applicable to the situation in less developed countries has largely been ignored. The economist stands fast by his principle of doctrinal purity. While admitting that non-economic factors have a bearing on economic growth, he claims that these fall within the province of other specialists, upon which he is reluctant to poach.

In order to achieve a deeper comprehension of the subject, I was obliged to do some reading in the other disciplines. While this study has provided me with new and useful insights, I am afraid I discovered that the performance of specialists in these other fields, political scientists and sociologists, is no better than that of the economists. There seems to be a state of mutual lack of comprehension between writers in these various disciplines. Each is interested in developing a consistent, logical and self-contained set of principles within his own domain with but scant regard and superficial understanding of knowledge in other disciplines. It is a depressing state of affairs, but I cannot presume to offer any solution.

I think I can best set out the problems of modernization as I see it from the point of view of a practising economist in one developing country, and a keen observer of the fortunes of other developing countries. It is unavoidable that I see the modernizing process in terms of economic growth with economic variables playing the dominant factor. But I will raise a number of non-economic issues whose understanding seems to be imperfect at this stage, at least by practitioners in the field.

Although the study of modernization and economic development received widespread attention since the end of World War II with the emergence of many newly independent states, the process of modernization itself, so far as it affects the countries of Asia, goes back several centuries. Indeed, if we wish to identify its genesis and want to nominate a birthday, I believe the 27 May 1498 has a special claim. That was the day Vasco da Gama arrived at the port of Calicut in south-west India. For it was the arrival of the European in Asia which set in train the process of social change which we today call modernization. However, it was not until several centuries after Vasco da Gama's arrival that the European presence began to make an enduring impact on the Asian scene. As K. M. Pannikar said, 'If by an act of God, the relations of Europe with Asia had ceased all of a sudden in 1748, little would have been left to show for two and a half centuries of furious activity'.

It is important to distinguish between the European impact before and after the second half of the eighteenth century. In the earlier period, the Europeans went there as traders. Their trading outposts existed by leave and licence of local rulers. They bought goods which were available in the East which they wanted, such as spices and sandalwood from Indonesia, silks and horses from Iran, cotton and spices from India. They paid for these by gold and silver and only to a negligible extent by manufactures as was to be the general practice in the later period. Apart from these traders, supplemented occasionally by zealous missionaries anxious to convert heathens to the true faith, Asian societies were left very much to themselves.

In the latter half of the eighteenth century, particularly in the nineteenth century, the pace of modernization of Europe itself gained momentum through the great technological and social changes we now call the Industrial Revolution. As a result, the nature of European interest in their trading outposts in the East underwent a profound change. The growing industries of Europe, supported by a rapidly advancing science and technology, required new types of raw materials on an increasing scale. They took the form of minerals as well as agricultural produce in tropical and sub-tropical areas of the East.

Political rivalry between European powers which their growing wealth encouraged accelerated the drive for Empire. Relationship between East and West took a different form, no longer as equals between trading parties, but as between overlord and subjects. Unlike the early period when European traders bought goods already available, in this period new industrial crops were introduced on a large-scale plantation basis and new mines developed by modern methods. So we have a whole series of new products grown or mined in the colonies of European countries — tea, coffee, rubber, sugar cane, jute, oil palm, tin, copper, oil and petroleum products and so on. To establish such a varied range of products as a large scale business, it was necessary to invest substantial amounts of capital. And of course to support all these activities, the colonial government had to introduce a wide range of infra-structure services such as seaports, roads, railways, telegraph and other means of communication.

So seaports were established through which the produce of these lands could be shipped to feed the burgeoning industries of Europe. From these seaports, radiated a network of railways and roads to take out the produce of the hinterland. Cities of substantial size grew at the site of these seaport and communication centres.

For the efficient conduct of business on modern lines, it was necessary to establish administrative and legal systems which would ensure the two requisites of orderly business. First, public security, law and order. Second, the enforcement of contracts. For investments in mines and plantations have a long gestation period, and the investor must be able to plan several years ahead with assurance.

While the top management of the communication systems as well as the administrative and legal apparatus could be manned by personnel sent out from the metropolitan country, these have to be supported by an army of lower level management, clerical and technical personnel. It would be wasteful given the primitive systems of communication by sea in those days, to bring these out from the homeland. So, an education system modelled more or less after the metropolitan country, teaching in the language of that country was introduced, sometimes by missionary effort and sometimes by the colonial government. In course of time, universities and technical teaching institutions were founded.

And as local residents benefited from the economic growth resulting from this infusion of Western capital and technology, they wanted their children to take full advantage of modern education not only in the local universities but also in universities in the metropolitan country.

So we see the seeds of modernization planted during this age of colonization in three principal fields. The first was in the establishment of plantations and mines supported by a modern communication system — seaports, railways, transportation, telegraph — leading to the growth of cities. Second, the introduction of modern administrative and legal systems. Third, the introduction and development of modern education systems.

While all this was going on, it should not be forgotten that this modernizing process was confined to certain geographical areas. I mentioned the seaports, the lines of communications and the administrative centres. We could also include hinterland areas opened up to cultivation of new cash crops as well as the new mining enterprises. For the rest of the country, the colonial government in general refrained as a matter of deliberate policy from upsetting the traditional social structure and reduced interference with local customs and institutions to the barest minimum.

To be sure, the process of acculturization initiated in the cities was bound to affect the countryside, but this was by way of side-effects and not by government design. The result was that subsistence agriculture, mainly the production of food crops, which was the most common occupation of countries in Asia before the advent of the West, remained outside the mainstream of development. There were exceptions to this rule such as, for instance, the 'Culture System', introduced by Van den Bosch in Indonesia in 1830. The object was to compel peasants in the subsistence sector in Java to grow cash crops. Initially a large number of crops was attempted; pepper, cinchona, cotton, indigo, etc. But only three — coffee, tea and sugar — survived. However, this was an exception to the general rule.

Subsistence peasant cultivation was of little economic value or commercial interest to the industrial West. No doubt peasants benefited from improved communication systems and possibly from agricultural extension services that were introduced here and there. They certainly felt the effect of improved public health measures which diminished the effect of

Malthusian checks on population growth. But the technique of production and the social system of village community life remained largely undisturbed by colonial governments, except when the need to raise revenue led to changes in the system of land tenure. A case in point was the Permanent Land Settlement introduced by Cornwallis in Bengal. As with Van den Bosch, revenue, not development, was the motivating force.

The general picture then in colonies at that time was one of the co-existence of modernity and tradition, with growing modern cities in the midst of a sea of rural traditional subsistence agriculture. This picture still remains true today.

The role of Asian colonies as providers of industrial raw materials and markets for manufactures is so well-known that people may think it too trite and commonplace an observation to merit attention. Yet it is worthwhile examining this role in some detail, because the subject is much misunderstood and its true implications have sometimes been missed. This as I shall show later, has had unfortunate consequences in the development plans of Asian countries in their post-independence era.

We can regard investment of Western capital and the application of technology in Asian countries to produce raw materials needed by European industries as creating 'surplus value' in the Marxist sense of the words. These economic activities, employing indigenous labour, produced a surplus value over and above what was required to maintain workers at subsistence level. Not only this, but this surplus value was translated into foreign exchange as the products were exported to the West. It is from this fund of surplus value embodied in foreign exchange earnings that enabled payments to be made on imports of goods and imports of capital equipment needed for modernizing the economy, as well as for remittance of profits earned by these foreign enterprises.

It would be wrong to conclude that the whole benefits of these activities accrued to foreigners, though they were undoubtedly the principal beneficiaries. Apart from workers engaged in these enterprises, there was often a substantial spill-over to local entrepreneurs and others who engaged in similar activities. For instance, rubber estates in Malaya were introduced by foreign enterprise. In course of time, local residents entered the field; these were not all capitalists. The peasant population also benefited, growing rubber in smallholdings as a supplement to their traditional activity.

When Asian countries achieved their independence after World War II, the leaders who headed the government of these states inherited both the modern and the traditional societies. But whereas colonial authorities, in general, had little reason to disturb the traditional order of things outside the modern money exchange economy, the local ruling elite were exposed to considerable pressure to improve the well-being of all their citizens, for those in the cities as well as those in the countryside.

Great expectations were raised that with the end of colonial rule, a liberated people would achieve not only a status of dignity in the world but also gain sufficient material advance for all citizens. In this way, they would put an end to the harsh poverty so many had to endure for so long.

Economic development plans were drawn up, sometimes with the help of foreign experts, but usually by indigenous effort, for the universities and the administrations of past decades and centuries had produced sufficient expertise.

An economic development plan is basically a programme of allotting capital investment among various sectors of the economy — agriculture, transportation, social services, manufacturing industries, mining, electric power, irrigation and so on.

Planners have to lay down a strategy of development if they are to make good and consistent decisions on resource allocation. Funds are limited; the demand for funds exceeds available supply many times over. Economic planners have to draw up criteria by which decisions on allocations can be made. And these criteria embody the strategy which planners believe to be the best way of achieving economic growth.

It is extremely dangerous to generalize on strategies adopted by countries with such varying backgrounds of historical experience and economic potential. However, I believe it is true that, in general, the position taken by Asian economists was as follows. First, they believed that since resources were limited in relation to demand, to spread resources evenly over all the sectors of the economy would not produce the best results. They believed that it was better to identify the crucial sectors of the economy whose development would stimulate general growth of the economy. It was there that the main effort should be mounted. To use economic jargon, planners preferred the strategy of encouraging the leading sector to the strategy of balanced growth.

The leading sector was identified as manufacturing industry. It was here that they pinned their hopes. They believed that it was the progress of manufacturing activities in the West and its near absence in the East that explained the disparity in wealth. The expansion of industry was expected to introduce new technology, new social attitudes, raise levels of existing skills, provide employment for the large numbers of unemployed or underemployed citizens. In short, industry would modernize and enrich. The general raising of the technological level of the countries, the spread of modern systems of production and management, all these, in the calculations of the planners, would not only generate economic growth but also help to bring about a rapid transformation of social attitudes, more consistent with the needs of modernizing societies.

The second common position taken by Asian economic planners of the early years was that they regarded the relationship of their country with the West during the colonial period — as a provider of raw materials and market for finished goods — as an unequal and unsatisfactory one. It symbolized colonial exploitation, and inequality between rich and poor nations. Why not convert these raw materials themselves into manufactured goods? Why not produce those goods traditionally imported from the West, and in this way save foreign exchange for more productive use?

All these different considerations, the decision to take the manufacturing industry as the leading sector, the policy of manufacturing goods that were formerly imported — import substitution in economic jargon — the political stigma of dependence on Western industries, all these combined to support the policy of industrialization based on supplying the domestic market as well as processing of raw materials formerly exported.

This course of action seemed to be in accord with the national aspirations of developing nations, and seemed consistent with commonsense and in accordance with the logic of economic development.

Yet, with hardly any exception, those countries which embarked on this line of development before long got into serious trouble. Instead of saving foreign exchange, as they substituted domestic manufactures for imported manufactures, they spent more foreign exchange than they earned. In the process, they got into chronic balance of payments trouble and increased the load of foreign debt to dangerous limits. The exceptions were those laggard countries which, while paying lip service to this policy, in practice did little to implement it.

The trouble experienced by developing countries in this respect is best illustrated by data on external public debts. This means foreign credits and loans which governments of these countries had borrowed and had to repay in foreign exchange. It excludes foreign credits and loans to private enterprise. By the end of 1969, total external public debts of developing countries amounted to US$60 billion. Over the last fifteen years foreign debts had grown at a compound rate of almost 15 per cent a year; that is, debts owed by poor countries to the rich doubled every five years.

Debt servicing, the payment of interest and repayment of capital, has been growing at the rate of more than 12 per cent a year. This is twice the rate of growth of exports of developing countries, and nearly three times the rate of growth of their GNP.

Servicing of foreign debts assumes an increasing proportion of export earnings of developing countries, and in many instances has passed the danger limit. There are no hard and fast rules which determine the safe proportion of debt servicing to export earnings. The World Bank has laid down a rule of thumb limit at 6 to 7 per cent. Several countries have already passed the 20 per cent limit, a good number fall in the 10 to 20 per cent range. The general average for all developing countries was above 9 per cent at a count made some years ago, and is probably well over 10 per cent now.

What went wrong? There is no one simple answer. Part of the trouble stemmed from sheer bad luck, such as crop failure due to droughts and floods, making it necessary to import large quantities of food thus dissipating foreign exchange resources. Another reason is the decline of prices of primary export commodities in relation to manufactured goods over the last decade or two. A third is deliberate trade discrimination by some wealthy countries against certain products of poor countries, for instance, textiles. But I believe that even allowing for these adverse factors beyond the control of developing countries, their performance could have been better if they had not embarked on the type of industrialization strategy that they did.

Industrialization based on import-substitution had proved a double-edged weapon. As a means of saving foreign exchange, it has been self-defeating. The reason is that machinery and equipment needed to establish these industries had to be imported from abroad. In many, probably most instances, the value of the output consumed at home, representing the maximum saving on foreign exchange, is less than the amount needed to pay for interest and instalment payments on machinery as well as for current purchases of spare parts needed for maintenance. This is particularly true of capital-intensive industries such as steel production, oil refineries, heavy chemical plants and other so called 'basic industries' which seem to have a fatal attraction for economic planners.

In addition to this, because countries are poor, the effective demand for these products is small, even in countries with large populations. It is therefore necessary to introduce some kind of licensing system for new industries in order to avoid over-capacity. The result has generally been the emergence of monopolistic practices, a lowering of efficiency, an increase in cost, with damaging effect on the economy, and practices such as padding of the labour force and executive personnel, which would not have happened under free market competition.

One economic effect of this kind of industrialization is that consumers have to pay more than if goods were imported. But this is probably less harmful than the non-economic effects. For one of the objectives of the leading sector strategy of development planning is to spread new technologies as well as new social attitudes appropriate to modern societies. These include respect for hard work, innovation, a meritocratic system of personnel selection and advancement, continuous striving for greater efficiency, in short achievement-orientation. With the feather-bedding and monopolistic practices made possible under high tariff protection of domestic markets, the drive to efficiency is blunted. Quite often business success depends on obtaining official permits and licences rather than on efficient production and management.

The balance of payments difficulties which afflicted most developing countries had other unfavourable side-effects. It was mentioned earlier that foreign exchange earnings resulting from the export of raw materials and other goods from developing countries represent a claim on the goods produced by the industrial West. In countries without balance of payments problems, exchange controls are either non-existent or lenient. Those who have local currencies are able to use these to buy imported goods from any country. When foreign exchange difficulties arise, it is necessary to introduce exchange controls, that is to ration foreign exchange through a system of permits. The result of this is that the Government becomes the sole arbiter of what goods may be imported, who may import them, in what amounts and under what conditions. This control endows contemporary governments of Asian states with a power of patronage of immeasurably greater range and variety than were possessed by the wealthiest monarchs of ancient civilizations. While the riches owned by these were confined to personal ornaments, household entourage and such like, exchange control decides who will have access to the whole range of goods and services produced by modern states, including foreign education and foreign travel. The wealth of ancient kings derived from taxes imposed on a peasant society and this has a built-in limit, for beyond a certain level of exaction, the kings risked a popular revolt.

But because foreign exchange earnings originate in the modern sector, the disposal of foreign exchange resources in any way that the government thinks fit, has but marginal effect on the peasant subsistence economy. Contemporary governments' powers of patronage are therefore less circumscribed by the risk of peasant revolt.

The risk here, however, is less in a general.election where democratic constitutions operate. However this does not necessarily encourage rational use of foreign exchange resources to promote economic growth. Other short-term purposes, such as strengthening the bond of loyalty and cohesion in the ranks of the governing party or creating short-term economic euphoria have obvious appeals. Even where democratic elections do not operate, those in power are also obliged to pay heed to the loyalties of supporters of their regime, that is, the soldiery.

It is, of course, not unknown for Prime Ministers and Presidents of modern states to phase the rhythm of monetary and fiscal policies in a manner most favourable to their electoral chances. The industrial economies of the West can withstand such temporary departures from financial rectitude. However, those of developing countries are too fragile.

It is here that the interaction of economic, political and sociological elements interact in a crucial way. Economic difficulties inhibit the full spread of modernizing attitudes and place severe strains on the political system. The political leadership in office are obliged to take defensive action to secure their power positions. In this way they are obliged to depart from rational economic policies which would give them the best long-term chances but which may compound their immediate troubles, because those call for unpopular measures. Once things go wrong, events in the economic, social and political fields interact in a cumulative way.

Unless arrested at some stage the process reduces the whole system into a pathological condition.

Despite the general picture of disarray in developing countries and increasing gloom evident in the literature about their future prospects, I remain fairly optimistic. I am, of course, taking the long view. The economic strategy adopted by Asian economists which I described, and which had led them into serious trouble, is, in my opinion, basically sound. Except in special cases, of which Malaysia is one, the strategy of favouring the leading sector, that is, the manufacturing industry, is the correct one. It is here that the surplus value is most quickly generated, both in terms of domestic production and foreign exchange earnings. The fact that many countries made mistakes in selection of industry does not invalidate the soundness of this approach. This is but a technical error resulting from faulty calculation of production and foreign exchange consequences. The remedy is to concentrate on export-oriented industries and on the development of minerals and export primary produce which had tended to have been neglected in the immediate post-independence era when such economic activities bore the taint of colonialism. Also the jet-age brings into the developing countries a source of foreign exchange earnings which they can tap with but little effort. This is the tourist trade. For a lucky few, there is the dazzling prospect of striking oil.

If economic variables were to be the decisive factor, there is every reason for optimism. The creation of wealth, which is what economic development is about, is basically a simple process. All it requires is the application of modern science and technology to production, whether in agriculture, mining or industry. The knowledge to do this has been built up over the last 200 years and is easily accessible. It only needs a moderate intelligence to absorb this knowledge and to apply it productively. What is more difficult to achieve is a social and political order that enables development to take place. Where a stable political system is achieved, progress can be spectacular, as the examples of South Korea, Taiwan and Hong Kong demonstrate. These have growth rates in the region of 15 per cent a year.

The threads of my argument may be summarized as follows, before I go on to the next stage.

i. The modernization process in Asian countries began several centuries ago under the impact of European colonization.

ii. Because colonies fulfilled special roles in relation to the metropolitan power, such modernization as took place was generally confined to the sea-ports, administrative and communication centres as well as hinterlands developed to produce raw materials.

iii. The result was a co-existence of modernity in the midst of a traditional agrarian society, by far the larger segment of society in most countries.

iv. Newly independent regimes were under pressure to accelerate the modernization process and chose as their principal instrument economic development plans in which the main effort was generally placed on industrial expansion based on import-substitution.

v. For a variety of reasons, these development plans encountered serious trouble, as a result of which economic and political troubles compounded each other.

vi. Despite the prevailing mood of pessimism, it is likely that developing countries will eventually achieve a break-through, adopting a modified form of the general economic strategy now in use. It is, however, unlikely that this time will arrive until they have established political institutions of sufficient strength and durability that will support the economic effort.

If we view the modernizing process in terms of a historical panorama, the development efforts in the post-independence age are but a continuation of processes which have their origins more than 200 years ago. Economic development in the age of imperialism had limited objectives. It proceeded within a strong framework of stable government, enabling these limited objectives to be reached with apparent ease. The post-war development plans had larger objectives and aimed at more ambitious rates of progress. Despite this, they are no more than a major variation of a theme, and not a fundamental change of course as some people erroneously believe.

But the greater effort which these larger objectives demanded did not have the support of the sturdy frame of political and administrative institutions of the colonial era. It is not surprising that the stresses and strains that they imposed on contemporary social and political systems resulted in the weaknesses which I have described. Political development differed from economic development. There was a major and abrupt discontinuity in the political process on the act of decolonization.

How could the other disciplines participate in what Myrdal called the great Asian Drama, other than as observers and chroniclers of events? Here I must speak with some diffidence as I am approaching an area in which I have no specialist knowledge. It is certainly easier to say what should not be done than to say what should be done and I will start from here.

In the course of my reading of sociological and other literature, I came across this observation. 'Efficiency and thrift, those two great Western virtues, are not such in the eyes of the peasant in Uttar Pradesh.' At the risk of being unkind and unfair to the author, may I suggest that the ethos and psyche of the peasant in Uttar Pradesh are of no great moment. Nor should thought be given as to how he could be modernized. If, by an Act of God, all the peasants the Uttar Pradesh were suddenly to be modernized, the result will probably be an unqualified calamity for that state. I believe that the social institutions, including the so-called traditional beliefs of man, are part of the total ecological environment. They keep man at peace with himself and in adequate harmony with his fellow-men, and enable him to endure a life which otherwise would be intolerable.

To remove all these, and introduce alien values and institutions would be to perpetrate a reckless act of cruelty, unless it is possible in this instance, to give the peasant what he will require for self-fulfilment — twenty to thirty times the land area he now possesses as well as access to tractors and all the paraphernalia of modern farming systems.

The time will no doubt come when peasants in Uttar Pradesh will be able to acquire these. But this will be the result of successful industrialization, the growth of cities and industrial concentrations, drawing into their systems an ever increasing labour supply from the countryside. This happened in Europe over the last two and a half centuries; it happened in Japan and doubtless it will happen in other developing countries in course of time.

It is better to leave the peasant and his quaint ways to the anthropologist. For those who are interested in the modernization process, the crucial area of study lies in the cities. It is here that the transformation is taking place and the interaction between old cultural systems and values and new ones takes on their most acute form. It is here that the development plans of economists place their greatest hopes. It will be here that the break-through to modernity for the whole nation will take place through the accumulation of wealth and the earning of surplus value on an ever increasing scale by the application of modern science and technology.

There are great problems of social adjustment of people brought up under a pre-industrial culture who have been drawn into the city to work under the hard discipline of wage employment. At all levels of the social ladder, conflict takes place between traditional customs and usage, and the requirements of efficiency of modern economic institutions, be they private firms, public utility, a government department or whatever. All this is familiar, but it looks to me, standing outside the specialization, that the applied research on these subjects needs to be supplemented by theoretical principles which will give coherence to an apparently bewildering array of experience.

Take another as an example. The system of education in developing countries will play a decisive role in the successful modernization of these societies. So will the mass media. These are the means whereby new values may be inculcated among those who will play leading roles in their societies. I may be unfair to the education authorities of developing nations, including that of my own, but I get the distinct impression that the principles that guide them in making practical decisions as to curriculum content, and indeed their understanding of the purpose of education, all these seem to be derived from the theories and practices of Western teaching institutions. Because Western societies do not experience the kind of culture and value conflicts common in modernizing societies, their education systems need not prepare pupils for such conflicts. As a result, the Asian intellectual is often a confused person and the process of education can be a traumatic experience.

Asian university students in the humanities are often accused by Western critics of lacking independence of thought, a critical faculty, and ability to relate what he learns to his environment. I suggest that it is this hiatus between what he learns and the real world around him that explains this shortcoming.

I suspect that it is this lack of comprehension of contemporary social processes, this absence of adequate preparation which should have been given in school, that contributes to the fragility of political institutions in the new states, especially those which are based on democratic elections. And unless we prepare the young adequately, it is unlikely that we shall achieve that durability and resilience of political institutions which have to underpin the economic development effort. Hitherto there has been a blithe assumption that the process of counting heads is sufficient to secure the kind of leadership that can successfully see modernizing societies through their difficult transition stage. There is not much in contemporary history to support such optimism. Nor is there much to rejoice over in other system of leadership selection such as the counting of guns instead of heads.

Here I am touching on some basic issues now largely ignored in Europe and America because of their irrelevance, but which agitated men's minds in the troubled days of antiquity. Plato and Confucius in the 5th century B.C., independently of each other, were concerned with the process by which societies chose their government and the qualities ruling elites should have. I suggest that the issues which they discussed are of deep relevance to the new states and that the disciplines of political science and sociology in these countries could usefully devote attention in this direction and seek a solution in the modern context.

PART III
Social Development and Modernization

6. Resistance to Change - From Whom?
W. F. WERTHEIM

I

IN the First World — the Western one — a rather simplistic picture of the Third World prevails. Within that picture the Westerners figure as the dynamic factor, those who want change and promote change. Inside the Third World it is again the most Westernized elements, the so-called 'elite', who are deemed to be the main exponents of a dynamism in pursuit of change. It is they on whom all hopes and expectations are set for introducing change in various fields, in a social environment which, according to that picture, is marked by inertia and stagnancy.

The broad masses of the peasants of Asia, Africa and Latin America are still considered to be dull and bound by traditions and superstition. Even Gunnar Myrdal does not escape this stereotype when writing: 'These masses are mostly passive, apathetic, and inarticulate' (Myrdal, 1970:62).

Over half a century ago a similar picture of Indonesian society was prevalent in the Netherlands. It was our duty, as a colonial power, to 'uplift' the indolent, spiritually immature 'native' population towards a higher level. The civil servants had to fight, as 'uplifters', against the sluggishness and the passive resistance on the part of people who did not realize what was good for them. The White Man's Burden was far from light, under such conditions, to those colonial officers who had to exert themselves in a tropical climate on behalf of a hardly co-operative native population.

The sceptical civil servant G.L. Gonggrijp gave expression to the frustrations among that group of benefactors to whom he belonged in the following words:

And as for 'uplift' — the Natives don't want to be 'uplifted'. The more I did my best to 'uplift' them, the more trying they thought me. I established banks to help them out of their debts, but it became apparent that they then had even more: besides their ordinary, run-of-the-mill debts they now also had their debts to the bank.

We know now since a long time that our so-called 'Ethical' policy in the Indies did not produce welfare for the broad mass of the peasantry. To quote a Dutch critic: that policy bore more bloom than fruit.[1]

We also now know that any colonial policy, in spite of all the flowery rationalizations and ethical slogans extolling the White Man's Burden, was designed in such a way that actually it was more appropriate to serve the colonial power's own interests than those of the native populations.

Nevertheless, in the present discussions on 'foreign aid', on our task in the Third World as Western intellectuals, on Community Development, similar tunes may be caught as at the time when the colonial character of one's policy was at least overtly admitted.

Again it is we Westerners who, together with a restricted group of Western-educated people in the Third World, are pretending to be the dynamic benefactors who are time and again being frustrated in the realization of the best of our intentions, by the 'resistance to change' prevalent among the poor peasant masses.

Still we are finding fault not with ourselves, but with the natives who keep refusing to understand us, who keep refusing to be 'uplifted' by us. And we forget to ask ourselves whether they have no valid reasons for refusing to be uplifted by us, with our methods.

Resistance to change is a topic on which in the past years a lot of paper has been spent. Generally 'resistance to change' on the part of the poor peasantry has been taken for granted. What remained to be done was to try to find sociological and psychological explanations for that resistance. One author on Community Development in theory and practice complains that exploitation and sub-human living conditions from which the peasants were suffering had made them timorous, suspicious, fatalistic and apathetic.

They have lost all hope, they lack all initiative or fear to exercise it, and they do not have the courage to break with the traditions which throttle them. To expect people who live under such conditions to take part in the efforts to improve their living standards at their own initiative is to expect the impossible.

The author concludes that the people need outside help in order to pull out of the morass (Buitron, 1961:14 ff).

Other authors have invented beautiful names for the factors which cause and maintain the prevalent apathy. George Foster, who did research in Mexico, insists on the scanty aspirations of the peasants, on the 'image of the limited good' prevalent among them. In his view the peasants do not want to achieve individual progress because, if they try to

[1]The expression is from the Dutch social-democrat J. E. Stokvis, an expert on Indonesia in the period between the two world wars.

acquire a disproportionate share in the available riches, they risk to incur jealousy and scorn (Foster, 1965:293 ff).

Banfield, whose research was concentrated on Southern Italy, advances another explanation for the slender preparedness among peasants to take part in development projects. In his view the main obstacle is not resistance to individual progress, but precisely a tendency to make the interests of one's own family prevail over those of the community — 'amoral familism', as he calls it. This amoral familism again produces a peasant distrust, which in its turn causes 'political incapacity', impotence to achieve progress through co-operation (Banfield, 1958).

There appears, therefore, to be a certain difference in stress between Banfield's and Foster's views, apart from possible differences caused by the fact that they are dealing with quite different regions. Whereas Foster, not without regret, observes that the Mexican peasants do not like the idea of achieving progress through personal effort, as small entrepreneurs, Banfield on the contrary deplores that South-Italian peasants stick to their small family farm and are averse from taking part in co-operatives undertaking community projects. Foster's view is evidently influenced by a typically American belief in 'free enterprise', the functioning of which he saw hampered in Mexico by the 'image of the limited good'.

Still more typically American is the position taken by Charles Erasmus, author of *Man takes Control*. Erasmus also undertook research in Mexico, where he found what he calls the '*encogido* syndrome', as source of the prevalent peasant distrust. The *encogido* is a special type of small peasant, a timid and withdrawn human being that avoids persons of a higher status except for a few who act as intermediaries between him and the broader society. The opposite personality is the *entron*, 'a person who pushes himself and is not afraid to interact with higher status persons for economically advantageous contacts'. It is the former, *encogido* type of peasants who are taking their present state of poverty for granted. It is they who do not want to push ahead, but who at the same time invidiously watch their neighbours, in order to keep them in their place. Everyone is bound to stick to a modest way of life, characterized by 'inconspicuous consumption'. 'Keeping the Joneses down' is how Erasmus describes this attitude, which he seems to view as more or less pathological, since it is contrary to the American ideal of 'keeping up with the Joneses'. The '*encogido* syndrome' is, according to Erasmus, a typical 'lower class' characteristic (Erasmus, 1968:70 ff).

In India it seems that Community Development workers also distinguish two types of peasants: those who run, who are receptive to new ideas and new techniques; and the mass of the people who are slow and inert, and move heavily. The former category, the so-called 'progressive' farmers, are the chickens. The slow ones are the ducks.

It is becoming clear now that all those who wish well for the poor peasants of the Third World are stumbling upon one universal obstacle:

peasant distrust. The only question one generally forgets to raise is whether this peasant distrust is not justified by scores of sad experiences and disappointments. Are the broad masses of the peasantry not right when they refuse to co-operate with projects that keep the existing social and political system intact? Is it not true that these projects aim at limited changes only which, according to their experience, merely benefit a thin upper layer of the rural society, which is already better off than the masses?

Recognition for having posed this question in a more fundamental manner is due to the well-known Dutch expert of Latin America, Gerrit Huizer, who in his recent doctoral dissertation deals with peasant unrest in that part of the world (Huizer, 1970). He shows that the so-called apathy and inertia of the peasants is narrowly linked up with a general atmosphere of repression which prevails in many countries of the Third World. It is not the poor neighbours of a peasant who primarily oppose his attempts to advance, but on the contrary those who have a stake in maintaining the existing conditions. With a wealth of examples, derived from his personal experience in Latin America and Sicily, Huizer shows that the poor peasants certainly are prepared to make an effort for a betterment of their lot whenever they expect a tangible effect from it. Maybe they are less interested than some American researchers in the individual type of economic competition which entails progress for a peasant at the expense of his neighbours. But they do readily join peasant unions whenever they see a prospect of a collective betterment of their lot before them, for example by enforcing agrarian reforms through which all of them will get a piece of land. They do know very well that the true obstacle standing in their way towards progress is situated in the repressive power of the prevalent political and social system under which they have to live, be it the *hacienda* system of Latin America, or the Indian caste system to which the higher, 'dominant' castes owe their economic power over the menial castes.

It is the rural gentry who know how 'to keep the Joneses down'. In a doctoral thesis on labour relationships in the Western part of rural India, J.C. Breman describes how a lower caste man, who was rash enough to enter the extremely profitable mango trade that had been thus far a monopoly of the dominant caste of Anavil Brahmins, was put in his proper place by these through threatening letters holding out the prospect of a raid at night (Breman, 1970:176). Huizer equally mentions examples for Latin America, of how *hacienda* owners attempt by all means, legal or illegal, to prevent poor peasants from taking to the cultivation of crops which could imply a competition for their own products (Huizer, 1970: 167).

In a mountain village of West Java not far from Bandung, the writer has been able to observe the obstruction poor peasants had to cope with, because they had attempted to rid themselves through their own effort of the dominance of a few landlords. In an earlier publication the Dutch rural sociologist Ten Dam had described how in the course of the national revolution in that village Chibodas, a group of land-labourers had tried to evade the power of the landlords by illegally occupying some forest land and cultivating food crops there, which at the same time could be considered to serve the revolutionary cause (Ten Dam, 1951). After the transfer of sovereignty from the Dutch to the Indonesian Republic the Forestry Service returned and claimed back the occupied land. As long as possible the illegal occupants tried to keep the freedom they had acquired for a short time through their own efforts, until the authorities made this definitely impossible.

When the writer arrived in the village in 1957 to see what had happened next, he found that a large group of landless peasants had registered a year previously for resettlement as independent small farmers, in South Sumatra. They had sold their scanty possessions and had been ready for departure a few months before his arrival. But the *transmigrasi* service had left them in the lurch. The promises were not kept, through some sloppiness or corruption the fare for their crossing had not been forthcoming, and the peasants had been forced to beg for work with the big landlords once more. Many of the villagers were convinced that the officials had sabotaged the resettlement plan in order to ensure cheap labour for the landlords.

Gradually we may realize where the true obstacles to change are to be found. It is those who benefit from the existing inequality and from the distress among the broad masses who, usually with some support from the authorities, oppose any attempt on the part of the underdogs to effectuate some basic change in their lot.

The impression that it is the poor masses which resist change, is being created by the fact that sometimes a government, supported by part of the better-off landowners in the Third World, takes an initiative to introduce projects allegedly intended to serve the interests of the common people. All such projects have in common that they aim at change on a limited scale. Under headings such as Community Development innovations are being introduced which are not directed towards a radical change of the prevalent conditions of power and ownership, but are intended to produce a few improvements of a more or less technical kind within the existing social and political framework: better planting methods, the use of fertilizers and insecticides, improved agricultural tools, etc. It is this type of small improvements, while the prevalent power structure is being kept intact, that meets with the usual peasant distrust which results in seeming apathy and passive resistance and is often interpreted as sluggishness, as resistance to change. But this peasant distrust is mostly based on a life-long experience with this type of restricted changes. This experience namely teaches that these improvements usually merely benefit the restricted group which is already better-off. The more prosperous peasants have sufficient land and capital, and generally also manpower at their disposal to try experiments, to buy fertilizers and insecticides at the lowered prices at which the authorities make them available as part of the Community Development programme. With government aid they are therefore able to establish a 'model farm', but their poor neighbours lack the means to follow the model. The welfare services in the Third World are generally 'betting on the strong' — on the *kulaks*, the wealthy peasants. The only consequence is, as appears from several field studies, for example in India, that these wealthier farmers are enabled through the improved techniques to exploit the poor masses of tenants or landless labourers still more efficiently than before.[1]

Peasant distrust has been sketched by Bailey in his studies on India in a most striking manner. The officials belong to the higher castes. They are far removed from the poor peasant masses, and only mix on a comparatively equal footing with a few rich landowners. The peasants and the functionaries have certain mutual stereotypes. The officials are viewing the peasants as stupid, indolent and greedy. 'They' do not know what is good for them, 'they' want things for nothing. On the other hand the peasants view the officials, including those belonging to the welfare services, as 'unpredictable, unsympathetic, ignorant, and immeasurably powerful'. 'They' do not understand 'our' problems (Bailey, 1957: 249ff and 253).

Ten Dam observed similar stereotypes among the poor *tanis* in West Java: to them the official is one who *melarang melulu*, who does nothing but forbid.

Peasant distrust of officials is known from all types of societies. But in countries where the poor peasants form a large majority this mood is being reinforced by a host of evil experiences. The distrust is a sound reaction to a type of change that does not lead to essential improvement, to real progress.

II

This leads us towards the extremely intricate problem of how the concept of 'progress' should be defined. After the concept of 'social evolution' had been more or less banished from scholarly literature for half a century — at least in the Western world — it is dawning at last upon social scientists that they cannot dispense with the concept of evolution. The whole 'development issue' presupposes an assessment of change in terms of 'progress'.

[1] I may refer to W. F. Wertheim, *East-West Parallels: Sociological Approaches to Modern Asia*, 1964, especially the final chapter ('Betting on the Strong'). See also S. C. Dube, *India's Changing Villages: Human Factors in Community Development*, 1958.

In the past years much time has been spent on discussions about 'modernization'. Implicitly it was always taken for granted that 'modernization' should be equated with 'progress'. 'Modernization' is then being conceived either as the technological advance, or as a social and psychological development towards an acceptance of unmistakably Western values, such as a high individual aspiration level, stress upon individual achievement and individual social upward mobility.

As a typical example of the way Westerners — Americans in particular — evaluate conditions in the Third World, I would like to mention the well-known work of Daniel Lerner, *The Passing of Traditional Society: Modernizing the Middle East*, which appeared in 1958. Through questionnaires the author attempted to discover how far some peoples of the Middle East had advanced on the ladder leading from Eastern backwardness unto the Walhalla of modernity. Some of the peoples were still living predominantly in their traditional society; a few others, among them Syria and Egypt, had got stuck somewhere half-way, and were therefore 'transitional societies'. Whereas their aspirations were Western ones, the achievements were thus far not consonant with the aspiration level. Finally there were a few peoples, such as the Turks, who were well on the way towards modernity.

What strikes us most is the naivety of the author's attempt to apply typically American values as a self-evident touchstone for modernity. A desire individually to advance, an urban way of life, are assessed as unmistakable signs of a modern attitude. The crowning folly was the way replies given to the question: 'Would the interviewee like to become a president of Turkey', were evaluated. A shepherd who was asked this question stared like a stuck pig — and by this he proved to be still wholly 'traditional'!

When resistance to 'change' comes up for discussion, it is generally this type of 'modernization' one has in mind. It is this type of change indeed, conceived in purely individualistic terms, which in the Third World often meets with peasant distrust. But this does not mean at all that the peasants do not want change. Change they do want — but in another direction. If we do not equate progress, evolution, with 'modernization' in the sense of Westernization but rather view it as part of the historical process set in motion by the human urge for emancipation and liberation from all kinds of oppressive chains, the concept of progress appears in a quite different light.

It is true that technological advance remains one aspect of the evolutionary progress, as a means to free ourselves from the limitations nature has set to human capabilities. But the great difference is that, in order to decide whether a distinct process should be viewed as progress, as a step towards social evolution, we should now ask ourselves to what extent it contributes to a liberation of thus far not utilized or suppressed human capacities. A liberation of ever broadening groups of mankind — the labour class, disprivileged races, subjected peoples, women, youth — all this is part and parcel of the world-wide emancipation process which forms the essence of the concept of evolution.

If we define the kinds of change leading towards progress in this way, it appears that it is often precisely the poor peasants who aspire at change. It is they who sometimes no longer follow evolutionary methods in order to achieve such a progress for the broad masses, but rather resort to revolutionary means. And it frequently occurs that it is the so-called 'elite' that resists this type of change, of progress.

The term 'elite', for the rest, is strongly associated with one's ideology. American sociologists and political scientists are highly interested in the elites of the Third World. To quote one American: 'We want to know whom to buy, and whom to kill'.

This leads us to the question, to what extent the resistances to change, that is to say, to fundamental change, is due to the impact of our own Western societies. In what way do we interfere in the situation in the Third World?

III

Already at the time of overt colonialism the colonial regimes were blamed for wanting artificially to keep native societies primitive. Under the guise of protection of the people against disturbing influences quite often a policy was followed that aimed at keeping the prevalent social structures intact. The traditional way of life of the primitive natives was often idealized, and a well-nigh museum-like care was devoted to maintaining old customs and traditions. This was especially true for areas where colonial regimes largely rested on the support of a native aristocracy, which was more or less mixed up in colonial exploitation — as was, for example, the case with the regents in Java, or with the Sultans on Sumatra's East coast.

As a matter of fact, of course there occurred a good deal of change. Utilization of natives as cheap manpower on plantations, in road-building and in the construction of bridges, implied a strong infringement upon the traditional social pattern and way of life. Occupying vast territories for plantations often robbed the native population of its real subsistence basis. In actual fact colonial policy therefore amounted to squaring the circle. There was, on the one hand, a wish to preserve old structures, socially and politically, as much as possible — on the other hand they were seriously impaired by the regime's economic activities. It was a matter of eating one's cake and having it. But under a colonial system eating always prevailed.

Basically neo-colonialism is also characterized by an artificially upholding of the existing social and political structures in the Third World.

In appearance and verbally the West supports change, equally in the countries of the Third World. But fundamentally the type of change, advocated and introduced from the West, is largely of the same kind as the one pursued by the so-called native elite: restricted change, leaving the existing social and political structures intact. We may even contend that the existing structures can often be maintained only by the grace of Western neo-colonialism taking on the guise of development aid.

For the position of the so-called elite is actually extremely we.. from a political point of view, as soon as it is being confronted with a surging broader popular resistance which, in the Third World, is predominantly a peasants' resistance. Quite a number of regimes in the Third World are increasingly based, not on a massive support among the peasantry, but on the arms and other means of coercion furnished by the West. Whereas, under a more or less populist regime, after the achievement of independence there still remains an effort to acquire an active, massive following among the peasantry (as was the case under Sukarno in Indonesia, or under Sihanouk in Cambodia, and as is still the case under Nyerere in Tanzania), after some time the total picture changes. While in the course of time populist regimes are being replaced by military dictatorships, the spontaneous support from the people fades away, and the regime has to base itself increasingly on so-called 'development aid', which finally gets decisive importance.

The most characteristic aspect of the type of change advocated by the West is the paramount stress laid upon technological solutions. The idea that a solution to issues like hunger and poverty can be found in technological innovation is narrowly connected with a typically Western view of world problems. A case in point is the present-day propaganda for a 'green revolution'.

In principle it is of course correct that food production could be considerably increased in many countries of the Third World through improved seeds and better planting methods. But usually it is overlooked that a practical application and the ultimate success of the innovation cannot be disconnected from the social environment where the new rice or wheat variety is being introduced. From a technical point of view, as is generally known, the new varieties could be successful only through a liberal application of fertilizers and insecticides. This problem is one that can still be solved by combining these together with the new seeds within one package furnished to the peasants. The problem becomes more complicated through the fact that the new seeds only thrive if there is optimal irrigation. And the construction of irrigation works is often dependent on social and political factors. And even if the works have been built, new problems arise. How can one ensure that the peasants will make an efficient use of the new irrigation facilities? In some areas in India (where a number of my students were undertaking research), a large majority of poor peasants did not make use of the available irrigation facilities.

But in fact even the utilization of the new seeds, fertilizers and insecticides cannot be dissociated from the total social structure. The wealthier peasants are the only ones who are in a position to make full use of the new possibilities. Again the green revolution in practice amounts to a 'betting on the strong'. In India the fear has already been officially expressed that the green revolution might result in a further polarization between rich and poor, and thus turn red.

And if an increased food production is being achieved, the question arises whether the additional yields will find enough prospective buyers. Market relationships are also narrowly connected with the prevalent power structure. One could well imagine that within a few years the prices of the food crops in such a country will decline to a point where for many growers no further incentive for cultivating the new varieties will exist any more.[1]

On the other hand, the massive experiments with the new varieties of rice in Indonesia, the failure of which has been recently officially admitted, teach us the lesson that if this application is not left to the free initiative of the peasantry, but is being imposed by the military through coercion, the results are becoming still more doubtful. In this connexion we have to note that in Indonesia the profits of the new seeds, and of the fertilizers and insecticides provided, largely accrued to a few big foreign concerns with which the Indonesian government had concluded contracts (Utrecht, 1970).

It is therefore understandable that distrust of the new type of colonialism, which aspires at making the countries of the Third World dependent upon Western technological know-how, is not only in evidence on the part of the peasantry in the Third World, but also on the part of progressive academics in that part of the world.[2] This type of export of technology is too often associated with positions of monopoly.

The French geographer Pierre Gourou rightly calls the present situation in the fields of science and technology still fully colonial (Gourou, 1966: 245).

The most glaring aspect of neo-colonialism, however, is the policy of preserving the prevalent *economic* structures. The existing pattern of exchange of raw materials against our finished industrial products remains in force, just as during the colonial period. The failure of the UNCTAD conferences has shown that the real resistances to basic change in the existing exchange pattern have to be looked for in the West. In spite of all the 'whitewash' about development aid, the preservation of the existing economic structures remains decisive for our policies.

[1]See for example Myrdal (1970: 123 ff) and Wharton (1969:468 ff).
[2]See for example Singh, 1969.

And on the rare occasions that the poor peasants in a certain country effectuate fundamental change, the Western 'resistance' to change assumes a more extreme form: that of napalm, fragmentation bombs and herbicides used against peoples who are impertinent enough to pursue *real* change, and who do not content themselves with the 'image of the limited good'.

For the First World is obsessed by the fear that the Third World, if it will really change, will not become part of the First but of the Second one.

Over fifty years ago Lenin wrote about progressive Asia and backward Europe. In 1970 it becomes clear that this was more than a sally. It was a prophecy.

7. Group Conflict and Class Formation in South-East Asia[1]

HANS-DIETER EVERS

I

ONE of the most difficult tasks faced by South-East Asian statesmen and scholars alike is to assess, understand and predict the major trends of social and political developments in the area. The task would be formidable in any society, in an area as complex as South-East Asia it appears to be doomed to failure right from the beginning. Should we then continue to study the 'golden road to modernity' by investigating isolated village communities, as Manning Nash and others have done, should we study the social history of particular small towns, like 'Modjokuto', and generalize from there (Geertz), or even explain the fate of nations through microscopic studies of the South-East Asian 'personality' (Pye, Philipps, Piker)? I feel there is still an almost unlimited need for further detailed and localized studies of the same high calibre as the work cited above. Nevertheless we cannot expect to understand the major trends of modernization in South-East Asia from these studies. To generalize from specific cases is methodologically dubious. Furthermore, major conflicts and changes are based on societal if not international frictions and processes. If we set out to study the modernization of societies I do not see why we should not concentrate directly on one subject and focus on societies and their structure rather than on villages, families or individuals.

[1]This paper was written while I was on sabbatical leave from Yale University on a senior faculty fellowship. Most of the ideas presented here were developed from 1958 to the present during field research projects on industrial entrepreneurs in Ceylon, Buddhist monks in Ceylon and Thailand, higher civil servants in Thailand and professionals in Indonesia and Malaysia. This selection of countries and groups has probably influenced my evaluation of trends of group and class formation in South-East Asia. I gratefully acknowledge that I discussed the paper with some of my fellows at the Institute of Southeast Asian Studies in Singapore who helped to weed out some of the major errors. I also benefited from a lively discussion after reading part of this paper at Columbia University in May 1971. I am to be blamed for those errors that remain.

Attempts to work in this direction are rare. Coedes' classical studies on the 'Indianization' of South-East Asia were not followed by similar works on 'Islamization', 'Westernization' or 'Modernization'. Boeke's theory of the development of a capitalist colonial economy and its dual structure and Benda's essay on 'the structure of South-East Asian history' stand out among the very few attempts to discover basic and long term trends in modern South-East Asia. Short of writing a monumental work on the modern history of South-East Asia, what methods could we use and what theories employ to detect, analyse and describe some of the major social and political trends in modernizing South-East Asia?

There appear to be two major options. The first is to utilize recent theories of modernization developed by American social scientists. I find most of them of little value. Lerner's communications theory, Marion Levy's and David Apter's rather abstract systems theories, Inkeles' modernization scales, and Talcott Parsons' neo-evolutionary paradigms appear to be too far removed from an empirical reality beset by society-wide conflicts, widespread political unrest, war, insurgency, starvation, massacres and racial strife. The second option, it appears to me, entails going back to theories developed along with empirical studies on the same topic in other societies and historical periods. Here the concern of social scientists with the modernization of European societies, the demise of its feudal past and the development of capitalist or socialist societies and political systems comes to mind. Weber's monumental work on rationalization, conflict and competition, the development of bureaucracies and the establishment of legal systems of domination appear to be as relevant today in South-East Asia as at the turn of the century in Europe. Durkheim's theories on the division of labour in society, Pareto's circulation of elites and Schumpeter's and Sombart's work on the rise of capitalism provide, together with the Marx, Engels and Lenin theories of conflict and development, a formidable arsenal to attack the problems of modern South-East Asian development.

Especially the theories of class and class conflict as societal (rather than partial) theories discussed by almost all the above-mentioned authors and developed by their followers give us the necessary tools already applied successfully elsewhere. The question then, of course, is: do we have class structures in South-East Asian societies or better, are classes sufficiently developed to warrant an analysis of major social and political processes in terms of class theory? In short, does a class theory fit the empirical reality of South-East Asian societies? There is no question about the existence of marked social inequality and conflict in South-East Asia. But is this social inequality structured into social classes and does conflict arise out of contradictions between classes?

It is my thesis that South-East Asian societies have already developed or are in the process of developing a rather specific type of class structure and that this class structure and its inherent conflicts provide the framework within which political activities and economic efforts will have to take place. In other words, the dynamics of class formation itself will influence if not determine future social, political and economic developments in the area. I have thus chosen the framework of a theory of class formation and class conflict not to prove or disprove the theory itself, but to analyse what I think is a major trend in the 'modernization' of South-East Asian societies.

Before I set out to explain my thesis let me anticipate some of the basic and major criticisms that have been levelled against attempts to discuss some South-East Asian societies in the framework of social class. The criticism runs approximately like this: a class structure is a typical European type of social organization born under very specific historical circumstances. To use a class model to analyse South-East Asian societies means forcing an alien way of thinking on a completely different cultural tradition and on a very differently organized social system. We would thus create an artificial society that only exists in the minds of foreign social scientists but bears no resemblance to social reality nor the thinking of its own members. Students of South-East Asian societies have, as far as they have commented on larger societal structures at all, tended to stress vertical links or patronage systems, superimposed on a more or less loosely structured peasant society. One recent study on Burma points out that 'below the national elite the social order is fairly undifferentiated and there is hardly a stratification approaching that of a class structure. People are not class conscious' (Lissak, 1970:72). For Indonesia vertical structures, in Indonesian called *aliran* (stream), have been described as the main structural principle of Indonesian society. A common religious or cultural value system rather than class consciousness is said to integrate different socio-economic group in each 'stream'. Class divisions are therefore non-existent, irrelevant or indistinguishable.[1]

For the case of Thailand Lucien Hanks has claimed that

efforts to depict social classes in Thai society flounder because of misconstruing the nature of this social order which resembles a military organization more than an occidental class type society. Like an army, Thai society has a hierarchy of fixed ranks which determine occupation, but one moves freely from occupation to occupation up and down the hierarchy (Hanks, 1962: 1252).

Though an army never struck me as a particularly flexible type of organization with a high degree of mobility from lower ranks into the officers corps, the implications of Hanks are clear: differences between integrated units and minutely differentiated ranks are important but not horizontally differentiated groups or classes.

Similar arguments are also very frequent among leaders of South-East Asian societies themselves. In recent interviews with local political party

[1]See Wertheim, 1959, Geertz, 1965, and Hindley, 1970, for recent discussions on this theme. Gunawan and van der Muijzenberg, 1967, described similar structures in the Netherlands.

leaders in Indonesia I was told by PNI members that differences and class distinctions were no longer in existence in Indonesia since the Dutch ruling class was abolished during the revolution. Views like this confirm Peter Worsley's description of what he calls 'populism' in Third World countries:

The societies of Asia and Africa are commonly seen by theorists in those countries not so much in terms of the class divisions that the Westerner almost instinctively begins to look for, but in terms of the common life-situation of whole populations which derives from their past and present tradition of village level democracy, and from the unifying experience of common political expression and economic impoverishment at the hands of foreign imperialists (Worsley, 1964: 130).

Though it is quite possible that Western social scientists have been influenced by the teachings of 'populist' political leaders or by discussions with intellectuals holding similar views, I do not necessarily want to allege that their statements confuse ideology with social reality (as in Evers, 1966). [1]Their observations that clearly distinguished classes did not exist in the respective South-East Asian countries at the time of their visit may very well be true. It would then perhaps be a misconstruction to describe the respective societies *at that very moment* in class terms. But it would certainly not be a valid assumption that a study of a society at any one particular point in time would give a fair description of the 'nature' (if, indeed, there is such a thing) of that society. A major characteristic of all South-East Asian societies is, after all, that they are changing and that this change is fairly rapid. My point, then, is that the often described fluidity or loose structure,[2] as well as the compartmentalization into vertical organizations, dual or multiple, into *alirans*, cliques and patronage systems are all aspects of rapid change and at times of the reorganization into an emerging class system. But this is an empirical question and I will have to put forward my thesis in the context of major social trends in some South-East Asian societies, after I have outlined the theoretical framework of my analysis.

[1]Professor Alatas objected to this statement during the seminar discussion. He felt I should not have retracted from my 1966 statement, made in relation to Thailand, but should have expanded it to include also Indonesia and other South-East Asian societies. South-East Asians themselves, Professor Alatas suggested, never had any doubts about the existence of a class structure, only foreign scholars blurred the issue. I would not quarrel with this point of view, except that I recognize the particular difficulties of anthropologists in analysing class structures within their normal theoretical instrumentarium. I would also admit that at certain times structural features other than classes are more relevant towards an understanding of a society at that time.

[2]A critical evaluation of the loose structure concept is the subject of a recent book and need not be repeated here: H. D. Evers, ed., *Loosely Structured Social Systems, Thailand in Comparative Perspective*, New Haven: Yale University Southeast Asian Studies, 1969.

II

The formation of classes is a slow historical process. Classes do not emerge over-night though dramatic events like wars or revolutions may speed up the process considerably. Even so, the positions making up a class have to be created and multiplied first.

We might look at a simple model to clarify this point.

Say we find a clearly developed class structure in a certain society at a certain time. There is an aristocratic upper class consisting of feudal and clerical nobles, monopolizing military power and control over land and dominating a fairly homogeneous peasantry. If we study the same society a few hundred years later, we may again find a strict class structure, but made up of completely different groups. Aristocrats and serfs have more or less disappeared. The upper class is made up of 'bourgeois capitalists', dominating an industrial proletariat. We are now faced by a question a Chinese historian might like to ask when he compares one firmly establish-ed dynasty with the next: what precisely happened in between two firmly patterned social and political structures? How did the transition take place? If in our case 'bourgeois capitalists' form the new upper class, when did the first person of this species make his dramatic appearance? And who was the first 'proletarian'?

Putting all this into less fictitious terms: any firmly established social order contains already the seeds of a new social structure in the form of individuals or groups who might under certain conditions at certain times grow and develop into larger units, groups or classes.

Class formation can thus be traced back to the individual level. Before a new class emerges there have to be new social positions sharing the same 'life chances', the same relation to the means of production and power and the same values. Here the connexion to what is now commonly called 'modernization' becomes apparent. The formation of new positions is, indeed, 'modernization'.

This process is usually described by evolutionary theorists as social differentiation (or by classical thinkers as an increasing division of labour).

Though no detailed studies on social differentiation in South-East Asia are available we can conclude from some statistical data and historical accounts that the process was fairly slow, until very recently, both in terms of new roles and in terms of persons filling the new positions. This is in-directly supported by the fact that the proportion of the non-agricultural section of the population of South-East Asian societies (with the exception of Singapore and West Malaysia) has not significantly risen, but has remained roughly at a 20 per cent level in contrast to earlier European developments.

In many cases the appearance of new roles has been quite sudden and those who take up these new positions had to go through a rigorous re-socialization process.[1] Large-scale organizations like bureaucracies, the colonial school system and armed forces usually provided forceful re-socialization agencies and were as such indispensable for modernization and the creation of modern positions.

In other words, the European experience of the gradual differentiation of social positions out of pre-modern society is not repeated in South-East Asia, but differentiation occurs primarily by importing role patterns or by their imposition on society from abroad, usually through the establishment of large-scale organizations. Modernization, social evolution and social differentiation are therefore largely foreign impositions on South-East Asian countries. Bureaucracies are patterned on Euro-American examples and differences are treated as deviations to be abolished, the medical profession subscribes to the ethics and standards of their counterparts in industrialized countries and factories hardly make any allowance for the different social background of their workers and try to achieve the same organizational standards as American factories. Modernization in the sense of role differentiation is therefore largely guided from outside and superimposed on a small section of the non-agrarian population.

As the number of positions for each occupational role increases, social mobility has to be high initially.[2] In fact during the first generation a new

[1]The psychological pressure and personal conflict accompanying the creation of new positions can be expressed in religious terms. There is generally in South-East Asia an increased interest in religion, exorcism and magic. Persons who have migrated to the cities to fill the new roles in the middle ranges of governmental and private bureaucracies seem to have lost their village or kinship connexions without having as yet developed an urban or occupational identity. To express their personal conflicts they turn to traditional means, black magic, and to relieve their anxiety they take part in exorcist rites or mystical practices. Spirit medium cults in Singapore, vows to town spirits (at *lak muang* temples) in Thailand, exorcism in Colombo, *kebatinan* groups in Java, and *keramat* veneration in Malaysian and Indonesian towns seem to attract more followers than ever before. As far as some preliminary studies show the new clients are predominantly second generation urban dwellers and occupants of a multitude of new middle level clerical and technical positions.
Some recent still unpublished studies are Gananath Obeyesekere's studies on exorcism in urban Ceylon, and the present writer's studies together with Arthur Stillman, Daniel Regan and Arman Moechtar, on a spirit temple in Bangkok and on traditional medical practitioners in Malaya and Sumatra. For Java, see Mulder, 1970.

[2]As Kamol Somvichian and Mokhzani remarked in their comments on this paper, mobility in the colonial period took partly the form of transferring an old strategic group or class, usually indigenous aristocracies, into new positions. This mobility can also be described as the modernization of a traditional elite. Modernization of the Thai bureaucracy started initially this way, higher training facilities in Malaya and the Netherlands East Indies were restricted to members of the nobility, and mandarins continued to take over government positions in French Indo-China. The expansion of lower level colonial bureaucracies and new professional positions, especially in conjunction with an expanding capitalist estate economy, increased, however, mobility from other groups. From the few available studies on this topic we can guess that social mobility into new positions tended to be high in most South-East Asian countries around the turn of the century, but declined before and during the economic depression of the late 1930s. See e.g. Furnivall (1939: 443) on Indonesia; Evers, 1966, on Thailand, and Evers, 1964 on Ceylon.

position is in existence there is 100 per cent in-flow into the new positions. Mobility for the whole society might not be high, but mobility in the newly emerging sector of the occupational structure has to show a very high rate. In the initial phases of modernization persons in modern positions tend therefore to be highly mobile people with all the characteristics associated with strong mobility.[1]

In the beginning the incumbents of new positions had probably very little in common. They might at best be seen as what Dahrendorf has termed 'quasi groups' (Dahrendorf, 1962). A sense of common identity is originally still overridden by an identity with the immediate social surroundings, the ethnic group, the kin group, or the stratum of origin.[2]

An awareness of the fact that members of a quasi group are affected in a similar way by the economic, social and political forces in a country is often created by dramatic events. The reduction in the number of civil servants in Thailand in 1924–7 or the reduction in business opportunities of Indonesian traders after a heavy influx of Chinese immigrants in the 1920s has developed a common identity and some form of internal organization (e.g. the foundation of Sarekat Islam).

Quasi groups are thus transformed into what I would like to call 'strategic groups', as they now become of strategic importance as groups for political development, for conflict situations, reform or revolution in their societies. They actively promote their own economic or political goals. They tend to support the activities of leaders, emerging out of their own ranks, or those leaders who are thought to represent their aspirations.

The strategic group is thus a *recruiting field* for political leadership and a political pressure group at the same time. I shall later return to an analysis of strategic group formation in South-East Asia, but might mention here that civil servants, the military, teachers, professionals and Chinese businessmen seem to have been the major strategic groups in modern South-East Asia.

An important condition for strategic group formation seems to be a sudden increase in the membership of a quasi group. An increase in size (not the absolute size as such) will put pressure on members to seek an appropriate share of wealth and power available in a society. (A sudden reduction in the available wealth might have a similar impact.) This will eventually always result in a conflict situation with other groups who either

---

[1] I have tried to analyse the relations between inter-generational mobility and the attitudes towards changes and cultural traditions in a research report entitled 'Higher Civil Servants in Thailand: Overseas Education, Mobility and Attitudes towards their own Cultural Tradition', Freiburg, Germany: Arnold Bergstraesser Institute, 1964.

[2] Striking examples emerged during a recent (1970) survey in a provincial town in Indonesia. There was a clear difference between an older generation of lawyers, who were very much involved in the welfare of their immediate community, in business transactions and religious affairs, but took little interest in the endeavours of the new generation of lawyers and their professional organization. Questions after common problems of professionals usually drew a blank with the older lawyers.

are on their way to increasing their share of scarce resources or are defending their old position.

The perception of potential conflict is certainly increased if members of strategic groups have what James Scott (1968) has called a 'constant pie orientation'. The endeavour of group members is in this case primarily directed at staking a claim to what is essentially perceived as a constant amount of goods, services, and positions. Enlarging the pie and appropriating the additions is not seen as a viable alternative. If indeed this constant pie orientation is as widespread as Scott claims, than it might help to explain the lack of social differentiation and the intensification of group conflict.

The ensuing conflict between groups may then, however, bring about awareness of a common interest, group cohesion and solidarity through the mechanism analysed in detail by Simmel and later by Lewis Coser in his book on the functions of conflict. This new or increased solidarity of the strategic group will be expressed in a distinct style of life and in the foundation of voluntary organizations. This in turn indicates that not only the person following a modern occupation himself, but his whole family becomes increasingly tied to the fate of his strategic group. Marriage within the strategic group and increasing self-recruitment reduce mobility into the group and strengthen group cohesion.

The political framework of group conflict is largely determined by the *sequence* in which strategic groups evolve. In a modernizing society whose old social and political order is doomed to disappear, new norms for political action have to be established. The first modern strategic group to emerge will have the most decisive influence on the new political culture. Once the rules of the game have been established and a distinct political style adopted, any future changes have to take account of the past structure. In most cases it will require a 'cultural revolution' to change the established political normative system. A recent book by Barrington Moore provides a good deal of material to back this view though its major theme is somewhat different. Moore concentrated his attention on several strategic groups, the landed gentry, the peasantry, the government administration, and the urban bourgeoisie. The rise of any of these to power in a revolution set the stage for the major different political systems in the modern world. His studies of Britain, France, Germany, the U.S., China, Japan, and India, lead him to discern three major routes to the modern world: a revolution from above by a combined gentry and bureaucracy led to fascism, a bourgeois revolution of the urban bourgeoisie to western style democracy, and a peasant revolution to communism. It is not so much the descriptive historical contents of Moore's work but the theoretical aspects, that are of interest here. The development of strategic groups, their struggle for dominance, and the identification of their interests and norms with what is to be the modernization process provides an excellent framework for analysing South-East Asian developments.

The process of group formation might very well be arrested and create a situation of confusion and long term conflict. An example is provided by Clifford Geertz. In his study on the social history of a Javanese town he describes the formation of strategic groups out of basic occupational groups. He then goes on to analyse how these what he calls 'first-order sociocultural groupings' are transformed, divided, rearranged in a time of revolution, political instability and economic depression into the already mentioned *aliran*. Strategic group formation meant modernization, the establishment of the *aliran* system a relapse into traditional patterns, without actually reestablishing an integrated traditional society. 'Both tradition and modernity seemed to be receding at an increasing rate, leaving only the relics of the first and the simulacrum of the second. With every shake of the kaleidoscope the past seemed further back and the future further ahead' (Geertz, 1965: 152).

This period of confusion, transformation and change, through which a number of South-East Asian countries have gone or are going, is precisely the period I have alluded to in the beginning. It would be misleading to interpret the nature or essence of any society on the basis of a flashlight photo in the darkness of turmoil and rapid change. If we adopt a long-term perspective there are signs that a new social structure will emerge. This new structure, I feel, will come about through a transformation of strategic groups into social classes, and I shall therefore try to present some theoretical propositions on this process of class formation in developing societies.

III

A rigid class structure and intensive class conflict are not very common phenomena. Basic patterns of structural conflict in a society can probably best be analysed as group conflicts between established and emerging strategic groups. Even if we can discern a fairly clearly developed class structure, there will nevertheless be remnants of strategic groups or newly emerging ones, both providing internal structure to classes.

In many cases strategic groups will dominate the social and political scene for prolonged periods of time until under certain conditions a class structure develops. In any case the dissolution of one class structure or a revolutionary change will always be preceded by the development of strategic groups, which will confuse the strict class pattern until a new class system emerges (if at all). The question then is how are strategic groups transformed into classes?

A class structure always presupposes a division into a ruling class and classes of those being ruled. It is of course perfectly possible that a society is dominated by a number of conflicting strategic groups. There seems to be, however, a tendency towards coalition. In fact coalitions and mergers of strategic groups controlling different shares of the societal wealth and power appear to be basic to class formation. Historical examples abound from the somewhat uneasy alliance between feudal nobility and clergy during European middle ages to the merger of civil service, big business and military elites analysed by C. Wright Mills for the U.S. The shift of the allegiance of the intellectuals from a ruling class to a subject class (e.g. an intellectuals — working class alliance) has been described as an important factor in the creation of a revolutionary situation by Crane Brinton. Pooling of resources to maintain the ruling position, exchange of personnel and common membership in organizations are some of the mechanism of coalition. A further aspect of class formation is the restriction or control of mobility into the new class. This is especially felt after a period of high mobility during the formation of strategic groups.

Conflict between classes is inherent in any society structured by class, as well as group conflict is inherent in a society structured by strategic groups. There are, however, various ways to reduce, channel or gloss over class conflict (Dahrendorf, 1959). One way is to transform class conflict into inter-personal competition by allowing social mobility and propagating an ideology of equal opportunity for all. This way is usually not open to South-East Asian societies, because opportunity for mobility is so obviously low and because intense inter-personal conflict is less likely in a society in which ethnic and family loyalties still loom large. An Asian solution is, however, provided in the form of clique and patronage systems. Disbursement of government funds and positions and sometimes sharing of dividends from corruption tend to keep patronage systems going for longer periods of time, though closing of downward patronage channels through closer integration of the upper class, economic crises or the creation of competitive patronage systems can endanger the precarious balance.[1] The main threat to such class systems is those *new* strategic groups that are difficult to integrate into patronage systems, like students or peasant movements.

I shall now turn to a similar loose discussion of some trends in group and class formation in South-East Asia.

IV

There is little doubt that class systems existed in South-East Asia before and during the colonial period. The colonial bureaucracies with their higher ranks formed together with the military officers, estate and big business managers or owners a caste-like upper class in firm control of the

[1]See Alatas, 1968, for a penetrating discussion of corruption.

TABLE 12
RURAL AND URBAN POPULATION IN SOUTH-EAST ASIA

Country	Per cent urban population 1970	Relative decrease of rural population 1950–1970 (percentage points)	Per cent of agricultural population 1970[1]
Brunei	44.1	—1.1	—
Burma	15.8	—2.9	64
Indonesia	17.9	—5.6	70
Khmer Republic	12.8	—4.9	76
Laos	13.4	—6.9	78
Malaysia			56
W. Malaysia	45.8	—21.5	—
Sabah	16.7	—3.5	—
Sarawak	19.0	—7.5	—
Philippines	23.2	—3.3	70
Portuguese Timor	10.4	—0.5	—
Singapore	100.0	—	8
Sri Lanka (Ceylon)	—	—	52
Thailand	13.0	—3.0	76
Vietnam, North	23.9	—16.1	78
Vietnam, South	26.1	—9.9	74

[1]Percentage figures are the same for economic active population in agriculture as per cent of the economically active population.

Sources: Col. 1 and 2 Kingsley Davis, *World Urbanization 1950–1970*, Vol. I. Berkeley, California (Institute of International Studies, University of California), 1969.
Col. 3 *FAO Production Yearbook 1971*, Table 4.

economic resources and political affairs of the colonies.[1] Also in pre-colonial society class lines were rigid enough. For Thailand Prince Damrong points out that 'Thai society was divided into two classes, the *nai* who constituted the governing class and the *phrai* who were governed'. Upward mobility, a recent study on the early Bangkok period adds, 'from the lower class ... to that of the governing class, i.e. the nobles and princes, appears to have been extremely difficult, except in time of war and irregular succession to the throne' (Akin Rabibhadana, 1969:155). However, the establishment of modern bureaucracies and modern professions in South-East Asia from the middle of the nineteenth century onward carried in itself the seed for the destruction of the pre-colonial and colonial stratification systems. The emergence of new strategic groups provided the leadership for nationalist movements, for multi-party systems, and the ensuing fluid situation of intense group conflict mentioned before.

There are some clearly discernible trends in strategic group formation and social change in South-East Asia. (1) As mentioned before there was no marked decline in the proportion of the agricultural population. Though figures are notoriously dubious there are indications that in some countries the percentage of people engaged in agriculture and fishing has actually risen at times.[2] The Indonesian agricultural population was estimated to account for 66 per cent of the total population in 1930, 67 per cent in 1965 and 70 per cent in 1970. *(FAO Production Yearbook 1965, 1969, 1970)*. In Thailand the respective figure dropped a mere 4 per cent from 82 in 1935 to 78 in 1965. For Malaysia we can register a decline by about 6 percentage points for the same period. Also in the Philippines the agricultural population was reduced only from 73 per cent in 1935 to an estimated 70 per cent in 1970.

The three South-East Asian countries with the lowest proportion of their work force in peasant agriculture are Singapore, Malaysia and Ceylon. The estate and mining workers, whose numbers rose rapidly earlier during this century, could become a considerable political force in Malaysia and Ceylon if they were organized in militant unions. Though the background of the communist uprising in the so-called Malayan Emergency is more complex, the attempt of the Communists to work through trade unions was a major factor in the post-war political scene. Most estate workers were effectively kept out of politics both in Malaysia and in Ceylon as they were isolated and treated as foreigners, but Colombo-based unions played and still play a major role in Ceylon politics. The 1971 uprising in Ceylon came, however, not as a working class movement, but appears to be almost completely a revolt of unemployed university

[1]For Indonesia see Wertheim, 1959.
[2]In Europe the decline of the agricultural population stopped briefly during the economic depression of the 1930s and in some areas (e.g. in Spain) farm labour actually increased, though for only a short period of time.

graduates, that means a strategic group of 'pre-professionals' and 'pre-bureaucrats'. It is interesting to note, however, that despite recent developments a system of parliamentary democracy is maintained and has functioned reasonably well in these countries characterized by a declining agricultural work force.

There have, of course, been substantial changes within the agricultural population like large-scale migration from North to South in Vietnam, Burma and Thailand, the growth of an agrarian estate proletariat in Malaya, Ceylon and parts of Indonesia and the Philippines, the increase in the number of tenants and impoverished peasants through mounting pressure on scarce agricultural resources, primarily land. The fact remains, however, that the agricultural work force still forms the majority of the South-East Asian population. If this trend is reversed, if the share of non-agricultural occupations rises, the repercussions for the overall structure of South-East Asian societies will be considerable. As I have mentioned before it will then be of primary importance for future political developments, which other groups develop first, which groups will use the strength of growing numbers to impress their interests and norms on the political system of the future.

(2) In the process of modernization, traditional strategic groups have steadily declined, at least until the 1950s, as their modern functional equivalents have increased in relative importance. We have thus a decrease in aristocrats and a rise of bureaucrats, a decrease in religious specialists and a rise in teachers and secular professionals. In Thailand for instance the share of Buddhist monks dropped from 21 per 1,000 of population in 1911 to 5.7 in 1965, while the share of teachers rose from 1.1 per 1,000 of population in 1925 to 5.5 in 1965 (see Table 13). In Indonesia the percentage of cabinet ministers using aristocratic titles dropped from 30 per cent in 1945–57 to 9 per cent in 1957–64 (Yasunaka, 1970:116). In general, the importance of traditional titles has been challenged by educational degrees.

Though members of the old aristocracy still play an important social and ritual role in Malaysia and Thailand, the only country where they are in formal positions of power is Laos, after the fall of Cambodia's Sihanouk. There has, however, been a reversal in this general trend in some countries. In South Vietnam the number of traditional Vietnamese medical practitioners has gone up considerably[1] (from 1,217 in 1951 to 3,049 in 1962 according to the Statistical Yearbook 1964–65), in Ceylon the Ayurvedic doctors have consolidated their ranks and became a major

[1]Mr. Mokhzani suggested in his comments on this paper that this revival might actually have a 'cushioning effect of modernization of the daily life of people in Southeast Asia'. Traditional medical practioners for instance 'help to re-interpret the changing situation in terms which are understood by the common man'.

TABLE 13

STRATEGIC GROUPS IN THAILAND, 1911–1965

(per 1,000 population)

Year	1,000 Population	Non-Agr. Labour	Gvt. Empl.	Buddh. Monks	Teachers	Lecturers, Prof.	University Stud.	Phys.	Legal Prof.
1911	8,266			21.0			0.0		
1915	8,783		8.7	16.1					
1920	9,511		8.8	12.2	1.1				
1925	10,599		8.2	11.5	1.1				
1930	11,918	(158)	6.6	10.8	1.7	0.01	0.8	0.03	
1935	13,788	(120)	6.1	8.9	3.3				
1940	15,331		7.3	6.4	4.0	0.01	1.1		
1945	16,737	(153)		9.0	4.2	0.03	1.5		
1950	19,635			6.8	(4.8)			0.10	
1955	22,762		8.3	6.1	5.2	0.09	1.9	0.12	0.06
1960	26,388	177	8.4	5.7	5.5	0.12	(1.5)	0.14	0.06
1965	30,591		8.6						

Note: Figures in brackets are estimates.
Source: Statistical Yearbook of Thailand and other Government publications.

political force during the past fifteen years and in Java a process of re-traditionalization seems to take place.[1] It is difficult to judge whether these structural underpinnings of cultural renaissance movements are the beginning of a new trend or rearguard actions before the ultimate collapse of a traditional way of life.

(3) The politically most important trend has been the rise of independent professionals, civil servants and military officers. The sequence of their emergence differs greatly among South-East Asian countries. I have already alluded to the importance of sequential patterns of development. Whereas higher civil servants and military officers have pre-established organizations which form their political constituencies, the independent professionals tend to establish their own organizations in the form of political parties or movements. Or seen from a different point of view, only one modernized section of the urban population, primarily free professionals, felt the necessity to form parties and back a multi-party system and parliamentary democracy. Leaders of national movements from Rizal, a doctor, to Sukarno, an engineer, have come from this strategic group of free professionals.

Independent professionals provide leadership for new political movements, as long as they are not co-opted as technocrats by bureaucratic regimes and controlled by the strait-jacket of disciplined large-scale organizations. As there is no large industrial proletariat as yet nor an established or sizeable middle class to act as a power base, their endeavours have often been doomed to failure as they were caught between the dilemma of using traditional appeals to draw peasant support (Indonesia, Ceylon) or to radicalize peasants for revolutionary movements (Vietnam).

The development of free professionals as a strategic group was relatively slow and was in some countries preceeded by a substantial growth of a government bureaucracy. The Philippines, Ceylon and Malaysia/Singapore are examples of countries where a large group of free professionals emerged fairly early. If we use the number of doctors as an index of professional development, these countries score very high before World War II: The Philippines had 29.8 per 100,000 population in 1960, Ceylon 15.9 in 1938 and Malaya (including Singapore) 14.0 in 1939.[2] French Indochina, the Netherlands Indies and Thailand had only about 1.7 doctors per 100,000 population before World War II (see Table 14).

[1]Both Prof. Sartono and Prof. Soejito of Gajah Mada University in Jogjakarta have expressed this view. See also J. A. N. Mulder, 'Perspektip terhadap modernisasi', *Basis* xx, 2 (1970): 34–40, who writes 'Proses masjarakat Djawa sekarang tjenderung ke re-tradisionalisasi' (p. 29).

[2]There were, however, only 99 advocates and solicitors registered in Malaya and Singapore in 1940. Most legal practitioners then were not registered. (Unpublished sources, National Archives, Kuala Lumpur.)

TABLE 14
PHYSICIANS PER 100,000 POPULATION IN
SELECTED SOUTH-EAST ASIAN COUNTRIES

	1903	1930–40	1950–52	1960	1966–70
Burma		9.3	11.9	9.1	10.4
Cambodia					4.5
Ceylon	3.5	15.5	16.9	22.2	27.0
Indonesia	0.7[1]	1.7[2]	1.5[2]	2.1[2]	3.6
Laos					6.0
West Malaysia		14.0	11.8	15.6	25.9
Singapore		—	—	—	65.8
Philippines		29.8	(18.0)[2]	(18.6)[2]	10.2
Thailand		1.3	8.3	12.0	11.9
Vietnam (S)			4.2	3.4	8.2
Vietnam (N)					
(French Indochina)		1.7			

1. Java and Madura only
2. Government service only

Sources: G. Myrdal, *Asian Drama*, Vol. III 1968, Tables 30.1 and 30.2; *Statistical Yearbooks* of S. Vietnam, Indonesia, Thailand; *U. N. Statistical Yearbook 1971.*

Though I do not want to imply that there is a direct causal effect between the early development of professional occupations and the functioning of parliamentary democracy, I would, however, suggest that the emergence of free professionals was one of the necessary preconditions. This argument is further strengthened by a perusal of literature on the social background of parliamentarians. Professionals have constantly provided a high percentage of party leaders and other functionaries in democracies. Further evidence is provided by comparative data on earlier developments of stratification systems in Western countries. In the middle of the nineteenth century the U.S. and England had a much higher proportion of professionals and a much lower proportion of government officials and military officers in their work force than for example Prussia and the German Reich. The growth of the government bureaucracy preceded that of the independent professions in Germany and thus contributed to an establishment of an authoritarian political system. Incidentally, the strategic group pattern in the U.S. today is in some aspects approaching the Prussian pattern of 1870.[1]

In South-East Asia these countries with an early development of a strong strategic group of professionals, namely, Ceylon, Malaysia, Singapore and the Philippines, were also able to establish and maintain a democratic system of government for a considerable length of time. In the other South-East Asian countries professional groups were preceded or overtaken by fast growing government bureaucracies and military forces.

Thailand belongs to this category. Modernization started in Thailand in the 1880s with reorganization of the traditional civil service and a sudden increase in the number of government employees. Social mobility must have been considerable as lower rank civil servants had to be recruited from rural areas (Evers, 1966, 1967). The higher ranks were filled primarily by members of the royal house and some powerful aristocratic families. Though great efforts went into the establishment of a modern educational system the development of professions was minimal. A medical school, opened in 1899, produced only 48 graduates between 1928 and 1931. There was no independent group of lawyers, architects or engineers, to speak of. The few Thai available were all absorbed by the civil service or the military.

The rapid expansion of the civil service came to a rather sudden halt about 1922 due to financial difficulties. The absolute number of government employees was reduced and the share of civil servants per 1,000 population dropped from 8.5 in 1922 to 5.8 in 1932 (see Figure 1).

[1]The sequential pattern of strategic group development is discussed and documented in the author's unpublished paper on 'Comparative Study of Social Stratification' read as a public lecture at Duke University in November 1969.

FIGURE 1

GROWTH OF THE THAI CIVIL SERVICE, 1918–1965

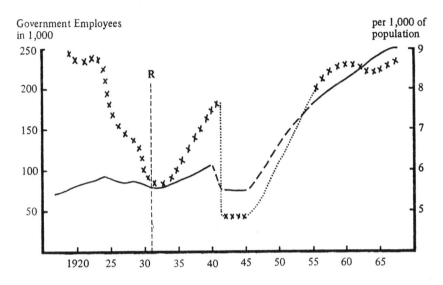

———— absolute figures, Government Employees
x x x x Government employees per 1,000 population.
R   Revolution of 1932, abolishing the absolute monarchy.

Dissatisfaction with reduced salaries, reduced chances of promotion and with the limit placed on upward mobility into the higher civil service positions, monopolized by the aristocracy, led to the 1932 revolution. This revolution was not a popular uprising, but a revolution of civil servants and military officers against a ruling aristocracy. The fruits of the revolution became apparent shortly thereafter. The rate of government officials per 1,000 population rose steeply from 5.5 in 1933 back to 8.5 in 1959.

A series of bloodless coups since 1932 did little to damage the basic structure of the Thai stratification system. Of much greater importance is, I would suggest, the rise of the strategic group of professionals. It is interesting to note that attempts to establish a workable political party system coincide with the rise of professionals in the early 1950s and during the past few years.[1]

The recent fall of Sihanouk and the royal Cambodian family in 1970 bears some resemblance to the Thai revolution of 1932. The coalition of

[1]Developments in Thailand are more fully discussed in a paper on 'Social Stratification and Political Development in Thailand', read at Cornell University in October 1969. The emergence and 'professionalization' of professions is now documented by the passing of several 'Professional Control Acts' (for architects in 1963, for engineers in 1965). There are estimated to be about 5,000 practising engineers and about 3,000 architects in Thailand (*The Investor*, Bangkok, Vol. 2, Nov. 1970: 1165).

civil servants and military officers, backed by the country's few dissatisfied intellectuals, deposed the prince somewhat reluctantly. If not for the Vietnamese war, Sihanouk and the royal aristocracy might have experienced the same fate as the Thai King in 1932: after some wavering among the revolutionaries he was allowed to stay as a constitutional monarch.

In Indonesia an early vigorous, though numerically small development of professions took place. As Indonesians were kept out of the higher civil service right to the end of Dutch rule (by 1940 there were only 221 Indonesians among 3,039 higher civil servants), the professions provided the major avenue to social mobility and the financial means for political activism. 'As opportunities for professional training expanded in the last two decades of colonial rule, many more dynamic students tended to seek professional careers where they had more independence from the colonial government' (Yasunaka, 1970:112). When, after independence, the Indonesian bureaucracy mushroomed, this trend was reversed. The percentage of professions in the Indonesian labour force fell from 1.0 per cent in 1930 to 0.7 per cent in 1953.

The low development of professionals in Indonesia is confirmed in a recent (1964/5) labour force survey. University educated professionals accounted for only 22 per 100,000 of the employed population. That means that before the war the South-East Asian countries listed above had already a higher proportion of physicians alone in their work force.[1]

Another strategic group, connecting rural society with the urban or national society is very important. This group consists often of traditional occupations like religious specialists and village headmen as well as modern ones like teachers, agricultural extension officers, police officers, and proctors. Paul Mus claims that in post-colonial Vietnam village leadership was actually the most progressive:

> The conservatism of the villagers used to be contrasted with the new aspirations of those relatively few urban intellectuals whose attitudes were moulded by contract with French culture. In the present situation, however, it is chiefly the conservative elements that seem to have congregated in the cities, while large areas of the countryside have resorted to armed resistance under leftist leadership (MacAlister and Mus, 1970: 70).

Primary school teachers appear to be the crucial elements within this group.

Their importance has gone up with their rising numbers both as a basis for social mobility into higher positions and as key figures in the struggle for the allegiance of the rural masses. They also seem to play a major role in what might appropriately be called 'cultural revolutions'.

A cultural revolution is here defined as a revolt against existing cultural values and a successful reversal of current trends of thought. It is concerned

[1]See: *Survey Sosial Ekonomi National Tahap Kedua* (November 1964 — Februari 1965), *Angkatan Kerdja Penduduk Indonesia (Ringkasan)*, Djarkarta: Biro Pusat Statistik, n.y. (ca. 1968), p. 100.

primarily with the field of education and language and finds its expression in a change of official language policies, the introduction of an indigenous language as the official language, the creation of a national language, changes in the language of instruction in schools and universities, a cultural revival, usually in the form of a renaissance or alleged renaissance of indigenous arts, values and philosophies. Of course cultural revolutions do not happen in a social vacuum. They are intimately connected with the formation of strategic groups especially those concerned with learning and teaching. The sudden change in numbers of teachers, students, religious specialists of various persuasions, apparently precedes a cultural revolution of this sort.

Especially primary school teachers, teaching in the vernaculars, tend to press for a 'national language policy' to ensure access to higher education and eventually higher civil service positions for themselves and their group. The Buddhist renaissance in Ceylon and the re-introduction of Sinhalese as the national language was preceded by a growth of primary school teachers and Ayurvedic physicians. Present developments in Malaysia and the pressure for Malay as the national language in civil service and higher education are also following a decade of rapid expansion of the group of Malay primary school teachers. Here again I stress that I do not claim that the growth of this particular strategic group *caused* the present Malay cultural movement but was a contributing factor or a social structural precondition.

After looking at the developments of some of the important strategic groups in South-East Asian societies, I would like to turn to the question of class formation itself.

V

The rise and the demise of various strategic groups during and after the struggle for independence created highly fragmented societies, in which these groups were competing for the inheritance of the vacated colonial power positions. Remnants of the old aristocracies wielded power and respect in some sections of the populations, but played no role whatsoever in others; professionals and employees, far from forming a 'middle class', had high status and power at times, but were divided by wealth.[1] Ethnic loyalties and religious ideologies added to the proliferation of groups and factions. This situation has already changed in some countries or is about

[1]Huntington is, I feel, quite mistaken, when he refers to these strategic groups as 'middle class', and writes: 'The true revolutionary class in most modernising societies is, of course, the middle class' (1968: 289). In most South-East Asian countries these groups were definitely at the top of the social hierarchy. Wertheim is much closer to the truth when he speaks of an 'intellectual and near-intellectual ruling class' in post-colonial Indonesia (1959: 165).

to lose its importance. A new and more unified class structure seems to emerge.

A first step towards class formation was often taken in the form of an economic policy of 'nationalization'. What in fact happened was a merger of the interests of a politically powerful strategic group and an economically strong group of businessman, who in South-East Asia are usually ethnic minorities, Chinese or Indians. Thus the Thai-ification programme of the Thai economy pursued vigorously after 1956 lead in fact to an involvement of the Thai military-bureaucratic elite in Chinese business ventures. The results were striking. Anti-Chinese drives stopped, the relations between government and business improved and both groups prospered. A ban on trade union activities, strict surveillance of popular Buddhist monks and an acquiescent peasantry, until recently not yet (except in the North-east) beset by landlessness and landlordism helped to stabilize the emergent class structure. The theory that social mobility into the higher civil service declined during that period (Evers, 1966; Evers and Silcock, 1967) leading to a fairly closed class structure, was confirmed by a recent Japanese Survey on Social Stratification in Bangkok. 'Intra-generational mobility in Bangkok cannot be called high from whatever angle it is investigated . . . . Accordingly Bangkok is a closed society', conclude the researchers in their 1970 report (Tominaga et al., 1970:3).

Similar alliances enhancing class formation could be found in Malaya. Already before independence, an attempt was made to pool the resources of the Malay political elite (and those remnants of the aristocracy that remain within it) with Chinese business interests.[1] The experiment was not so much endangered in 1969 by factional strife within this alliance but by racial·tension and strife within the lower class whose aspirations for social mobility into higher positions were fanned but not fulfilled.

In Burma and in Indonesia the alliance between military-bureaucratic groups and non-indigenous business interest did not materialize. The Burmanization policy lead to a more or less forceful removal of Indians and Chinese with economically disastrous results.[2] Anti-Chinese politics in Indonesia led to a decline of Chinese small business though some reversal of this policy can be sensed at the moment. The alliance which helps to stabilize the military-bureaucratic groups in Indonesia, as well as in Thailand and South Vietnam is now contracted with foreigners, which make the Chinese business community less important. Especially in South Vietnam, the massive American intervention has backed one of the strategic groups,

[1]In the economic field the co-operation is most aptly demonstrated in the logging business, where members of the Malay aristocratic or bureaucratic elites provide licenses and Chinese businessmen capital and know-how. The 1969 race riots between Malays and Chinese were obviously a lower class phenomenon.

[2]The politics of Burmanization are described by Holmes, 1967. Violence against Chinese erupted again in 1967. Whether the new U Nu led UNLF will indirectly cause an alliance of Ne Win's military group and Chinese or foreign business groups remains to be seen.

military officers, to such an extent that this group has seen no necessity to seek alliances among other strategic groups like the Buddhist clergy, professionals or students.

In Thailand American military aid had become very important. Access to this source of support has probably strengthened the power of the military ruling class to such an extent that Thailand remained without the usual *coup d'etat* for so long.

On the whole international aid, especially American military aid, has contributed largely to the establishment and consolidation of a strong upper class which is able to ensure law and order and suppress rebellions.[1]

The most spectacular process of class formation has been going on in Indonesia for some time. Here the military themselves have branched out and filled the most important positions in the higher civil service and the economy, legitimized by the ideology of the 'civil mission of the armed forces' (Gavi, 1968).

The possible formation of a unified lower class, attempted by the PKI, was successfully inhibited by religious strategic groups and the army. Professionals and intellectuals are co-opted and neutralized as technocrats, are tightly controlled as *golongan karya* (functional groups of Indonesian parliaments), or form part of a widespread patronage system. Political parties, still patterned on the old *aliran* system, are so far not seen as a threat to the power of the ruling military elite.

The resumption of foreign aid and the influx of foreign capital has helped considerably in the formation of a unified upper class. Foreign companies have provided executive positions and are frequently blamed for providing substantial sums as bribes to higher government officials. As foreign companies operate on a profit basis, these sums are used to achieve a reduction of taxes and duties or are charged to the Indonesian government through higher fees and prices. Inflated rents for housing foreigners provide an additional source of income for the new upper class. Foreign investors and aid agencies serve thus as a channel for the redistribution of the Indonesian GNP into the upper class. As most of the new ventures are in the extraction industries, like oil, mining or logging, their direct effect on the creation of new occupations is probably small. Though no recent empirical studies on social stratification in Djakarta have come to my attention, a mere observation of Djakarta life today gives an indication of present trends. Ecologically, upper class and lower class districts are

[1]Among other factors described below substantial US-AID investment guarantees covering the risk of 'expropriation, war, revolution, insurrection' (Jan. 1967, Indonesia) create a definite interest on the part of the US government in maintaining a stable, capitalist-inclined, friendly government, in power. Several American political scientists have actively supported this policy in their works. To cite but one example: Chalmers A. Johnson, *Revolutionary Change* (Boston: Little, Brown and Co., 1966, pp. 119–20) argues for the need to measure 'disequilibrated conditions' which promote revolutions. 'Practically speaking, an index of disequilibrium would provide a means of warning a legitimate elite of the possibility of revolution, thereby alerting it to the need for both policies of social change and military counter-insurgency preparations.'

clearly separated. The mansions, luxury cars and lavish functions of the new upper class provide a vivid contrast to the slum areas of recent migrants and the crowded housing areas of minor government officials. Though the living standard of some middle income groups seems to be rising, the cultural, social and economic distance to the new upper class is definitely increasing. Judging from samples of marriage patterns and careers of upper class children, self-recruitment and closure seems to be the trend. The re-traditionalization of Javanese rural and small town population, mentioned before, is thus contrasted by an increasingly Western life-style of the upper class. But these are only speculations on recent developments which should be checked by survey data.

Also elsewhere in South-East Asia the international dimensions of class formation are becoming more and more apparent. A host of foreign experts, business partners, embassy personnel and military advisers have become an integral part of the new upper class. They intermingle freely with the indigenous elite and tend to live in the same residential areas of the metropolitan cities. The colonial 'European city' and 'native quarter' is frequently replaced by culturally and socially equally differentiated upper and lower class districts.

VI

If we abstract even further from the extremely rich tapestry of South-East Asian social structures and events the analysis warrants, I think, some ideal typical conclusions. The first is, in a way, a paradox. 'Modernization' has produced a trend towards the development of a new, rigid class structure. By creating and consolidating a new upper class, the modernization process is, however, eventually arrested or at least retarded. 'Modernization' and the material fruits of modernization are increasingly concentrated within the new upper class. Perhaps South-East Asian societies tend to develop features similar to a number of Latin American countries. Economic development is concentrated in the large urban centres,[1] foreign political and economic influence is strong, and the overall development low. Modernization has produced its own barriers.

The second conclusion is that the period after independence tended to be characterized by intense conflict between groups and factions. Many of these groups shared ruling class features: they had access to power and wealth and they dominated large-scale organizations (like parties, bureaucracies, armies or business companies). But they were fragmented,

[1] I have discussed this process in a short paper read at the International Conference on Southeast Asian Studies in Kuala Lumpur, 23–26 February 1972: 'Urban Involution: The Social Structure of Southeast Asian Towns', Working Papers, No. 2, Dept. of Sociology, University of Singapore, Singapore, 1972.

often by ethnic, cultural or religious identities. After classes are consolidated by alliances as described above, the direction of conflict tends to shift: conflict between groups declines and conflict between the new upper class and the peasant or urban masses tends to arise. Instead of the ousting of rival factions we will have insurgency instead of *coup d'etat* revolutions. How far reality will approximate or has already approximated to this type of social and political development remains to be seen from further research.

8. Social Rank, Status-Honour and Social Class Consciousness Amongst the Malays[1]

A. KAHAR BADOR

I

WRITING on the study of social stratification and social mobility in Malaya in 1965, B.A.R. Mokhzani remarked that until then there had been no systematic study made of social stratification and social mobility in Malaya. Except for a single study that carried the title of social stratification (available then only as an M.A. typescript)[2] and several studies on various aspects of Malayan (almost exclusively Malay) life in which references to the problem of social stratification were made, there was a conspicuous absence of materials published on the subject. Mokhzani suggested two major reasons that contributed to the lack of material on this specific subject as well as in the more general sociological-anthropological subjects of inquiry; firstly, the absence of an academic department of sociology and anthropology in the Malayan universities and, secondly, the 'cultural' orientation of the past writers on Malayan subjects.

Seven years have since elapsed since Mokhzani made the above remarks. In some important respects in Malaysia to-day, sociology and anthropology have made great strides. By being established as an independent academic discipline in the School of Comparative Social Sciences in the

[1]The fieldwork research for this study was made feasible through a grant provided by the London-Cornell Project for Chinese and South-East Asian Societies with funds from the Nuffield and Carnegie Foundations to which go my sincere thanks. My sincere thanks also go to the Wenner-Gren Foundation for Anthropological Resarch for making their funds available to me, through the good offices of Professor Raymond Firth, at the London School of Economics and Political Science, during the period of preparation to go into the field, and for a further period after returning to the School to write up the material gathered. I wish also to thank the Negeri Sembilan Government and the Lee Foundation for their financial contributions. I would also wish to thank the many people in the State of Perak whose inestimable help and friendship facilitated my work while in the field.

[2]This M.S. has been published later. See Hussin Ali, 1965.

new University of Penang (established in 1968), and the institution of a Department of Anthropology and Sociology in the even more recently established Universiti Kebangsaan in Kuala Lumpur in 1970 and in the University of Malaya in 1971, anthropology and sociology have now been given their long overdue recognition.

The overall situation of sociological-anthropological studies to-day is, however, not much further advanced than it was five years ago. It is true that in the meantime there have been more studies brought out either by students from the University of Malaya which exist in the form of either Academic Exercises in part fulfilment of the B.A. degree or in unpublished thesis typescript for the M.A. degree submitted mainly in the Department of Malay Studies,[1] or by other research workers sponsored by overseas institutions from United Kingdom, United States or Australia. But as far as I am aware those studies have focused almost entirely on problems other than the specific problem of social stratification.

This lack of concern for the study of social stratification may be traced to two principal causes. Firstly, it is a reflection of the state of development of sociological-anthropological studies in the country which has been indicated earlier. Secondly, there seems to have been a lack of interest on social stratification itself as a problem for research by the research workers; they have been attracted by other problems or aspects of Malaysian life. This, in turn, might have been partly due to the lack of theoretical orientation towards stratification as a social phenomenon worthy of inquiry and, partly because there seems to be a tacit feeling amongst the research workers themselves that stratification, especially in terms of class stratification in the Marxian sense, is not such a pervasive and glaring social phenomenon as obtained in the industrialized western societies as the literature on the subject has shown. Comparatively speaking, there is some truth in the latter assumption. The nature and form of social stratification as well as the degree or intensity of its manifestation in the Malaysian situation are not comparable to, or at least, is different from its manifestation that generally characterize the industrialized western societies.

This is, of course, not to say that the phenomenon does not exist or that it is in any sense less real to the people of the country. Those studies mentioned by Mokhzani in his paper cited above have amply shown that some form of stratification does exist even at the presumably most homogeneous level of society, namely the rural village communities in the country (Swift 1965, Husin Ali 1965). In my own study of the Malays in the state of Perak, although the focus of my interest was on some other problem, it was evident that some form of stratification does prevail amongst the various categories of the people that came within the focus of

[1]This is because the Department of Malay Studies has been offering a number of courses of sociological-anthropological nature ever since its inception. But as to be expected such courses have not been systematically organized as sociological-anthropological courses as understood in the established University departments of Anthropology and Sociology elsewhere.

my research (Kahar Bador 1967, 1970). Those studies, especially the one by Gullick (1958), have shown clearly that amongst the Malays there existed a system of social stratification which, from the contemporary point of view, may be called the traditional Malay system of stratification.

I propose to examine here the inter-relations between the traditional Malay social stratification system and power groups with particular reference to the Malays in the State of Perak, Malaysia. It is my hypothesis that in a situation in which the traditional social stratification system of a society, for various reasons, is still regarded as culturally valid by its members, the social group with the highest status-honour indices in that society, e.g. the royalty and aristocracy together, are able to hold their position at the top of the social status hierarchy while relinquishing political power to a newly-emerged group of leaders of 'lowly/common' origins by making use of the status-honour system to advantage. It is hoped that by the end of this paper by examining the situation in the Malay society in Perak this hypothesis would be borne out. Admittedly this hypothesis may be of limited applicability but it would have served its purpose if it is found to have yielded an adequate explanation of the situation as it prevailed amongst the Malays in Perak. By extension, and with suitable modifications, I think it could be used adequately in explaining the situation amongst the Malays as a whole.

In order to find out to what extent this hypothesis is valid in the specific context of the Malay society in Perak, it would be necessary firstly to give a description of the traditional social stratification system as it still prevails in the Malay society in the state of Perak. It is against this background that the validity of the hypothesis would be tested. It would in fact involve an examination of the Malay notions of social rank, status-honour and social class consciousness, their manifestation and implications which would, it is hoped, be made clear by the end of this paper.

II

The general features of the early Malay stratification system as obtained around the 1890s are already quite adequately given in the literature.[1] To a large and significant extent the system as described by Gullick (1958) still operates today, though the gross cultural — social political and economic — changes and developments have left their imprint upon the system, affecting it considerably. Historically, the situation in Perak represents to a considerable extent the closest attempts by the later Malay

[1]One of the more complete and readily available sources of information on the division in the Malay society in the early period, approximately at about the time when the British intervened in the affairs of the Malay States in the 1890s is the study by Gullick (1958), which used historical data '... in the same fashion as an anthropologist uses material obtained by contemporary fieldwork' (p.1).

States to recreate their political systems involving divisions of society in terms of power and status dimensions after the earlier Malacca Kingdom model. Indeed, the genealogy of the ruling family of Perak claims direct lineal descent from the last of the Malacca Sultans who escaped to Sumatra from the Portuguese conquerors of Malacca in 1511 A.D.

As a social phenomenon, the stratification system of any society has several well-known dimensions. Of these dimensions the most frequently observed are power (in any form), occupation, class and status-honour. In the Malay situation these elements do exist though the extent of manifestation of each compared to the other varies. However, two of these dimensions, viz. power and status-honour, seem to be more emphasized from time to time in the history of the Malays. Thus, to talk about the Malay stratification system inevitably leads one to discuss also these two mainsprings of the system. At some risks of begging the chicken-and-egg question, it may be stated that insofar as the Malays are concerned status-honour or social prestige seems to be more a reflection or derivative of institutionalized power positions, at least initially, than the other way round.

Hence, the most significant feature of the traditional Malay stratification system is that it is closely woven into the fabric of the traditional political institution. The structure of the political institution of the Sultanate therefore pervades the structuring of the stratification system of the society into several clear categories of people.

The classification of people that prevails in the entire Malay society is thus to be found amongst the Perak Malays also. There is therefore the classification of the people (i.e. only the Malays are being referred hereto) into the three well-known categories of *rajas*, *orang besar* and *orang kebanyakan* ('common people'). Traditionally, each of these categories corresponds to the position it occupies in the structuring of power positions in the institution of the Sultanate with the Raja forming the apex of the hierarchy.

III

Recruitment into the *Raja* group is possible only through being born into it from a *Raja* father regardless of whether the mother is a *Raja* or not. Thus, *Raja* is always used as an honorific prefix to some other name to indicate either, verbally or in writing, membership of the *raja* group. The prefix *Raja* being patronymic, the offspring of a marriage between a non-*Raja* male to a *Raja* female would not inherit or be allowed to use the prefix before his or her name. Further the marriage of a non-*Raja* female to a *Raja* male does not make her a *Raja* even if she is the Consort of the

Sultan. In Perak, the title given to a 'commoner' Consort of the *Sultan* is *Raja Permaisuri*, which distinguishes her 'commoner' birth from a Consort of '*Raja* blood' to whom only the title of *Raja Perempuan* may be given. There is therefore no 'formula' in the Malay situation that corresponds, for instance, to the European royal proclamation by which means a 'commoner' woman on marrying a Prince could 'become a Princess'.

Internally, the *Raja* group is differentiated into those who hold ranked offices and titles and those who do not. In Perak, these ranked offices and titles are, namely, the *Sultan* (including his Consorts), *Raja Muda, Raja Di-Hilir* and the four 'Titled Princes' (*Raja2 Yang Bergelar*) in that descending order. These ranked *Rajas* below the *Sultan* also constitute an hierarchical order of succession to the throne, i.e. to the position of *Sultan* with the most junior ranked 'Titled Prince' bringing up the rear. They are in fact considered collectively as 'Heirs to the Throne'.

Around the four rank orders of *Raja* mentioned are the other members of the *Raja* group related to them in varying degrees of genealogical proximity. But the 'core' or 'inner circle' of the *Raja* group consists only of a sub-group that is collectively known as *Waris Negeri* (lit. 'Heirs of State'). As a term, however, *Waris Negeri* consists of a rather broad category of *Raja*. It includes not only the reigning *Sultan* and his descendants, but also the patrilineal descendants of former *Sultans* as well as those of former 'Heirs to the Throne'. The number in theory therefore can be large indeed seeing that the present *Sultan* is the 33rd in the line and, further, especially since there is an absence of any definite formulation of principle of genealogical distance beyond which a *Raja* ceases to be a *Waris Negeri*.

However, an attempt at codifying and limiting the interpretation of the *Waris Negeri* was made in the State Constitution, 1948, which defines the *Waris Negeri* to include only the

...direct male lineal descendant acknowledged to be legitimately and lawfully begotten, of the body and flesh of the Eighteenth Sultan ... and professing the Muslim Religion of the Shafei Muzahab.

However, this legal definition is still wide enough to include all the patri-lineal descendants of the past fifteen *Sultans* (the present one being the 33rd *Sultan*) over a period of the last century and a half. What is certain, there-fore, is that all the ranked *Rajas* do belong to the sub-group, the 'inner circle' or 'core' included in the *Waris Negeri* category.

Not much can be said about the non-ranked or ordinary *Rajas* except that each and every one of them carries the honorific prefix, *Raja*, before his or her proper name, e.g. Raja Ahmad, which denotes that he is patri-lineally descended from a father who also bears the honorific prefix of *Raja*. In other words he is not a 'commoner' (orang kebanyakan). Collec-tively the ordinary *Rajas* may be said to be basking in the reflected high status-honour and prestige of the ranked orders of *Rajas* mentioned earlier.

IV

The Malay term *Orang Besar* (lit. 'Big Men') is a very common term used by the Malays when referring to certain categories of people who possess certain attributes of high value in their social-cultural configuration of values. But to attempt to give a precise definition of who or what is an *orang besar* is not as easy as it may seem. What is certain is that the category of persons regarded as *orang besar* are in possession of a bundle of attributes or qualities which are highly valued. These attributes may be the incumbency of 'leading positions' or roles regarded as of some crucial importance for the social and political life of the people; they may be occupants of certain highly ranked positions in possession of some form of power and influence in the direction and execution of public affairs, or; they may be just formal functionaries who are highly ranked by the people. Or finally, all these attributes are bundled together in some imprecise fashion as being in the possession of the so-called *orang besar*. Hence, the term *orang besar* is really in the nature of an omnibus descriptive category applied to persons who have such attributes as given above.

In terms of the hierarchy of status-honour and prestige and often in terms of institutionalized power positions, the *orang besar* ranks in theory below the *Raja*. Indeed, in the early days the terms *orang besar* followed closely any mention of *Raja*, thus: *Raja2 dan Orang2 Besar*, used to refer collectively to the 'Rulers' and their traditional 'Big Men' (literal translation of *Orang Besar*) when discussing the affairs of State. With the emergence of a new group of leaders of non-*Raja* or non-*Orang Besar* ancestry, the meaning of the term *orang besar* has since widened to include also those in the new categories.

In the situation in Perak, the category of *orang besar*, insofar as the traditional role structure is concerned, is further internally differentiated into *Orang Besar Negeri* which is constituted by the Four Chiefs who are in the 1st Rank Order and the Eight Chiefs of the 2nd Rank Order. Only these two rank orders may be classified as *Orang Besar Negeri* while the remaining 16 Lesser Chiefs and 32 Minor Chiefs are merely referred to as Orang Besar 16 (lit. the 16 'Big Men') and *Orang Besar 32* (lit. the 32 'Big Men').

The term *Orang Besar* without any qualification would thus include the traditional hierarchy of *Orang Besar* as well as others who in other ways are regarded as possessing the bundle of attributes or qualities mentioned earlier. The latter category would include more specifically officials in the higher echelon of the Government service and also political leaders mainly those who have managed to gain the seats of political administrative power in the State or Federal Government through the process of democratic elections. While the Government officials are together referred to as *Pegawai Kerajaan*, the elected representatives to the *Dewan Perhimpunan Undangan Negeri* (State Legislative Assembly) and those elected to the Federal Parliament are referred to as *Yang Berhormat* (the Honourable ...).

The traditional *Orang2 Besar* as a whole are 'commoners' but not of the 'common people' (*orang kebanyakan*). They are differentiated from the *Raja* group because they are not descendants in the male line of *Raja* ancestry. And *Raja* as a patronymic being ascribed only by birth the 'commoner' *Orang Besar* may in theory never acquire the Raja's appellation. (In the early history of some other Malay Sultanates, however, it did happen that some powerful 'commoner' chiefs/*Orang2 Besar* did manage to declare themselves as Raja of the state and eventually his descendants 'became' *Raja* and were accepted as such. For example, the ancestor and founder of the dynasty of the present Sultan of Johore and that of Pahang). On the other hand, these *Orang2 Besar* are differentiated from the 'common people' by their mainly hereditary and illustrious rank orders with grandiose titles and offices by virtue of their positions in the traditional authority structure of the Sultanate. In the hierarchy of the traditional rank orders they come below the 'Titled Princes' in a series of fixed order of precedence with the Four 'Chiefs' forming the 1st Rank order and the 32 'chiefs' bringing up the rear.

Like the *Raja* group recruitment into the traditional *Orang Besar* is mainly by ascriptive criteria though not perhaps as rigid as the former. A person is a member of the group by virtue of being born of *Orang Besar* families. Unlike the *Raja* their offspring do not possess any distinguishing honorific prefix. But as a group they are nevertheless distinguishably 'aristocratic' or 'of the nobility' in terms of other socially recognized criteria, e.g. in their style of life and in the use of certain distinctive forms of address in speaking to them. In this latter case they are like the *Raja*; the difference lies in the terminologies used. To address a *Raja* one addresses him as *Tuanku* if he is the *Sultan*, or *Tengku* for the others and refers to oneself as *patek* (also *pacal yang hina*, meaning 'your subject and lowly serf'); to address an *Orang Besar* the terms of address are '*Dato*' for him and '*hamba Dato*' for oneself. In the case of the *Orang Besar Negeri* only the term of address is *Tengku* — a practice which obtains only in the case of Perak nobility.

V

The *orang2 kebanyakan* are the 'common people' who possess none of the attributes nor the pretensions of the *Raja* or *Orang Besar*. In the hierarchical ranking order of the traditional stratification system in the society they represent the lowest stratum. It is in this stratum that the mass of the Malays are to be found. They constitute the *rakyat*, the 'subjects' of the royal Ruler. They are the people who, in the peasant society, till the soil, grow the food and tend the animals either for their own subsistence living or for cash income; they are the peasantry. They may be tending their own land or as a tenant farmer to landlords amongst whose ranks the *Orang Besar* and the *Raja* are often to be found. What is certain is that they earn a living through soiling their hands, while the *Raja* and the *Orang Besar* have other means of livelihood.

Besides the peasantry, and especially with the increasing opportunity of wage earning mainly as 'government servants' in the various government and semi-government administrative structures, those *orang kebanyakan* who have been lucky to have had varying degrees of education are also to be found as 'government servants'. This was a new occupational category, the higher rungs of which until around the 1920s were reserved by the then British administration for offspring of the royalty or aristocracy, but in which presently people of motley parentage are to be found employed as long as the basic achievemental criteria of education is fulfilled. A number of the earlier recruits have indeed risen to the top of the occupational ladder and distinguished themselves as civil servants, administrators, doctors, judges, etc.

The nature of the traditional Malay social stratification system as it still prevails may be summarized as follows:

(1) the traditional stratification system is based fundamentally on ascriptive criteria of birth with descent for such purposes being given patrilineal emphasis;

(2) it is a rigid ranking order and especially in the case of the *Raja* group it is almost caste-like;

(3) these social status distinctions are not bridgeable by 'social-climbing' through any other means except by occasional marriage and then mainly (in the case of the *Raja* only) by a male of higher status with a female of a lower status order;

(4) the *Raja* and *Orang Besar* groups have in common possession certain symbols of legitimacy which serve as their 'character' of existence. This constitutes the cultural tradition of the Malays that lies rooted in the immemorial past. This fact and the fact that it has been going on for centuries and that there are certain 'supernatural' attributes supposedly in their origins lent to it the sanctity of an order that is regarded in term of high status-honour and prestige. Some of these are (Kahar Bador, 1970):

(a) the possession of hereditary titles and offices;

(b) the possession of 'instruments' of office, which in the case of the chiefs consist of a 'letter of appointment' (*surat kuasa/tauliah*) under the seal of the Sultan;

(c) the possession of insignia of title and office consisting mainly of traditional symbol of authority like a *keris* (Malay dagger) usually of some antiquity and purported to possess 'supernatural qualities' which have been passed in hereditary manner;

(d) the ceremonials and rituals surrounding the taking of title and office also with certain 'supernatural' implication;

(5) the rank orders of *Rajas* and *Orang2 Besar* have a common entitlement to the receipt of 'political allowances' paid out of the State Treasury and determined either generally or specifically by the State Legislative Assembly. The amount varies in accordance with the rank of a particular *Raja* or *Orang Besar* in the hierarchy. This allowance originally represented payment commuted by the British administration in lieu of the revenue and taxation they used to derive from and levy upon the population in their respective territories over which they held sway. In addition, if the *Raja* (in few cases in fact) or the *Orang Besar* concurrently holds office as a 'District Chief' (*Orang Besar Jajahan*), which again is mainly hereditary, then he also receives a 'District Chiefs' allowance. Other perquisites of title and office holding include an official residence and a government loan to purchase a car for use, rather similar to those of a senior civil servant;

(6) finally, the *Rajas* and *Orang2 Besar* are often involved in interlocking relations of kinship and affinity with one another, either actually or putatively. There is thus inter-marriage amongst families who regard one another as belonging to the same *bangsa* (lit. it means 'race' but in this context it connotes social rank and social status). That is, there is implicit and explicit expression that they all belong to more or less the same stratum of people with high social rank, status and prestige.

The most significant features of the traditional structuring of roles in the Sultanate as a socio-political system are that positions in the rank orders of an otherwise political hierarchy have come to denote collectively an index of high social status and prestige. With the *Sultan* at the apex of the socio-political hierarchy, social status, rank and prestige are defined in a constellation of increasing social distance of a lower rank order with the 'commoners' representing the lowest stratum. This rigidity tends to be tempered only by various kinds of affiliation with the *Sultan* or the *Orang Besar*, the most important being kinship extended more or less bilaterally, royal grace for services rendered and even proximity in residence which gives greater opportunity in getting into royal service.

In this manner then, the personnel in the *Raja-Orang Besar* hierarchy and through them members of their families, over the period of many generations, have come to represent the 'top' in the social stratification system. Each of the groups represents really a 'status group' in the Weberian sense[1] whose role incumbency is determined by a fundamentally similar 'status-situation'.

In Malay society then, the more important element emphasized in the present day context is stratification by social honour or prestige which gives rise to the formation of status groups basing their claims to such regard upon certain highly regarded cultural characteristics which are mainly symbolic in form and function. In other words the Malay stratification system conforms more to Weber's conception of stratification by status rather than to that of Karl Marx in which stratification is based upon class distinctions which, in turn, are founded upon relationships to the means of production. There are undoubtedly elements of class distinctions as understood in the Marxian sense in the Malay situation, like the peasantry as opposed to the *Orang Besar* or *Raja* groups. But these seem to have been subsumed under the more complex status-situation in the Weberian sense.

The mainspring of this stratification by status system rests on the traditional Malay conception of the Sultanate as a socio-political system. Basic in the theory of the Sultanate is that the *Sultan* is the 'Fountain of all Honours' and the 'Ultimate owner of the Soil' and that he alone may confer titles and dignities. The point is that it is not enough to be powerful but that such realities of power, be it political-administrative, economic or in any other form, must be given due recognition by or 'be honoured' in terms of the traditional status-honour indices before such a position becomes legitimized or validated. In practical terms, this involves the conferment of titles and insignia of office by the Sultan from whom, as the 'Fount of Nobility' such validation may only emanate. The *Sultan* (or Royal Ruler) is Sovereign and he embodies the Malay notion of *Daulat* involving, traditionally, the notions of sanctity, sacredness or inviolability attaching to the person of the *Sultan* and even extended to his residences. In earlier days the notion of *Daulat* involved also a belief in some supernatural power that would act in retribution when royal dignity was outraged. Such a belief was then the ultimate sanction that was embodied in the notion of royal majesty. Today, there is still some lingering belief in this supernatural potency of royal majesty. But to all intents and purposes this has largely become rationalized into a pattern of expected behaviour that rests on the 'sanctity' of immemorial tradition. Thus the conventions in speech, terms of address and special mannerisms in respect of behaviour towards the *Sultan* and the traditional *Orang Besar* are still couched in terms of ultimate courtesy and extreme deference. Especially on formal or ceremonial occasions they are adhered to most punctiliously. In sum, therefore, it may be stated that the traditional status-rank orders

[1]By 'status group' I mean persons whose role incumbency is determined by fundamentally similar 'status-situation'. By 'status-situation', I mean the component elements that determine conditions or situations of prestige or social status of individuals and groups. One particular 'status-situation' is differentiated from others by the exclusiveness of the elements that distinguish it from other similar groups.

are still regarded as the collective index of high social status and prestige although they may be largely symbolic in function.

These then are the complex of cultural values that underly the traditional stratification system of the Malays stemming from the structuring of roles associated with the Sultanate as a socio-political institution that have persisted throughout the several centuries of Malay social and political life. It is against this background of persistence and continuity in the highly regarded cultural tradition that we may now turn to examine the interrelations between such a system of stratification and power groups in the contemporary situation which has been the consequence of and response to the gross cultural — social, political and economic — changes experienced by the society. Politically, the most important of these changes has been firstly the taking over of political-administrative power from the traditional authorities by the British administration from the 1890s and secondly, the constitutional transfer of such powers to the democratically elected leadership within the framework of Constitutional Monarchy after the British model which was formally established with Independence of the country in 1957.

VI

The modern components of the political-administrative structures of power and authority are constituted by two major types, firstly, the government administrative bureaucracy and secondly, the 'People's Representatives' (*Wakil Rakyat*) as constituted in the State Legislative Assembly.

The context of the roles and functions of the bureaucracy is the framework of the administration of the State, while the context of the roles and functions of the 'People's Representatives' is the Government of the State through the fully elected State Legislative Assembly. It is sufficient to refer to the category of roles in the Government administrative bureaucracy only in respect of the 'officer category' or the Higher Civil Servants — the category of general administrative officers as opposed to the professional administrative officers like engineers, doctors, etc. The reason for this is mainly an empirical one, which is the fact that the Malay officers predominate in the former category while in the latter category their number is insignificantly small.

1. *The Higher Civil Servants*

The State of Perak, like all other constituent States in the Federation of Malaysia, has its own State Government and administration. A written Constitution, the Laws of the Constitution of the State of Perak, 1948, specifies the form and functions of government and codifies the position of the Sultan as a 'Constitutional Ruler' within the framework of parliamentary democracy after the British model. The administrative bureaucracy is thus serving under a fully elected Government.

The executive control of the administration of the State is maintained by the State Secretariat in the capital of the State at Ipoh. The Secretariat is headed by the most Senior Civil Servant in the State who is designated as the State Secretary. For legal advice on matters of legislation and administration there is the State Legal Adviser and the principal officer in charge of the financial affairs of the State is the State Financial Officer. While the State Secretary and the State Financial Officer are senior officers of the Federation Malayan Civil Service, the State Legal Adviser is on the Federation Legal/Judiciary Service. All the other administrative officers in the State are also officers on the Federation Establishment.

For administrative purposes, the State is divided into eight districts, the larger ones in turn being further divided into Sub-Districts. These Districts are graded in some order of importance which is reflected in the seniority of the grade of its chief administrative officer, the District Officer. A District Officer usually has several other administrative officers as assistants and deputy assistants. Locally, these officers are commonly referred to by the initials of their designated officers, thus: D.O. (District Officer), C.A.D.O. (Chief Assistant District Officer), A.D.O. (Assistant District Officer) and D.A.D.O. (Deputy Assistant District Officer).

The Officers from the State Secretary downwards constitute the hierarchy of administrative officers for purposes of carrying out the administrative will of the State Government. But, sociologically, what is significant is that the hierarchy of authority roles also indicates the social status positions of the incumbents that transcend their purely official roles. The initials of the designated officers at the District level especially have become terms of address expressive of polite and respectful behaviour towards them. Thus these initials have come to possess a symbolic significance not only as designations of positions of the officers in their 'official' capacities; but also in the general non-official life of the District to which they are assigned.

These administrative officers, together with their professional/technical colleagues, constitute an important category of persons to whom the rest of the people refer collectively as *pegawai kerajaan* (lit. 'government officers'). Together they have come to be included in the omnibus category of *orang besar* (lit. 'big man'), but as a sub-category which may be called the 'modern' *orang besar* as opposed to the 'traditional' *orang besar* described earlier.

Internally, however, the Higher Civil Service is hierarchically stratified into the Malayan Civil Service (MCS) and the Malay Administrative Service (MAS), which in reality constitute the senior and junior divisions respectively of one civil service structure. In the public service terminology of the Federation, the MCS is on the Division I of the Federal Establishment and the MAS is on the Division II. Each division is further subdivided into various grades in an hierarchical order. These distinctions, which are characteristic of any bureaucracy, mark off individual personnel within the Service and are of extreme importance in the structuring of roles in the Civil Service. But, outwardly they constitute the first category of 'modern' *orang besar* with whom the populace have had to deal.

Recruitment into the Higher Civil Service is clearly based on achievement criteria which insist on the possession of a certificate or diploma showing evidence of the minimum educational qualification required of candidates for appointment. This usually involves a formal educational achievement in English medium schools with the minimum level being the Overseas Cambridge School Certificate with a higher than a pass standard in the English language subject. Those with a University degree (general or pass only) can gain direct entry into the MAS cadet rank, and those with an Honours degree directly into the MCS cadet rank. But what is significant in the context of the Malay society is that these officers have had the benefit of English education, which signifies 'quality' or higher educational achievement than others. Recruitment into the Service itself is conducted by an independent Public Service Commission of the Federation.

An examination of the social background of the Higher Civil Services personnel in the State reveals certain important features.[1] These may be summed up briefly as follows:

  i. the number of officers in the ranks of the Service who have any aristocratic/royal connexion is negligible. At the time of fieldwork in 1964/5, out of a total of 52 MAS and MCS officers only 6 have the honorific prefix of *Tunku*, *Raja* or *Ungku* before their proper names;

  ii. they all possess the minimum educational qualification for entry into the Civil Service;

  iii. a sizeable number of them had also previously seen service in other Government Services;

  iv. on the whole they are comparatively young; the average was found to be 35.9 years for the MCS, and 28.6 years for the MAS.

Other features of the Higher Civil Service personnel are firstly, like all their colleagues in other equivalent Services of the Government bureaucracy, they enjoy comparatively high salaries and several material fringe benefits which enable them to lead a style of life that is above the average for the majority of the Malays.

Secondly, like any bureaucracy in general, the Service constitutes a career with a high degree of security and that each officer's position at the various levels confer upon him high prestige and social esteem corresponding to his position in the hierarchy in relation with his clients, the members of the public.

---

[1]For details see my earlier study (1970). Only a summary of the administrative structure of roles in authority positions which has a bearing upon the topic of this paper is given here.

Finally, the personnel in the Higher Civil Service constitute a solidary group of people. There is evident a sense as well as expressions of belonging together to a corporate body which is structurally and organizationally placed in authority roles of great importance in the government and administration of the State, affecting the lives of the people in various ways.

The Higher Civil Service personnel therefore are in possession of the bundle of attributes and qualities which are highly valued by the people. This led them to categorize or call the Higher Civil Servants also as *orang besar*, which usage represents really an extension of the traditional appellation. They thus constitute a ranking order or stratum of the society by virtue of the fact that all its members have similar chances to gain the things and experiences that are generally highly valued.

The mainsprings of their high prestige and status-honour are undoubtedly legitimate power or authority vested in their roles and, secondly, the nature of their occupation. But while power *per se* does not always lend prestige, e.g. the armed robber directing the cashier of a bank to empty the till, the role-performance of the incumbents of legitimate, i.e. social power or authority, roles often commands prestige from the other party involved in the interaction especially if such roles have already a long tradition of legitimacy. This is the case with the Higher Civil Service in Perak (and in Malaysia as a whole) in which there is already a significantly long tradition stemming from its initial creation by the British administration soon after their intervention in the affairs of the Malay States in 1890s.

The Higher Civil Service is also an occupation since it consists of a set of activities pursued regularly as a major source of income. But, it is in the nature of the occupation involving no soiled hands but rather performing roles and functions of high value that the prestige of the Service rests. Thus, as an occupation, the Higher Civil Service personnel belongs to a single class position, but because as an occupation it carries an expected quota of prestige, on and off the job, the same personnel also belongs to one status position.

In sum, therefore, the Higher Civil Service personnel represent a new/ modern *orang besar* stratum in the society in which class position and *status* position involve one another with executive-administrative authority as the underpinnings of the stratum. Based upon his class position, he derives regular income from his occupation as a Higher Civil Servant which is above the average for the majority of Malays. By means of this high and regular income he could afford a style of life to satisfy or enhance his status-position. For, it is in the consumption pattern and style of life that their status position is clearly manifested.

2. *The 'People's Representative'*

The other new/'modern' category of *orang besar* is constituted by the roles in the authority structures of the democratically elected Government of the State. These roles are subsumed under the State Legislative Assembly which is composed of members of the political party in power and the members of the Opposition parties. The membership of this most 'modern' category of *orang besar* is thus composed of individuals who, through their political competence in popularly based political parties, have risen to occupy the leading roles in the most 'modern' institution in the society, i.e. that of a parliamentary democratic system of government and administration within the framework of a constitutional monarchy as institutionalized in the State Legislative Assembly (*Dewan Perhimpunan Undangan Negeri*).

The emergence of a really effective form of articulate and popular political participation amongst the Malays really occurred during the post-war reconstruction period (1945–48) during the Malayan Union episode. The seeds of political awakening, however, had already grown much earlier before the war, though their public manifestation was effectively prescribed by the British Colonial regime.

It is necessary here only to highlight some of the new but highly significant developments of the future 'People's Representative' arising out of the major and country-wide Malay popular protest against the Malayan Union proposals in 1945 that threatened the *status quo* concerning the whole conception of the Malay Rulers as the embodiment of sovereignty (at least in theory) and the position of the Malays as the indigenous community. Briefly, it was the first time that all sections of the Malay community — from the *Raja* and *Orang Besar* to the ordinary people — participated actively together in national political issues. Hitherto, such 'high politics' had been regarded and exercised by virtue of the pre-emptive rights or prerogatives of the *Raja* and *Orang Besar* groups. The top leadership of the national mass political party, the UMNO (United Malays National Organization) which was the one major party formed then, was still drawn almost entirely from the ranks of the English educated members of the Malay aristocracy, the *Raja* and *Orang Besar* families, i.e. the traditional leaders of the Malays. But in the second rung of the leadership at least, there were already members from the 'Common People's' family background.

The Malays in the State of Perak, in common with those in other States, also made their political contribution in those early years. Led by one of her senior civil servants, who was also concurrently one of the 'Eight Chiefs' of the 2nd Rank (Dato' Panglima Bukit Gantang Haji Abdul Wahab, a barrister qualified in the United Kingdom) the *Perikatan Melayu Perak* (PMP — Malay National Association of Perak) was formed with the Dato' as leader. And this local political party was affiliated to UMNO in the foundation years. Subsequently, it broke away and with the premature death of the Dato' later the party died a natural death. In other words, there was still the same continuity in the beginnings of the role of the traditional, but *cum* achievement based *orang besar* as the 'People's

Representative'. In Perak, since almost all such 'traditional-modern' leaders compromised their positions by associating with their kinsman, the said Dato', the latter's demise and the consequent natural death of his party, also laid the top positions open to contest by the 'true' 'People's Representative' of 'commoner' origins, who had faithfully stuck to UMNO in the State.

However, the new role of 'People's Representative' had to await the subsequent years of transitional period of political development before it could really play its part fully. This emergent role really came into its own after the 1959 first General Elections to the State Assembly (and Federal Parliament) were held.

Thus, amongst the Malays as a whole, a new category of *orang besar* ('big/important person') consisting of those political leaders who got elected into the State Assembly (or Federal Parliament) came into being fully. To the existing Malay political lexicon, the new terms *Wakil Rakyat* ('People's Representative') and *Yang Berhormat* ('the Honourable Member') have been added as new honorific terms of address. Together with the two earlier categories of *Orang Besar, Raja/Orang Besar* and the *Pegawai Kerajaan* (the Higher Civil Servants) the *Wakil Rakyat* have since formed what may be described as a triadic patterning of status, class and authority roles closely involved with one another.

In the role of the 'People's Representative' two distinctions need to be made, i.e. those who are merely Assemblymen, and those who in addition are also appointed as members of the State Executive Council headed by the *Menteri Besar* (Chief Minister) which body really constitutes the Government of the State. In terms of power and authority and status differentials the latter category constitute the top positions in the State.

Recruitment into the role of the 'People's Representative' is implicit in the nature of the mass political party structure in an democratically elected system of Government. Hence we need not dwell further upon it here. But what is of great significance is the characteristics in the social background of those political-administrative decision-makers which bear upon the problem of status and power/authority configurations in the State.

Firstly, the most significant feature revealed by an examination of the membership of the State Assemblies of 1959 and 1964, is that Representatives of 'Common people' background have been dominant, almost to the entire exclusion of the nobility. In other words real political power has almost completely passed into the hands of the 'Common people's representatives or leaders'. Secondly, in terms of formal or quality education on the whole their level of achievement is lower than the members of the Higher Civil Service or even the traditional aristocracy. Thirdly, by comparison with the generally youthful bureaucrats on one side and the generally rather elderly traditional aristocracy, especially the Chiefs, their average age falls somewhere in between. Fourthly, in terms of occupational or other experience their background is rather chequered excepting for the fact that they seemed to have made politics their vocation. Hence to be an elected 'People's Representative' has become to them their 'profession' approaching close to a career and occupation that are to be diligently maintained and perpetuated. This last is based on the fact that they are paid a regular income and enjoy other material fringe benefits which, in a large number of cases, have meant an enhancement in their material standard and style of living.

VII

In the beginning of this paper I stated my hypothesis that in a situation in which the traditional social stratification system of a society is still regarded as culturally valid, for various reasons, by the members of that society, it is possible for the social groups with the highest status-honour indices in that society — e.g. the royalty and aristocracy — to maintain its status positions while relinquishing actual political power to an emergent group of leaders of 'common' origins by making use to advantage the cultural configuration of evaluation of the status-honour system. The big question is, of course, how is this possible? And if so in what ways?

In the first place, the answer to this is that the necessary conditions of continuing validity of the traditional system and the differentials in the power position, social class and status situations in the two opposing categories must be fulfilled. These conditions seem to me to be quite adequately met in the example described at some length earlier. The traditional divisions of the society still persist and are still regarded as culturally valid. The social status distance between the *Raja/Orang Besar* and the *'Orang Kebanyakan'* origins have not been narrowed by the acquisition of seats or positions of power and authority. As has been described above, in terms of real political-administrative and executive power, the Civil Servants and the 'People's Representative', especially those in the State Executive Council capped by the *Menteri Besar*, have vested in them instruments of exercising such power and authority in accordance with the policies that they themselves enact. And one could have presumed that power or authority or what these might yield would be adequate rewards for them.

But what seems to be missing from resting on such positions alone is the validation or legitimization in terms of cultural values with which they are familiar and into which they have been basically socialized. Hence, the necessity to seek validation in terms of or after the traditional model of indices of high status-honours. On their part, the traditional holders do not really wish to absorb these 'new men' and thereby lose the symbolic meaning of their position. But, on the other hand, they fully realize that for the polity to function in as harmonious a fashion as possible as well as out of sheer practical considerations, the implications of persisting and maintaining a caste-like rigidity in social distinctions could be detrimental to their position. Hence, a compromise has been worked out. A system of honours and dignities after the traditional model has been instituted by which means the *Sultan* as 'the *Fount of Nobility*' creates life *Datos* and other 'Honours' and 'Awards'. By these means, being a 'People's Representative' or a Civil Servant for some length of time not only brings about cumulative increment in the style of life, but for the more successful or lucky few they also provide a channel for a new kind of status-honour increment as well. Thus an initially 'lowly/common' origin could be compensated for in this manner. In other words, the system allows for a stamp to be put on base metal.

In this manner, therefore, these new *Datos* including the non-Malays (for the system applies to all) who have been similarly 'ennobled' by the *Sultan* for distinguished services rendered, now constitute a category of what I term as the 'new style aristocracy' vying for the symbols of high status-honour with the old established aristocracy. By the creation of a system based upon the traditional model the traditional aristocracy is still able to uphold its position especially since there is still persistence and perpetuation of the predominantly ascriptive criteria as opposed to the achievemental ones amongst them. They are still conscious of their origins and this social status and social class consciousness manifest themselves now and again when some individuals in the 'new aristocracy' presume a little more beyond the niceties of etiquette and other expressive behaviour consonant with their positions.

PART IV
Religion, Ideology and Modernization

9. Religion and Modernization in South-East Asia[1]

SYED HUSSEIN ALATAS

I

THE relation between religion and modernization in South-East Asia is a theme of such a complex nature that a discussion of any of its various aspects would necessitate a preliminary methodological and conceptual clarification. Such a clarification is further necessitated by the fact that modernization as a historical and contemporary phenomenon has been treated by scholars from different disciplines using concepts as political modernization, economic modernization, technological modernization, military modernization, educational modernization, administrative modernization, and so forth. It becomes almost the general practice to employ the concept modernization in a diffused and ambiguous manner. The ambiguity and diffuseness of the concept lies in the fact that no distinction or differentiation is accomplished between the numerous phenomena. This has resulted in the following:

(1) *The identification of modernization with different types of social change.* Various types of social change were regarded as modernization, some of which were the conditions and effects of modernization, rather than the essential process as such.[2]

(2) *The identification of modernization with Westernization, implicitly or explicitly.* A clear instance of explicit identification is Toynbee's concep-

[1]This chapter is an extract from my paper published in the *Archives Européennes de Sociologie,* Tome XI, 2 (1970). I should like to thank the editor for permission to reprint the paper.

[2]Based on several researches on modernizations, J. W. Hall summarized at least 32 characteristic features of modernization from the political, social, economic and intellectual spheres, as part of his attempt to define modernization. Notwithstanding its usefulness and comprehensiveness, yet in a few instances, he failed to distinguish between the essential process of modernization and some of its effects. The weakening of religious and cultural dogmas is one of the suggested characteristics which is in reality only an effect relative to time and place. See J. W. Hall, 1965.

tion of modernization.[1] Chitoshi Yanaga, a historian of modern Japan, lumped the concepts modernization and Westernization together evidently induced by the historical instances he dealt with, in a chapter called 'Acceleration of Modernization and Westernization' (Yanaga, 1949).

(3) *The identification of modernization with the constitutional and democratic form of government based on the Western European model.* An implicit identification is clearly shown by Eisenstadt when he considered the failures of constitutional democracy in Indonesia, Pakistan, Burma and the Sudan as 'breakdown in modernization'. He regarded the attempts of Nazism as 'demodernization', the rise of militarism in modern Japan as 'a breakdown' (Eisenstadt, 1964). It is obvious that his concept of modernization is somewhat narrow and misses the essential nature of the process.

(4) *The emphasis on a particular aspect or process of modern society as the essential core of modernization.* Here too there is an implicit identification with the Western model. The industrial and capitalistic aspects of Western society are then considered as the basic ingredients of modernization.

(5) *The confusion of the term modernization with the process of arriving at modernity,* that is, pertaining to the modern world. In this sense anything novel created at the present time is modern, like modern ballroom dancing, modern fashion, modern music, modern art, modern individualism, modern family, etc. Here too the model is usually Western society.

In view of the prevailing ambiguity of the term modernization the following definition is suggested to be used within the context of this paper. *Modernization is the process by which modern scientific knowledge covering all aspects of human life is introduced at varying degree, first in the Western civilization, and later diffused to the non-Western world, by different methods and groups with the ultimate purpose of achieving a better and more satisfactory life in the broadest sense of the term, as accepted by the society concerned.* The traits of modern scientific knowledge are the following: (a) the objectification of nature; (b) the assumption of laws and regularities in nature explainable in terms of a rational and empirical approach divorced from magic, religious dogma and philosophical systems; (c) the recourse to experimentation to assess the validity of suggested explanations; (d) the use of signs and abstract concepts; (e) the maintenance of a critical and enquiring spirit; (f) the search for truth for

---

[1]'Today the whole world is bent on being modern; but this agreeable word "modern" is a euphemism. It is a substitute for the less agreeable word "western" ' (Toynbee, 1962: 24). The motive for using the word modern instead of Western for the introduction of science and democracy is merely to save face for 'it goes against the grain to admit that one's own ancestral way of life is not adequate to the situation in which one now finds oneself' (Toynbee, 1962: 24).

its own sake;[1] (g) the employment of and concern for definite methods (h) the use and discovery of inanimate energy for further developments.

The characteristics of modernization listed by several scholars are ultimately dominated by one basic process: the development and application of modern science. Industrialization is after all the accomplishment of modern science based on the use of inanimate power and innumerable invention. The banking system, double entry book-keeping and the transaction of modern business, are all the results of scientific inventions. They are the application of modern science to human affairs.[2]

The sets of criteria to classify modernization will depend on the foci of interest.[3] We can then have modernization of the constitutional democratic type, of the totalitarian type, of the autocratic type, etc. Similarly, we can classify modernization with reference to other foci of interest in all fields of human endeavour. One instance which may be viewed in terms of modernization is the modernization of feudalism. Unfortunately there is no surviving modernized feudal society that could serve as our instance. But we can point to historical instances of such modernization. The feudal society of the Tokugawa period in Japan did attempt some modernization in certain sectors conceived as significant by the then ruling power. Plans for military reforms were drawn up in 1862 by the Tokugawa Shogunate, though the achievement was not impressive. Modernization of the army and navy developed rapidly at the end of the Tokugawa period under the impact of foreign countries.[4] Interest in Western learning was shown by

[1]These traits are each subject to further elaboration. We have, however, to stress that only recourse to actual concrete historical instances can express adequately what is meant by modern science. It should involve the entire corpus of knowledge related to modern science and its origin in Western Europe from at least the seventeenth century. Only then will the differentiating traits between modern science and its precursors be made clear. The invention of the steam engine, the discovery of electricity, the microscope, and a host of other things are specifically unique traits of modern science and technology.

[2]Rustow and Ward (1964: 4) have hinted at the possibility that the central aspect of modernization as a historical phenomenon is man's rapidly increasing control of the forces of nature. The following is their view of modernization: 'Modernization as a historical concept includes such specific aspects of change as industrialization of the economy or secularization of ideas, but it is not limited to these. It involves a marked increase in geographic and social mobility, a spread of secular, scientific, and technical education, a transition from ascribed to achieved status, an increase in material standards of living and many related and subsidiary phenomena. Rough numerical measures of modernization are provided, in our century, by the ratio of inanimate to animate energy used in the economy, the proportion of the working force employed in secondary and tertiary rather than primary production (that is, in manufacturing and services, as opposed to agriculture and fishing), the degree of urbanization, the extent of literacy, the circulation of mass media, the gross national product per capita, and the length of life expectancy at birth' (Rustow and Ward 1964: 3-4).

[3]Norman Jacobs, in his *The Origin of Modern Capitalism and Eastern Asia* (1958) suggested that Japan and Western Europe belong to the same basic type of modern capitalism while India and China belong to another. The criteria of classification are certain historical and structural factors facilitating the rise of modern capitalism in Japan and Western Europe at the period of take-off.

[4]In the eyes of Shinga (1956) feudal restrictions prevented the successful completion of the modernization process in the Tokugawa period.

- the Tokugawa Shogun Yoshimune (1716–1745), who was fond of astronomy. The first frictional electric machine was brought by the Dutch in 1770 and was soon imitated and multiplied. In 1823, a German physician, von Siebold, attached to a Dutch merchant ship trained many Japanese in the medical profession (Kawaki, 1931). With the overthrow of the Tokugawa Regime after the Restoration of 1868, the break with the feudal past was by no means complete despite several changes in the social, economic, political and educational fields. The political order of Japanese society, based on the sacral absolutism of the Emperor, may be viewed as the modernized version of feudalism, wherein science, industry and technology, together with the social structural adjustments, were made to serve the needs and privileges of the ruling group whose basic values were derived from the feudal past.

The second consequence derived from our conception of modernization is the need to distinguish it from Westernization. Though it is true that the basic ingredients of modernization are derived from the West, nevertheless it is possible to consider them as autonomous cultural elements which are subject to diffusion without necessarily being accompanied by Western culture. If they are, the reasons are to be sought elsewhere rather than in the intrinsic nature of the process of modernization. We are compelled by the nature of cultural diffusion to make this distinction. In the case of the history of Europe this distinction has never been questioned. When Europe adopted many technological, scientific, philosophical and material elements of the Islamic civilization during the Middle Ages, this adoption has never been characterized as Islamization or Arabicization, and rightly so. The adoption of those elements were not accompanied by a wholesale introduction of Islamic customs, morals, philosophy, rituals, rites of passage, values, habits, etc., though in certain areas like Spain and Sicily there were considerable Arabic Islamic influence accompanying the diffusion of science and technology.[1]

The third consequence of our conception of modernization is that although modernization can refer to numerous phenomena not everything can be modernized, and some such things are magic, and certain forms of religion. Any attempt to introduce modern science and technology into their spheres of activities would lead to their dissolution. On the surface the inclusion of scientific elements into their activities may give the impression of modernization but in reality this is not the case.[2]

The fourth consequence from our conception of modernization is to distinguish its effects. Not all effects of modernization, whether the pro-

[1]From Asian history the only country we can think of in which modernization and large-scale Westernization went hand in hand is the Philippines. It is the only Asian country profoundly and consistently influenced by Western culture for the last four centuries (Phelan, 1959).

[2]An instance where modernization was well-nigh impossible was the religion of the Toradjas in Central Celebes, Indonesia (Adriani, 1932).

cess is initiated from within or from without, can be viewed as the modernized results of such a process. An instance at hand is the cargo-cults of New Guinea which Firth (1964: 112–13) has characterized as a mere delusion and fantasy. The introduction of modern goods and system of transportation initiated among natives an adjustive reaction which was not based on reality-orientation, as evidenced by the belief that their ancestors would soon return in ships and aeroplanes laden with goods.[1] Though the rise of the cult was the effect of modern Western rule, and though the objects and goals desired were modern, it can hardly be said that the cult movement was a modernization of the traditional religion. The aspects of the traditional outlook which provided the basis for the cults were not concerned with modernization in the sense we understand it.

Having stated some preliminary observations on the nature of modernization it is by now clear what shall be understood under the term modernization. This chapter concentrates on the relationship between religion and modernization in South-East Asia centering around scientific and economic development. Some of the problems posed by Max Weber shall be discussed.[2] We may start with enquiring whether religion encourages or hinders modernization. Three possibilities can be suggested, (1) that it hinders modernization, (2) that it encourages modernization, and (3) that it is neutral. The data derived from the South-East Asian setting in particular and the Asian one in general point to the fact that it is impossible to sustain any generalization after concretely analysing cases of each specific religion such as Islam and Buddhism. In the case of the great world religions such as Islam, Christianity and Buddhism in South-East Asia we may suggest that in some places they are neutral, in some places they encourage but nowhere do they hinder modernization and economic development. The reason why it has sometimes been suggested that religion hinders economic development is to a great extent due to the following factors:

(a) That the observer is not familiar with the religion concerned, its teaching and doctrinal structure as conceived by the participants.

(b) That the observer is not aware of the influence of other factors extraneous to the religion concerned, sometimes in conflict with it, but responsible for the phenomena impeding modernization.

(c) That the observer is not sufficiently aware of the dynamics of social and cultural interaction when it comes to the interaction between religion and its cultural and social setting.

(d) That the observer draws his conclusion from a limited amount of data.

[1]There is a host of literature on the subject. Among those dealing with the interpretation of such movements see Inglis, 1957, and Stanner, 1958, may be noted.

[2]Elsewhere I had discussed Weber's thesis on religion and the rise of capitalism with reference to South-East Asia (Alatas, 1963, 1965).

II

There is one instance at hand to illustrate the general statements made thus far. It has been suggested by some that Islam in Malaysia impedes the economic development of the Malays through its emphasis on what Weber calls otherworldly asceticism. Though the portrayal of condition may be correct, the conclusion is not. It has been stressed that Malay religious teachers often point to the future life as the abode of ultimate happiness for the faithful while this world is ephemeral and transient. It is argued that this inhibited the Malay Muslims from vigorous economic action in comparison with their Chinese neighbours.[1] The total population of West Malaysia is approximately 8,801,399 according to the latest census (1970). More detailed figures are available for 1957, when 3,125,000 were Malays (49.8%), 2,334,000 Chinese (37.3%), 707,000 Indians (11.3%) and 112,000 Others (1.8%). The distribution in urban centres was as follows:

Malays	Chinese	Indians	Others	Total
604,000	1,704,000	286,000	74,000	2,668,000
22.6%	63.9%	10.7%	2.8%	100%

The occupational distribution of the ethnic or racial groups according to the 1957 Census Report is shown in Table 15.

As apparent from the occupational distribution the Chinese community in West Malaysia are concentrated in manufacturing, commerce, salesmanship, craft, quarrying, mining, building and construction, and in executive and managerial professions. They also concentrate in the professional and technical fields if we exclude the nurses, midwives and teachers included in the total figures under the census classification heading.

The Malays[2] excel in the field of agriculture, the services, and unemployment. In the services it is mainly government service with a high concentration in the police and the army. In the private sector the highest concentration is in rice cultivation (more than one-third of the total economically active), next comes rubber cultivation, small-holding (approximately one-quarter of the total economically active), and finally fishing (approximately one twenty-fifth of those economically active).

[1] I am unable to trace one or two published statements made several years back, but from time to time this opinion emerges in discussions among Malaysian intellectuals.

[2] Under the term Malay is included the 41,400 aborigines. For detailed information on the occupational census of the Malays and Chinese, see Fell, 1957.

TABLE 15

OCCUPATIONAL DISTRIBUTION: 1957 REPORT,
BY ETHNIC AND RACIAL GROUPS

Occupation	Malays	Chinese	Indians	Others	Total
Professional, Technical and Related Occupations	41.0	38.1	11.0	9.9	100.0
Administrative, Executive and Managerial Occupations (excluding those in agricultural and retail trade)	17.5	62.3	12.3	8.0	100.0*
Clerical Occupations	27.1	46.2	19.8	6.8	100.0*
Sales and Related Occupations	15.9	66.0	16.8	1.2	100.0*
Agricultural Occupations	62.1	24.3	12.8	0.8	100.0
Miners, Quarrymen and Related Occupations	7.8	86.0	4.9	1.3	100.0
Transport and Communication Occupations	41.7	40.3	16.0	2.0	100.0
Craftsmen Production Process Workers and Labourers n.e.c.	23.7	55.7	19.7	1.0	100.0*
Service, Sport, Entertainment and Recreation Occupations	39.7	33.3	12.8	14.2	100.0
Total Gainfully Employed	47.2	35.7	14.4	2.6	100.0*
Persons not working but looking for work	50.1	33.4	14.8	1.7	100.0
TOTAL Economically Active	47.3	35.7	14.5	2.6	100.0*

*Totals do not add up to 100% because of rounding.

In the case of the Chinese the highest concentration is in rubber cultivation (more than one-third of the total economically active), next comes commerce (more than one-fifth of the total economically active), then sales and related occupation (more than one-sixth of the total economically active), and finally manufacturing (approximately one-seventh of the total economically active).

Among the Chinese community the traits which Weber suggested as belonging to the modern capitalist spirit are well pronounced. Frugality and diligence are highly prized. The making of money and success in life are emphasized, accompanied by a disciplined effort, long range planning, and a rational ordering of life. Their religion and philosophy of life are very much associated with wealth.

In the case of the Malay community the above traits are lacking as far as the commercial and industrial aspects of social life are concerned. This lack was then attributed to Islam. Nothing is further from the truth for the following reasons:

(a) The teachings of Islam encourage diligence, frugality, discipline, a rational approach within the ends and means context, active participation in commerce and industry. Mohammed was the only one among the great founders of religion who was himself a trader. The spiritual leaders of the Islamic world such as the famous Imams and Sufis were mostly people who derived their livelihood from trade and industry. Islam was spread to South-East Asia by traders. From the teaching, as well as the history of Islam, there are sufficient sources of inspiration and directives for a vigorous entrepreneuring life. There is also the doctrine of the calling, in a sense. A man who succeeds to acquire wealth through honest and diligent effort is favoured by God.[1]

(b) The South Indian Muslims in Malaya developed an energetic and rational approach towards business. The discipline and organization of life centered around their business activity are obvious. They dominated the retail trade in tobacco distribution and money changing. Together with the Chinese they participated significantly in the bookselling, the restaurant and the grocery businesses. The South Indian Muslims belong to the same religion, the same school of thought (mazhab Shafei) and the same mystical orders as the Malays. If Islam inhibits rational economic action, there is no reason why the South Indian Muslims in Malaya should be otherwise than are the Malays. Similarly we can suggest the same implication concerning the Syrian Muslim businessmen, the Bohra Ismailis of Bombay, and the rest of the Muslim business world.[2]

[1]In this connexion, Weber's writings on Islam are, on the whole, absolutely untrustworthy. So are many of his remarks on Buddhism. He misses even the elementary knowledge of the religion and its historical facts. There is hardly a more disfigured picture of Islam than that depicted by Weber (1964).

[2]A quotation from an authority may be helpful here. 'Islamic law favours every practical activity, and holds in great esteem agriculture, commerce, and every kind of work; it censures all those who burden others with their maintenance, requires every man to keep himself by the produce of his own labour, and does not despise any sort of work whereby man may make himself independent of others' (Santillana, 1931: 289).

(c) A section of the Minangkabau, Bugis and Achehnese Muslims of Indonesia has developed a different economic ethos and activity from the Malays. The traits of modern economic striving are present among them. They belonged to the same cultural background, religion and feudal structure, but yet developed a different economic ethic. Religion (Islam) cannot be the reason why one is not the same as others.

(d) Large sections of South-East Asian societies whose religion is not Islam exhibited the same traits as the Malays do towards modern economic action. They share a common system of values clearly expressed in their hierarchical evaluation of occupations. This common pattern of occupational grading is shared by many countries in Asia and South-East Asia with different religious backgrounds. An instance from Ceylon, the following may be noted:

(i) Wage earning and entrepreneurial activity, except cultivation, in private business is conceived as grossly inferior in status to an equivalent occupation in government establishments.

(ii) Work or productivity as such does not have normative significance. Thus idleness and unproductive work or activity lack negative moral qualification.

(iii) Non-agricultural manual employment, even when not vocational, is generally regarded as degrading.

(iv) Consumption rather than investment direct thrift and savings.

(v) Wealth in land is considered more honourable and secure than capital investment.[1]

It is this value system, a hangover from the feudal past and consolidated by colonial influence, that forms the greatest obstacle to modernization in contemporary South-East Asia. Other factors are to my mind less determining. The problem however remains as far as religion and modernization is concerned. What is the role of religion in sustaining or changing this value system? In the past the great religions such as Hinduism, Buddhism, Christianity and Islam had become part of the feudal or pre-modern fabrics of social life. They had accommodated to themselves different economic ethics, and different outlooks towards science and technology. When there is a change towards modernization, to what extent shall their influence be decisive in support of it? To answer this question we shall have to descend to a more concrete and microanalytic level of analysis, for ultimately the processes of modernization operate along those lines.

[1]As Bryce Ryan (1964) noted, the above values characterizing the Sinhalese status-achievement-work ethos has no support in religion comparable to the Protestant support of Capitalism. The support comes from the cultural and institutional background rather than Buddhism. Buddhism does not hinder the emergence of modern capitalist values, though it does not suggest them. Empirical evidence on this point is found in H. D. Evers' study on the emergence of a class of industrial entrepreneurs in Ceylon (Evers, 1964).

It has been stressed by Weber (1951: 199) that Chinese magical-animism with the vested interest of its practitioners completely prevented the advent of indigenous modern enterprises in communication and industry. 'In general one may say that every sort of rationalization of the archaic empirical knowledge and craft in China has woven towards a magic image of the world' (Weber, 1951: 196). Medicine and pharmacology were rationalized in an animistic direction. Astrology were connected with archaic meteorology. Forms of mountains, heights, rocks, plains, trees, grass, and waters have been considered geomantically significant such that 'a single piece of rock by its form could protect whole areas against the attacks of evil demons' (Weber, 1951: 198). Death, burial, construction works, and other items required geomantic control. A new funeral place might disturb all the spirits of the tombs and cause terrible misfortunes. The above approach towards existence prevented the objectification of nature, the pre-condition for the development of technology.

Family piety based on animism was the strongest influence on Chinese conduct. It facilitated and controlled the strong cohesion of the sib associations. Weber also noted the absence, in the Confucian ethic, of the tension between nature and deity, ethical demand and human shortcoming, consciousness of sin and need for salvation, action on earth and compensation in the beyond, religious duty and the social reality. There was hence, 'no leverage for influencing conduct through inner forces freed of tradition and convention' (Weber, 1951: 236).

The Puritan ethic was in contrast to the Confucian. It objectified man's duties as a creature of God. The religious duty towards the hidden and supra-mundane God made the Puritan appraise human relations, including the nearest in life, as mere means and expression of a mentality reaching beyond the concrete environment. Its ethic was universal and not particularistic. It was committed to a sacred cause or idea, while the Confucian was not. Stressing his point, Weber said, 'For the economic mentality, the personalist principle was undoubtedly as great a barrier to impersonal matter of factness. It tended to tie the individual ever anew to his sib members and to bind him to the manner of the sib, in any case to 'persons' instead of functional tasks ('enterprises')' (Weber, 1951: 236–7). The barrier to the rational economic mentality was intimately connected with Chinese religion. It was an obstacle maintained by the ruling and educated class. Protestantism and the ethical religions shattered the fetters of the sib. It established a community of faith rather than blood. 'From the economic viewpoint it meant basing business confidence upon the ethical qualities of the individual proven in his impersonal, vocational work' (Weber, 1951: 237).

We need not take issue with Weber on his description of Chinese religion. But we may challenge his assessment of Chinese religion and philosophy as an impediment to the rise of modern capitalism. Weber had definitely exaggerated the significance of religion while he played down the significance of other factors. This can be shown with the instances from Malaysia. Given a differential historical, sociological and economic background, the same Chinese religion and values not only did not hamper the rise of the modern capitalist spirit, but positively promoted it. We have shown in Table 15 that the Chinese excel in those areas of action requiring functional and rational qualifications, in the entrepreneurial and managerial fields, in the commercial and industrial sectors, and in the modern professions. The influence of religion and culture is channelled through the following:

(a) Money and the idea of money dominate the religious practices of the Chinese more than the other communities in Malaysia. A considerable amount of money is burnt annually in the form of paper money imported from China. Singapore alone spends some millions of dollars (Malaysian) a year. Paper money is allegedly remitted to the dead by burning it. Paper money is used as offerings in temples. Devotion to the dead ancestor, a very important duty, involved the idea of money. This acts as a strong incentive to possess money.

(b) The obligation to honour the dead ancestors in this world by raising one's status here requires wealth and good deeds. With wealth it is possible to build a temple and reserve a family graveyard.

(c) Impressive public and private events such as the celebration of the New Year, weddings and funerals, and the commemoration of the dead are strongly associated with wealth and money.

(d) Many influential taboos and symbols are associated with wealth and good luck. It is considered undesirable to sweep the house on the first day of Chinese New Year as this may have the effect of driving away prosperity. Golden colour is much desired; a Chinese orange symbolizes wealth; carp symbolizes profit and surplus; the New Year's cake (*nien koh*) symbolizes success and increase in status.

There are numerous other instances in Chinese religious life wherein wealth and prosperity figure prominently. The area of religious life covers the worship of gods who are expected to bestow some return favours, the worship of natural forces, belief in the retribution of good and evil, in occult practices and in fortune-telling. The predominance of the ideas of wealth, honour, status, and good-health in the motivational structure of Chinese religions intensify the need for achievement in those areas. Possessing a strong motivational drive for wealth, honour, status, good health, the ability to express piety and devotion for the family and ancestors, are certainly the decisive cultural factors capable of releasing a vigorous economic action. Given the proper social and economic backgrounds, they become a significant moving factor, no matter how irrational their ultimate philosophical and metaphysical anchorage seems to us.

Judging from the experience of the Chinese in Malaya, whose religion and traditional values were derived from the mainland of China, it is clear that Weber's generalization on the negative influence of Chinese religion and values on capitalist action and entrepreneurial activity, cannot be defended. Given a different setting the same religion and values, however incongruent they may be in form and spirit, with natural science and its fundamental attitudes, can be a great contributing factor in the emergence and development of the modern capitalist spirit and the process of modern-ization that goes with it.

From the history of the Chinese in Malaysia, showing their active participation in the spread of modern capitalism in this part of the world, which is also the integral part of modernization in this area, we may deduce the following conclusion: we have to classify types of magical-animism into those favourable to modernization and those inhibitive towards modernization, in addition to those which are neutral. Many interested scholars, in their enthusiasm for Weber's thesis, have focused their attention primarily on the prophetic religions or the rationalistic reformist religions of Asia, without paying much heed to Asian folk religions. This has led to an over-simplification of issues, in some instances.

The suggestion that Chinese religion has contributed positively to modernization and economic development in Malaysia, despite its magical-animistic tendency which is diametrically opposed to the rational and empirical outlook of science, would compel us to follow a further line of inquiry. Why is it that the Malays, with a religion by far much more in harmony with the precepts of the natural sciences and the values of economic development lag far behind the Chinese in both areas, while the Chinese succeeded in achieving a tremendous amount of support from their religion which had not been a driving force for the pursuit of science and modernization in their own homeland? The answers are to be sought in the historical and sociological backgrounds of the two communities respectively. There were different factors operating. They formed the significant causative factors belonging to different types. The first to note is the change of the political and social environment as experienced by the Chinese immigrants and their immediate descendants. The second is the fact of their being immigrants having to struggle for survival under conditions of hardship. The third is that within the new environment the Chinese religion and tradition became a positive force in favour of modernization and economic development. The fourth is that Malaysia itself offered ample scope for Chinese labour and entrepreneurship. This is very clear particularly from the latter part of the nineteenth century to the subsequent decades.

The political and social environment created by the British in Singapore, Malacca and Penang, with their emphasis on free trade, the rule of law, and orderly administration, had given the necessary peace and security to enable the process of modernization and economic development to take place without hindrances. A rather significant effect of this development is the change in the status system. In the traditional Chinese society the intellectuals, educated government officials and teachers ranked highest in the occupational status hierarchy. The businessmen were below them and the landed gentry. In Malaysia, however, the businessmen, the successful entrepreneur, rank highest. After their death the possibility of deification is there provided they merited the honour. The most apparent deification was that of Sheng Ming (1822–1862), the Chinese leader of Sungei Ujong. He was a good and successful manager of business as well as a settler of disputes. He became an apprentice at the age of fifteen under a general merchant in China for fourteen years after which he migrated to Malaya. After his murder in 1862, a deification cult developed around him. In 1882, his friend and blood brother Yap Ah Loy, another well-known Chinese pioneer and miner of Kuala Lumpur, erected a temple, in his honour, the Hsien Szu Shih Yeh, in Kuala Lumpur, which has since become a famous centre of worship. Yap Ah Loy himself was eventually deified.[1] They became the patrons of tin miners all over Malaya. Yap Ah Loy was a great influence in establishing peace and order in Kuala Lumpur, in building commerce and industry, roads, hospitals, schools and temples.

The deification of Yap Ah Loy, the tin miner and successful business-man, and his blood brother Cheng Ming Li, also a successful businessman, is the religious sanction for the new status system which exerted a consider-able influence on the motivation of subsequent generations. The historical, sociological, economic and political conditions in Malaysia did not restrain the growth of modernization and capitalist development among the Chinese community.

It was the reverse conditions that checked the rise of modern capitalism in China. The geography of the country did not encourage land or mari-time trade, natural harbours being few, especially in the north. There were few trading neighbours within easy reach to encourage commercial enterprise to give rise to a class of adventurous seafarers.[2] Mountains and deserts discouraged travel, and trade routes were few and difficult. The land did not produce the surplus which could expand trade. There was no stimulation in the form of demand for luxuries in the mass of the frugal population. Incessant toil required by subsistence crops engaged most of their attention. On the social side the duty of sons to stay at home for the support of old parents and grandparents prevented mobility. Money was rarely needed by the bulk of the population, despite the fact that the earliest coins and the first bank-note were known to have been used in China.[3]

[1]This temple now includes the deification of three pioneering leaders of Chinese settlers, Sheng Ming Li, Chung Lai and Yap Ah Loy himself. On this subject see Middlebrooke, 1951 and Suing, 1965.

[2]The Emperor Yong Lu had discouraged his subjects from pursuing trade as a pro-fession. His edict of 30 July 1402 A.D. prohibited private trade overseas (Wang, 1964: 100).

[3]Authentic bank-notes in paper were mentioned in the time of Emperor Hsien Tsung c. A.D. 800 (Quiggin, 1949: 200, 248).

From the government side there was no leadership in the direction of economic development. Its taxes and restraint on free export trade hampered the growth of entrepreneurship of the kind which was so important in Britain's industrialization. Thus the lack of stimuli from foreign trade, new technology, and government encouragement, together with the social system thwarted the development of capitalism and modernization.[1] There are numerous other factors which can be suggested, but suffice it to say that they fall within the domain of the non-religious. They are such factors that obstructed the rise of modern capitalism in China. The absence of such restraining factors in Malaysia from the nineteenth century and thereafter provided the Chinese immigrants with the opportunities they did not have at home. In the beginning there were difficulties here and there, but with the decline of power of the Malay sultanates and the accompanying substitution by British influence and eventually rule, the proper political context was created. There was however no vigorous or extensive capitalist action among the Malays. We shall now explain why such a phenomenon did not occur. There were at least four main reasons, the most significant of which was the despotic nature of Malay rule, the other three being the small size of the country and population, the geographical barriers, and the social values.

Previous to the latter part of the nineteenth century, things had remained the same among the Malays for successive centuries. Consequently observations made in the early nineteenth century could very well apply to centuries before that. There were extremely few technological changes or innovations, or even assimilation of the kind that created significant social changes. The cannon and the musket were introduced to Malaysia and South-East Asia from outside but these had no revolutionary effect in the sense that the stirrup had in Western Europe (White, 1962). Before 1874, much of mainland Malaya (West Malaysia) was not directly affected by changes introduced from outside with the exception of Penang, Malacca and Singapore. It was in this unaffected area, particularly in the east coast of Malaya, that observations on the conditions of life in the feudal Malay society were made by Abdullah bin Abdul Kadir Munshi, the first modern Malay Muslim with a reformist tendency. He was born in Malacca in 1796 and died in Mecca in 1854 while on pilgrimage. In 1838 he was sent to Kelantan from Singapore to deliver some letters to the rajas of Kelantan and the Chinese headman there. The rajas were engaged in a succession of wars with each other. His record of this journey was however completed in 1852 (Abdullah, 1961). In 1843 he completed his memoir which was first printed in 1849 (Abdullah, 1949). He had worked as a secretary and research assistant to Raffles, the founder of Singapore. His case is interesting because it is the first one known in this area of a local citizen

[1]For a comprehensive and detailed summary of the impediments to capitalism and modernization, see Fairbank, Reischauer and Craig, 1965: 88–116.

consciously sensing the problem of modernization and attempting to analyse the backwardness of his own community.

There were three main lines of thought followed by Abdullah. These were (1) that traditional Malay society was bogged down by vice and oppression condemned by Islam; (2) that British rule was just and progressive; and (3) that the Malays should abandon their traditional shackles and the vices of their ruling class, that they hold fast to their religion, and adopt the knowledge and virtues of the British. It is clear that in his rejection of certain elements in Malay life and in his adoption of certain elements from modern British life as he saw them, he employed Islamic values as his criteria for selection. Here is then a clear instance of convergence between Islam and modernization. What Abdullah recommended was not Anglicization of the Malays, but certain values and science pertaining to the phenomenon of modernization.

During his journey to Kelantan in 1838, he was appalled at the degraded condition of the Malays in Trengganu, Pahang and Kelantan. These states were not reduced to destitution by plunder or natural catastrophes but by the rapaciousness of their ruling houses. How did it happen? Abdullah described the mechanism. Whenever a person accumulated wealth it attracted the attention of the ruler and his henchmen. The wealth would be seized by direct or indirect means. This state of affairs stifled the growth of any incentive to acquire more than was necessary. There was continuous terror. The subjects lived in a state of fear. There were several prohibitions impressing upon the people to remain inferior. They were not allowed to use an umbrella in the royal village, they were not allowed to use shoes and yellow dresses (Abdullah, 1949: 23–25). Then there was the frequent warfare between the rulers and their rivals. Their subjects were compelled to do the fighting and at the same time to feed themselves. The warfare which Abdullah witnessed was a tiring and drawn out one about which people from neither side were enthusiastic. It was a conflict imposed upon them by their rulers. Being a small place, a family could find its members present in the different localities having to support opposing factions. Hence the low morale. Those involved tried their best to conceal themselves, in dug out trenches. Four or five shots were fired a day. Though the rate of casualty was low, the effect on trade and farming was tremendous.

In addition to such warfare and royal oppression, there was the ravage on property and freedom caused by a powerful class of parasites, the friends and bondsmen *(hamba raja)* of the ruler. Many of these bondsmen came from the criminal class. If a person was guilty of a serious crime, one way to avoid punishment was to run to the ruler and declare himself as his slave. Thereafter no one dared to touch him. There were, on the whole, two classes of slaves amongst the Malays, the ordinary slaves *(abdi)* and the debtor-slaves *(orang berhutang)* (Aminuddin, 1966). The institution of slavery was greatly abused by the ruling class.

Having considered the political situation in the Malay states and its effect on economic action and social progress, it may be asked why there was no resistance among the population to overthrow the ancient regime. Three factors came into play here. The country was divided into several small states, each with a small population, divided by rivers and jungles which did not make communication easy. Control by the ruling classes was not difficult as far as their direct subjects were concerned. But these same factors encouraged anarchy among the chiefs and rulers. A strong central authority was difficult to establish. Nevertheless the contenders in the game of power were able to enforce efficient control in their respective areas. One of the states, Perak, the second biggest in West Malaysia (Malaya) has an area of 7,980 sq. miles. In 1879 its Malay population was estimated at 56,632, of which 3,050 were slaves. There were at least 28 chiefs, minor chiefs and rajas exercising effective control on the daily life of their subjects. We can safely consider that each one would have at least 100 loyal supporters, both family members and hirelings. The 28 persons with their 2,800 supporters could easily enforce control on the daily life of 56,632 people without leaders to resist and impeded by geographical barriers. Moreover out of the total Malay population only a section of them were adult males. Each chief with their 100 supporters could very well control effectively an average area of 275 sq. miles, most of which was uninhabited.[1]

Side by side with the above factors, there was the value system of traditional Malay society which condemned rebellion and stressed the attitude of absolute loyalty, no matter what the ruler was, an autocrat, a tyrant, or a benevolent monarch.[2] Uprisings and peasant rebellions which had dotted the history of Europe during successive centuries were unknown to have occurred in Malay history, before the twentieth century, though known to have happened quite frequently in the history of Islam.

Considering the factors which had been cited to explain the stagnation of Malay society prior to the expansion of British rule, it is apparent that Islam had not been the cause of that stagnation even if we take the interpretation of Islam current in those periods. Discrepancies between Islam and magical-animism, between Islam and gambling of which the Malays were very fond, between Islam and opium smoking, between Islam and forced marriages or concubinage practised by the rulers, between Islam and the avoidance of learning deplored by Abdullah to which he attributed the oppression of the rulers, and numerous other instances, are too obvious to require further proofs. With the exception of ritual and the law of

---

[1]The figures of the number of chiefs and population were derived from Aminuddin bin Baki, 1966.

[2]On this see the classical Malay historical text, *Sejarah Melayu*, written probably not earlier then the sixteenth century by an anonymous author. See also *Hikayat Hang Tuah*.

inheritance, the other main values and teachings of Islam had been violated, particularly those with reference to the acquisition of knowledge and wealth, order and justice in society.

III

We may thus arrive at the following conclusion. In the case where the values of religion and modernization converge, the impeding factors towards modernization are clearly to be sought elsewhere. Should that not be the case we may then suggest, as Weber did, that the impeding factors originate in religion provided we can trace it to the doctrinal structure. Nonetheless the problem is not as simple as all that for even in cases where the values of religion are not converging with those of modernization, these values can indirectly promote modernization, or become neutralized by other values emerging from the context of action. The latter can be a theme of an interesting enquiry.

10 Islam as an Agent of Modernization: An Episode in Kelantan History[1]

WILLIAM R. ROFF

In December 1915, the Kelantan State Council, upon Malay initiative, resolved upon the creation of a Council of Religion and Malay Custom (*Majlis Ugama dan Isti'adat Melayu*), the Sultan, Muhammad IV, stating shortly thereafter that the *Majlis* would have responsibility for 'all matters pertaining to the Islamic religion which may bring benefit to the people of this Our State and increase the welfare of Kelantan', and that one of its principal tasks would be to 'raise Kelantan to a status consonant with that of other advanced States'.

The *Majlis* so formed was the culmination of and inheritor to a complex process of bureaucratization of Islam that had been under way for some decades — a process that had never been completely dissociated from the politics of the state, but in any case embodied a uniquely Malay response (or more accurately a Kelantan response) to the challenges of the time. I should like to sketch very briefly what seem to me to be some of the stages of this essentially administrative process.

Kelantan in the nineteenth century was in only a limited sense a centralized polity. For much of the century, authority outside the capital, Kota Bharu, is said to have been exercised largely by the *Imam* of village *surau*. The *surau* was the ritual centre of rural Islam, the prayer house for daily and Friday prayers, the focus of all specifically Islamic ritual involving the community at large, the village school, and more generally a place of resort for the piously inclined. The *Imam*, leaders of the religious community, were responsible for the proper conduct of Friday prayers in their *surau*, performance of marriage and funeral rites, and the arbitration within their *mukim* or parish area of legal disputes involving Islam,

[1]An expanded version of this chapter is being published in William R. Roff (ed.), *Kelantan: Religion, Society and Politics in a Malay State*, forthcoming.

especially over land and the division of property. Maintenance of *surau* buildings, and subsistence of *surau* officials, was met by the surrender of *zakat* alms or taxation by the members of the *mukim*. From around the 1870s, district headmen known, on the Siamese model, as *To'Kweng*, were appointed throughout much of the Kelantan plain. Some partitioning of local authority with the *Imam* appears to have taken place at this time, but the basic unit of civil administration for land and other matters remained the *mukim surau*, the *To'Kweng* had no ritual functions comparable in importance to those of the *Imam*, and the authority of the latter remained paramount in the rural areas. *Imam* were seldom effectively responsible to the centre, but there did reside at the capital both a state *Mufti* and a *Hakim* — the former exercising judicial rather than merely consultative functions (assisted by a *Kathi*) in a *Shari'a* Court administering largely Muslim personal law; the latter acting as judge in what was primarily a criminal court in which a mixture of Islamic and customary law was administered.

The fifty year reign of Sultan Muhammad II, which ended in 1886, saw some strengthening of central institutions in the state, probably including those associated with religion, but the details of this are not clear. Following his death, Kelantan entered upon some twenty years of political confusion, during which a number of developments significant for the administration of Islam took place, which can be reasonably well documented.

First, there ensued a period of religious severity or revival under the influence of the minister known as Maha Menteri, from about 1888 until the latter's death in 1894. This was characterized by strict insistence on observance of the *Shari'a* law (especially concerning moral laxity and ritual observance), public readings of *hadith* literature by the *Mufti*, prohibition of traditional theatre, and enforcement of attendance at Friday prayers in the local *surau*. Administration of these regulations was assisted by a new emphasis upon centralized control of the *Imam* and other *surau* officials, and was accompanied by a more general administrative penetration of village society. This period of re-emphasis upon Islam may be seen as having been in some measure a response to the cultural as well as the political threat to Kelantan independence which existed at this time. The Kelantanese were not unaware of the implications of the British political advance in the western states of the peninsula; they were equally sensitive to renewed Siamese pressure from the north; and the constant intrigue round the throne presented an additional threat from within. Islam for many, and especially an Islam revivified by increased contact with the Hejaz and with refugee *ulama* from Siamese Patani, appeared to offer at least a partial recipe for resistance to disintegration.

Secondly, beginning in 1903, some of the political uncertainty which had characterized these years was resolved by the appointment (as a result of a British-Siamese agreement) of a Siamese 'Adviser' of British nationality,

W.A. Graham, who embarked on a programme of administrative re-organization of the state. Though forbidden by treaty to interfere in matters concerning Islam, Graham in fact wrought considerable change in this sphere. To summarize, between about 1905 and 1909, continuing tendencies already begun, he built a much stronger secular and centrally controlled administration at the village level, thus resolving the growing tension between *Imam* and *To'Kweng* in favour of the latter; and secondly, he succeeded in delimiting the powers of the *Shari'a* Court while strengthening in legislative terms its authority. Concerning the first of these developments, the *Imam* were removed altogether (at least in theory) from revenue collection and land administration, and restricted to what Graham called the 'spiritual control' of their parishioners. Concerning the second, *Shari'a* Court jurisdiction was set firmly within the context of Western-style procedures and the boundaries of its jurisdiction established (in some cases extended by being made explicit). The principle of having a separate 'religious court' was given a wholly new emphasis, it being established also that the powers of this court were properly to be defined by statutory enactment — a notion foreign to *Shari'a* law.

During the same period, fresh and more efficient provision was made for the regulation of *surau* and their officials, collection and disbursement of the *zakat*, and much else, mostly under the administrative oversight of the *Mufti*. This marked the real beginning of the accretion to the office of *Mufti* (which also acted now as appeal court from the *Shari'a* Court) of very substantial administrative authority — a process that was to increase in the decade following.

Though the principal beneficiary of the political and administrative centralization that took place under Graham was unquestionably the ruler, Muhammad IV, certain structural tensions resulted — between ruler and *Shari'a* Court on the one hand, and between ruler and *Mufti* on the other.

From 1909, Kelantan came under direct British control. The policies pursued by the first British Advisers did not differ significantly from those of Graham, though two developments affecting Islam may be noted. *Shari'a* Court powers were limited, and the administrative authority of the *Mufti* was greatly enlarged. Concerning the court, its powers to deal with land inheritance and other property matters were greatly reduced — significantly, with the active concurrence of the ruler — and it became in effect (and ultimately in name) little more than the *Kathi*'s court for the capital and its immediate district. Concerning the *Mufti*, a young and energetic man, representative and leader of a new generation of *ulama*, it may be noted that he now became a salaried member of the administrative establishment, with a growing staff of subordinates — fifteen by the year 1914. The *Mufti* thus found himself possessed of considerable conjoint powers, as apex of the *Shari'a* court system (which now included two additional district *kathi*'s courts) and state jurisconsult, and as a leading functionary within the Western structure of government.

Increasing tension between the Sultan and the *Mufti* was evident by 1915. In that year, coincidentally, occurred the Pasir Puteh Revolt. It is not possible to discuss the revolt here, but it is pertinent to observe that there is some evidence that it reflected elements of disaffection against the throne as well as against the British. Its conclusion found Muhammad IV anxious to see to the bases of his own authority in the state, and to listen to the councils of the young minister who rose to power at this time, Dato' Stia.

The *Majlis Ugama*, to which we now return, appears to have been the brainchild of Dato' Stia and another young man, recently returned from some years in Mecca, Dato' Jaya. The *Majlis* was to be at once a means of restating the ruler's authority over his people and their welfare, principally by way of Islam, and instrumentally by control of the grass-roots of power (then as in the nineteenth century), the *Imam* of village *surau*; an assertion that Islam itself was not to be relegated to the subsidiary role allocated to it by the British; and a vehicle for the modernization of the state as a whole. It also provided a convenient means of restricting the growing power of the *Mufti*, by, in effect, putting the governance of Islam and of Islamic institutions into committee.

Briefly, the *Majlis* was to have twelve members — the proportion of *alim* to non-*alim* remarkably high when contrasted with those *ad hoc* committees of State Councils which in other states performed analogous if much attenuated functions. Of the greatest importance, it was to be financially autonomous, deriving its revenue from the collection and retention of two-fifths of all *zakat* surrendered in the state — the proportion known as 'the ruler's share' and customarily distributed by him to the three main mosques of the state and the remainder of the canonically determined deserving categories. The *Mufti*, pointedly, was not made a member of the *Majlis*, and this office was the prime institutional loser as a result of the creation of the *Majlis*, all powers of control over *surau* and their officials and over parish Islam in general, being transferred to the new council, which likewise became the final court of appeal from the *Shari'a* and *kathi*'s courts.

How, then, did the *Majlis* use the resources of power and money now at its disposal — and by 1920 it was grossing some $60,000 (Malayan) annually, only a small proportion of which went on recurrent expenditure?

Part of its custodial function related to the maintenance of morality, good behaviour and the proper practice of Islam in the state, and it pursued these ends with some fervour. But the generation of 1916 was not that of 1886, and a new breed of *ulama* had appeared, conscious of the social roots of social disorder and anxious to promote change rather than merely increase fervour. In consequence, the *Majlis*, in addition to interesting itself in a number of fairly pressing contemporary concerns —

ranging from proposals for the offering of financial inducements for marriage to prostitutes, and the incineration of night-soil, to the prevention of recidivism by the provision of religious instruction in jail — developed far-reaching and imaginative plans for the provision of English, Arabic and Malay education in the state, opening a tripartite *Madrasah* in Kota Bharu in 1917 and other schools later, with mixed secular and religious curricula, and prompting the then British Adviser to propose the transfer of all education in the state (at that time a mere handful of government vernacular schools) to the auspices of the *Majlis*, a proposal rapidly disallowed by the High Commissioner in Singapore. Ancillary to these endeavours, the *Majlis* also started a press for publication of school text books and other works, a translation section, and a fortnightly journal which soon acquired a considerable reputation among Malay intellectuals throughout the peninsula.

In the field of economic development, aware that its powers must in the long run be limited by its income, and that this in turn was wholly dependent on the rice crop (from which all *zakat* taxation was derived), the *Majlis* sought to maximize its returns and provide for the future by embarking on institutional entrepreneurship — though its proposals for the purchase of land to develop as a rubber estate were in the long run to be quashed by the British Adviser as running undue risks with public funds.

By 1920, it may reasonably be said, the Kelantan *Majlis Ugama* had wrought the beginnings of a social revolution, and though this was to be to some extent deflected in the years that followed, it continued to wield great power, providing institutional support not only for the ruler but for the strategic group of new men associated with its early years, who were henceforth to dominate the politics of the state. It has been discussed here, however, primarily as an indigenous agent of directed social change, utilizing the institutions of Islam, wedded to Western bureaucratic forms, to further what were clearly perceived by its progenitors as the interests of the state as a whole.

Beyond trying to analyse, if in rather sketchy fashion, the intricacies of administrative change and development during the crucial 'contact years' of Kelantan's modern history, and in particular to trace the strain of insistent self-determination that ran throughout, this paper has also been concerned, by implication, to suggest two general points. The first and the more obvious is precisely that elements of institutional continuity in the modernization of traditional societies should not be underrated and certainly cannot be ignored. The second is prompted by the reflection that perhaps too much attention has been paid in the past, where the modernization of specifically Islamic traditional societies has been concerned, to the dramatic clash of rival ideologies and the rubrics of 'reformism', and too little to the more mundane but often sinewy detail of administrative institutionalization and bureaucratization, which must lie at the root, if not necessarily at the heart, of much social change.

11 The Scarcity of Identity: The Relation between Religious Identity and National Identity[1]

JOSEPH B. TAMNEY

I

ONE important part of the modernization process is to develop a sound policy about the allocation of involvement or identity (for now, we use the two terms interchangeably). Should citizens become completely involved in the nation? Or should public policy seek to balance involvements in the nation, religion, ethnic group and family? Hildred Geertz (1963:77) described a 'good' policy for Indonesia as follows: 'If Indonesia is to survive ... it must create for itself a new national organization and a coherent national identity, one which at the same time rests on a multiplicity of local community forms and identities'. Easily said. But is there a limit to the number of communities with which a person can identify? And does national identity retain its intensity when a person spreads his identity to embrace several communities? These are some of the questions relevant to modernization that remain unanswered. Beyond them is the more basic question: is involvement scarce?

Some authors clearly say 'no'. For instance, Elder (1964: 48), on the basis of research done in India, has written: 'one can apparently add national identity to one's other loyalties without detracting from those other loyalties. A good family man and a devout follower of his religion can still be nationally loyal.' But it is doubtful if Elder's evidence justified his conclusion. National loyalty was measured by whether or not a person referred to the nation in answering two open-ended questions, one of which went as follows: 'What is the best and finest thing you could do in

[1] I would like to thank the following people for their invaluable help in carrying out this project: Bernie Go, Amudi Pasaribu, Johannes Erwin, J. C. Tamba, Janus Umrie and Chuah Toh Chai. Many other people were helpful; I wish I had the space to list them all. Financial or material assistance was received from the following: The Ateneo de Manila Research Council, the Institute of Southeast Asian Studies (Nanyang University), and COEMAR (United Presbyterian Church, U.S.A.).

your life?' Responses to such questions are interesting, but easily influenced by the circumstances in which the question is asked. In other words, we have doubts about the validity of Elder's method. Of course, Elder may be right, but obviously more research is needed.

MacDougall (1970: 7) reports a study done by university students; the sample was composed of Secondary 4 students in Singapore. One finding of the study is that the students have equally high loyalty to their race and to their nation. This would suggest that involvement is not scarce. But loyalty is not involvement. Involvement refers to a sense of oneness with an object. People can be loyal without being highly involved. When you are a citizen (or a member of any human collectivity), you tend to be loyal automatically, i.e. you need some powerful incentive to make you disloyal or a traitor. Loyalty reflects more the absence of alternatives than the intensity of involvement.

Not all existing research goes against the idea that involvement is scarce. The present writer found that the extent to which students were upset by the assassination of President Kennedy was slightly but significantly related in a negative manner to their degree of involvement with their parents, i.e. the students more involved with their parents were less affected by the assassination (Tamney, 1969). The study assumed that those who were less affected were less involved with Kennedy. I concluded, therefore, that the study did suggest an inverse relationship between familial involvement and involvement with Kennedy, and this supported the scarcity idea. However, there are valid methodological objections to this research. For example, is it valid to assume that the assassination-reaction measures student involvement with Kennedy?

We shall not attempt to review all relevant research. The state of the question whether identity is scarce is, we believe, indicated by Tajfel's (1970: 122) analysis of a recent Unesco-sponsored conference on ethnic and national loyalties — 'in one of the discussions at Cannes two general propositions, both derived from empirical evidence, were set side by side: (1) 'positive ingroup attitudes are related to negative outgroup attitudes' (i.e. there is an inverse relationship); and (2) 'ingroup attitudes are extended to attitudes toward outgroups, so that the two are directly related'. As they say, more research is needed. But research alone is not enough. We must begin to specify the conditions under which an inverse relationship between any two involvements would be expected and those under which it would not.

The purposes of this chapter, therefore, are (1) to elaborate on the scarcity approach, especially considering the conditions under which it is not likely to hold, and (2) to present data meant to test the elaborated theory.

II

When most people suggest that there is an inverse relationship between involvements,[1] they have in mind the fact that leaders often create solidarity by inciting people against a common enemy. For instance, it is suggested that one result of the recent China-Russia confrontation was that it helped unify China after the Cultural Revolution. If true, this would mean that China-involvement would be inversely related to Russia-involvement.[2] But in such situations the inverse relationship is not due to any inherent scarcity of involvement, but to official propaganda. Such examples are not relevant to this paper. The basic hypothesis we want to explore is as follows: the greater the involvement in any one object, the less *it is possible* for people to become involved in other objects.

Why might this be true? Following Freud, Slater (1963: 349) has clearly stated an important theoretical position: 'If we assume a finite quantity of libido in every individual, then it follows that the greater the emotional involvement in the dyad, the greater will be the cathectic withdrawal from other objects.' Slater argues for the inherent scarcity of involvement.

Everyone recognizes the limitations of time. But Slater assumes that in fact once a person is involved with another, in some sense this other person is never forgotten. For instance, Slater (1963: 341) writes, 'so long as an individual cathects more than one object he will be unable to achieve a complete absence of libidinal tension....' The foundation of the scarcity hypothesis is fixation. Slater seems to suggest that once we are involved in an object, a certain amount of fixation always exists, i.e. a certain amount of interest is always invested in that object although we may not be fully conscious of this investment. Scarcity would mean that we never completely forget an object at any moment of our lives. Certainly Freud and the analysts who have followed him have encountered sick people for whom the idea of fixation made sense. For instance, a rejected child might never be able to completely forget this rejection, and at some level

[1]Support for the scarcity approach is, also, found in Turk's (1970: 14) analysis not of individuals, as in Tamney's study, but of organizations. One conclusion of the study is as follows — 'local integration proved to be inversely associated with extralocal integration. Once the influences of other sources of variation were removed, the number of national headquarters was shown to have a *negative* effect upon the mention [by informants] of community-wide associations.' The question arises why this inverse relationship. Turk does not answer it. One possible reason is that identity is scarce, so that when people become involved in national organizations, they lose interest in the local community with which they can no longer identify.

[2]Involvement can be either positive (pleasant) or negative (punishing). In this paper we limit involvement to mean positive involvement. But if involvement is scarce, and if involvement can be either positive or negative, then a policy of creating nationalism by stimulating hatred towards a common enemy can only have a limited success. If the assumptions are correct, to the extent people hated the enemy they could not love their own country.

of consciousness might actually be continually working on reaching some 'solution' to this problem of rejection; such a person would indeed be fixated on his parents. But does the idea of fixation have relevance to the majority of people? Perhaps for most people the amount of interest invested in objects which are below the level of full consciousness might be so little as to not be a practical problem.

Another explanation of why involvement might be scarce is suggested by Erikson's discussion of 'identity'. Until now we have assumed that 'involvement' and 'identity' refer to the same phenomenon. However, this is not exactly true. Identity implies involvement, but involvement does not imply identity. A person can be involved with something, but not have thought about it. The individual might not be self-conscious about the involvement and therefore it would not be part of the person's identity. Moreover, someone might be involved with another, but will seek to deny the involvement, as a result of which the involvement will not be a part of a person's self-concept or identity. For instance, adolescents are involved with their parents. Yet, because they want to be free, they might reject this involvement. As a result if one were to ask them to define themselves they might not even mention their status as a child, or if they do mention it, give it low priority. A person's identity, then, is not a true reflection of his pattern of involvement. The identity contains those involvements that are self-conscious and accepted. Still the fact that identity is dependent on involvement means that Slater's analysis should apply to identity, i.e. we believe it is meaningful to talk about the scarcity of identity because of fixation. But introducing the concept of identity allows us to go beyond Slater and to make use of Erikson's work.

Erikson (1968) implies that identity-confusion is a painful condition, and that if this is to be avoided individuals must integrate the components of their identity. Integration means establishing a hierarchy of identity-components, which in turn depends on societal integration. Society must have arranged its roles in a neat hierarchy, so that each person's identity, reflecting this hierarchy, would be integrated. Erikson's stress on hierarchy suggests that identity-components cannot be equally valued. Rather, they must be ranked. As a result the more important any one object, the less likely that other objects will be important.

Erikson's approach might seem fruitless to people familiar with the 'third world'. What characterizes the latter is not a hierarchy of roles, but a confusion of roles and of identity. Hildred Geertz (1963: 17) describes Indonesian city-dwellers as 'bicultural', following regional cultures in religious and familial matters and metropolitan cultures in politics and economics. Coughlin (1960: 204) claims that the 'overseas Chinese have a double identity, both Chinese and Southeast Asian...'. In Thailand the Chinese prepare Thai food, wear Thai costumes, and use Thai magic; at the same time they like Western music and dancing, and go to Western films; yet, at least some of them remain Chinese. Reading about South-

East Asia leads outsiders to speculate on the frequency of 'split personali-
ties' in the region. How can the people overcome the seemingly high
degree of identity-confusion in the region? But, of course, the existence
of multiple identities does not necessarily mean identity-confusion. Each
identity can be institutionally segregated from the others, e.g. Thai at
work, Chinese at home, Western in places of leisure. But Erikson's
analysis definitely suggests that these identities must be rank-ordered, as
indeed they might be. The crucial test of Erikson's work is not whether
people have more than one identity, but whether the elements of a person's
total self are hierarchically organized.

Although the analyses of Slater and Erikson are quite different, they
both predict the same process. Slater talks of cathectic energy and Erikson
of value, but both energy and value are considered by the respective
authors to be scarce commodities. Both theorists, therefore, suggest that
to the extent a person is identified with one object, the probability that
another object will be important declines.

A truly adequate test of this hypothesis at the present moment seems
impossible. For instance to accurately predict using Erikson's approach
the extent to which a person values his national identity we would have to
know: (1) how many gradations of value does a person recognize; some
people might consider one identity-element truly important, and all the
others of equal secondary importance; other people might make 3 or 4
distinctions; and (2) the value of all identity-elements other than the ones
we are trying to predict; for instance, to predict the importance of national
identity, we should collect information about ethnic, religious, familial,
regional identities as well as about the importance of jobs, hobbies, voluntary associations and various personal relationships; such a complete
inventory is out of the question. Moreover, it might not be worthwhile to
make the effort necessary to meet these conditions. It would seem practical,
at first, to perform admittedly crude tests of the scarcity idea to find out if
there seems to be any empirical justification for more refined investigations.

III

Conditions under which the scarcity hypothesis would not be valid would
be as follows: (1) *de facto* identity of the differently named groups; the
Batak Protestant Christian Church is composed mainly of Toba Bataks;
there is a *de facto* identity between the Church and the ethnic group, therefore we would not expect an inverse relation between the degree of identification with the religion and the degree of identification with the ethnic
group; in people's minds these two names would refer to the same material
objects; (2) symbolic identity of two groups; it has been suggested that at
the beginning of the Indonesian independence movement Islam was the

symbol for nationalism; Islam and Indonesia were closely related concepts; in such a situation we would not expect an inverse relationship between the degree of national identity and the extent of religious identity; and (3) role-linkage between the groups; if a Catholic was told that to be a good Catholic, he must be a good citizen and sacrifice for his country, then we might expect a positive relation between religious and national identities. Consideration of role-linkage reminds us that role-conflict can produce a negative relation between identities but not for the reasons discussed in this paper. For example, a Catholic might believe that as a Catholic he could not support a government that favoured a liberal abortion law. If this was widespread, there would be an inverse relation between religious and national identity, but not because involvement is inherently scarce or because value is scarce, but because of a specific historical conflict between church and state.

IV

The research reported here attempted to test the hypothesis that to the extent people identified with a religious collectivity, they were less likely to identify with the nation. The study was designed so that the effect of membership in two different religions, Islam and Christianity, could be investigated. Moreover, the effect of each religion was studied in at least two different nations. Finally, since ethnic identity is often of a critical importance in the development of national identity, the effect of ethnicity will be controlled in this analysis.

The research involved the study of students at the following universities: University of the Philippines (data collected, August 1969), Nommensen University, Medan, Sumatra (April, 1970), Sriwidjaya University, Palembang, Sumatra (August 1970), Nanyang University and the University of Singapore (May-June 1970). A description of the sample is contained in Table 16. At each university students were given a self-administered questionnaire. At the Sumatran universities the questionnaire was in Indonesian, at Nanyang University it was in Chinese. At the other universities it was in English.[1]

At the University of the Philippines, Nanyang University and the University of Singapore I helped in administrating almost all the questionnaires. At Sriwidjaya the questionnaire was administered by several staff

---

[1] I would like to express my appreciation for the help received in translating the questionnaire from the following persons: Sartono Kartodirdjo, Mohd. Rosjid Manan, M. A. Nawawi, John Buxton, William Liddle, James Peacock, Chuah Toh Chai, Chiew Seen Kong, and Miss Wang Cheng Yeng. Both the Indonesian and Chinese versions of the questionnaire were back-translated and modified before being used. Of course, the translations may not be perfect; for instance, some minor modifications were not re-backtranslated.

TABLE 16

CHARACTERISTICS OF STUDY SAMPLES: IDENTITY SURVEY

Place of Data Collection	Citizenship	Ethnicity	Religion
1. Nommensen University (211)	Indonesian (210) Other (1)	Chinese[1] (14)	Roman Catholic (7) Protestant (5) Other (2)
		Non-Chinese (197)	Islam (31) Roman Catholic (10) Protestant (135) Other (21)
2. Sriwidjaya University (139)	Indonesian (139)	Chinese (15)	Islam (4) Roman Catholic (7) Other (4)
		Non-Chinese (124)	Islam (115) Protestant (2) Other (7)
3. University of the Philippines (354)	Philippines (306)	Chinese[2] (51)	Islam (1) Roman Catholic (28) Protestant (9) Other (13)
		Non-Chinese (255)	Islam (5) Roman Catholic (203) Protestant (21) Other (26)
	Other Response (48)	Chinese (35)	Roman Catholic (11) Protestant (11) Other (13)
		Non-Chinese (13)	Roman Catholic (6) Protestant (1) Other (6)

[1]'Chinese' means those who answered a question which began 'Chinese Only'. 'Non-Chinese' in this table means the people who did not respond to this question.

[2]Includes 2 cases of people who did not answer the 'Chinese Only' question, but whose mother speaks Chinese. For the other samples such people are considered non-Chinese for purposes of this table.

Place of Data Collection	*Citizenship*	*Ethnicity*	*Religion*
4. Nanyang University (275)	Singapore (196)	Chinese (196)	Roman Catholic (32) Protestant (20) Other (144)
	Malaysia (48)	Chinese (48)	Roman Catholic (1) Protestant (11) Other (36)
	Other[3] (31)	Chinese (31)	Roman Catholic (2) Protestant (8) Other (21)
5. University of Singapore (452)	Singapore (396)	Chinese (289)	Islam (2) Roman Catholic (61) Protestant (80) Other (146)
		Malays[4] (74)	Islam (62) Roman Catholic (6) Other (6)
		Other[5] (33)	Islam (4) Roman Catholic (5) Protestant (7) Other (17)
	Malaysia (45)	Chinese (25)	Roman Catholic (13) Protestant (3) Other (9)
		Malays (13)	Islam (11) Protestant (1) Other (1)
		Other (7) Other (11)	Islam (2) Roman Catholic (7) Protestant (1) Other (8)

TOTALS:
Total sample — 1,431
Islam — 237
Catholic — 399
Protestant — 315

[3]27 are 'stateless'.

[4]For purposes of this table 'Malay' means the respondent is not 'Chinese' and the mother speaks Malay but not any Indian or Pakistani language. The category could contain a few people who are not really Malays, e.g. Arabs, Eurasians, or Europeans.

[5]This would include Indians, Pakistanis and Europeans.

members to one large class. Most of the students at Sriwidjaya were in military uniform, being in the process of receiving military training as part of their university programme. At Nommensen the questionnaire was administered by a senior student with the help of a faculty member. For most people the questionnaire took from 45 minutes to 1½ hours to complete, except in the Indonesian universities where some of the students took 2½ hours to complete the questionnaire.

The students tended to come from the social science faculties. The Philippines sample is the most diversified from an academic point-of-view. On the other hand, all the students at the Indonesian universities were from either Economics or Business Administration.

Most of the students filled out the questionnaire during a class period. But in some cases students completed questionnaires under supervision but outside class hours. A very small number of students completed the questionnaires in an unsupervised situation.

The measurement of religious indentity is based on responses to three questions. Respondents were asked how they felt about each of these statements: (1) 'I would prefer *to marry* a person who has the same religion as myself'; (2) 'I would prefer to work for a boss who has the same religion as myself'; and (3) 'I would prefer my close friends to have the same religion as myself'. These questions were scattered about the questionnaire. Each question was followed by five responses: 'strongly agree', 'somewhat agree', 'somewhat disagree', 'strongly disagree', and 'religious orientation not relevant'. 'Strongly agree' was scored 1, 'somewhat agree' was scored 2, and the other three responses were treated as the same category and scored 3. The range of the religious identity score, therefore, was from 3 (high identity) to 9 (low identity).

In our work we will consider three religious categories: Muslim, Roman Catholic, and Protestant. Whether a respondent belonged to one of these categories was determined by his/her response to this question: 'which category comes closest to expressing your present religious orientation?' The categories offered were: Islam, Roman Catholicism, Other Christian, Traditional Chinese Beliefs, Buddhism, Traditional Religion, Religiously Indifferent, Anti-religious, Interested in religion, but belong to no one religion, and Other. The category 'Other Christian' is hereafter called 'Protestant'.

We justified our measure of intensity of religious identity as follows: if religion is an important part of a person's identity he will use it as a criterion in reacting to others. So, if people believe that their religion is not relevant in evaluating marital partners, friends or bosses, we assume that a religion cannot be an important part of their self-concept. Preferring to be with people of the same religion does not mean people are prejudiced, but we believe it does mean that their religion is an important part of their identity.

National identity is measured by the respondents' willingness to sacrifice for their government. It would be inappropriate to use basically the same three questions for measuring religious and national identity. It is meaningful to ask our respondents how important it is to marry someone of the same faith, because it is possible for him *not* to do so. But, for instance, to ask an Indonesian how important it is to marry an Indonesian, is to ask what can truly be called a purely 'academic' question. We chose to base the measure of national identity on a willingness to sacrifice for the government.

But why focus on the government? In South-East Asia nations are not ethnic groups. A nation is not equated with one historical tradition. Rather all the nations are new. Under such conditions the nation, in peoples' minds, is the state or government. The nation is the political system, or so we assumed. With this perspective it made sense to us to measure national identity in terms of willingness to sacrifice for the national government.

The actual questions used in this paper were part of a set of six questions. The set was introduced by the following paragraph: 'At times national governments demand sacrifices from the people. To achieve their political and economic goals, political leaders must sometimes ask much from their people. Which of the following things would you be willing to give up in order to help your national government achieve its objectives.' For present purposes two questions from the set have been used: (1) 'Would you be willing to give up or to lose a respected position in your community which you had earned by years of hard work to help your government?' (Item 1 in set of 6); and (2) 'Would you be willing to give your life to help your government?' (Item 5). Each question was followed by 3 responses: I am sure I would be willing, I probably would be willing, and I do not think I would be willing. The first response was scored 1, the second 2, and the third 3. Thus, the range of scores was from 2 (high willingness) to 6 (low willingness).

The idea that national identity and a willingness to sacrifice for governmental policy are related is not unique to this study. For example, Doob (1964: 6) defined nationalism as follows: 'the set of more or less uniform demands (1) which people in a society share, (2) which arise from their patriotism, (3) for which justifications exist and can be readily expressed, (4) which incline them to make personal sacrifices on behalf of their government's aims, and (5) which may or may not lead to appropriate action.' If people are willing to sacrifice themselves, narrowly defined, for some collectivity as the state, we assume it because they identify with the nation. In other words, only those people will be willing to die for the state who will live in the state.

More specifically, then, our basic hypothesis is: to the extent people use religion as a criterion for association with others, they will not be willing to sacrifice for their government.

The theoretical prediction, however, must be modified in light of our historical understanding. It has been stated that conditions such as *de facto* identity, symbolic identity, and role-linkages affect the usefulness of the scarcity approach. Our task, therefore, is to decide the extent to which these conditions exist in Indonesia, the Philippines, and Singapore regarding the relation between national governments and the Muslim, Catholic and Protestant collectivities in these countries.

V

In none of the countries we focused on — Indonesia, the Philippines, and Singapore — is there one official state religion.[1] It is true that in 1956 President Ramon Magsaysay dedicated the Philippines to the Sacred Heart of Jesus, but this seems to have been an isolated act of only momentary, political significance. In Indonesia there are religious political parties representing Islam, Roman Catholicism and Protestantism. None of them dominate the national government, making quite clear that state and religion are separate. In both the Philippines and Singapore separation of church and state is a basic principle of government structure. A *de facto* identity of a religion and the state is not, therefore, self-evident in the countries studied.

But there are degrees of identity. How can we measure the degree to which a religion and a state are identical in the minds of people? When Park and Burgess discussed the fusion of social groups they emphasized the importance of a common history: 'Assimilation is a process of inter-penetration and fusion in which persons and groups acquire the memories, sentiments, and attitudes of other persons or groups, and, by sharing their experience and history, are incorporated with them in a common cultural life' (quoted in Gould and Kolb, 1964: 38). To the extent groups share a common history, we would expect them to be experienced as identical.[2]

A second indicator of identity would be indigenization, i.e. the degree of structural independence of foreigners.

Let us briefly discuss, then, the extent of historical overlap between Islam and Christianity and the nations studied as well as the degree of indigenization of these religions.

Islam was studied in Sumatra and Singapore. Clearly, the history of Islam predates the history of these nations. There is no question of complete identity. On the other hand in both places the spread of Islam was based on the conversions of rulers and their peoples (on Sumatra see

[1]Islam is the state religion of Malaysia, from where a part of the sample comes.

[2]This approach seems similar to Young's (1970) analysis in which he relates solidarity to distinctiveness of 'meaning areas' or 'social symbols'. We would suggest that the distinctiveness of symbols is dependent on the distinctiveness of histories.

Nicholsen, 1965, on Malaya consult Rauf, 1964). Islam became part of the social history of the Malays and Sumatrans, or at least of some of the peoples living in Sumatra such as those from South Sumatra, the area from which our Muslim Indonesian sample comes. Rauf suggests that the mass conversions to Islam might have represented a reaction to a religious-moral crisis stemming from the downfall of the Sriwidjaya empire — 'The political disintegration resulting in social disequilibrium and the breakdown of religious authority apparently created a vacuum which was filled by the Islamic faith' (Rauf, 1964: 84). Referring to Sumatra Nicholsen (1965: 40) suggests that the spread of Islam was a means of showing opposition to the Portuguese. The advent of Islam seems to have been a socially significant event. Conversion to Islam marks a stage in the social history of Malays and South Sumatrans.[1]

Granted that Islam is part of the history of Malays and South Sumatrans, but to what extent are these ethnic groups part of the history of the nations within which they reside? It seems to us that the histories of the new nations of the Malay archipelago are the histories of the ethnic groups composing these nations. We suggest, therefore, that to the extent a religion is part of the history of an ethnic group in the region, it can be considered part of the national history.

Of course, not all ethnic groups are considered by themselves or by others to be equally part of a nation. For instance, the Malays in Singapore or the Chinese in the Philippines or Indonesia probably feel less a part of the nation than other ethnic groups in those nations.

Christianity was studied in three countries — Indonesia, the Philippines, and Singapore. The percentage of Christians in each country is as follows: Indonesia — 6.3 per cent; the Philippines — 92 per cent, Singapore — 6 per cent. (Anderson, 1968: 5; Nyce, 1970: 102).

Considering Singapore first, Christianity in this country seems the opposite of Islam among the Malays. Most of the Singaporean Christians are Chinese who joined the churches individually or as a family. One important reason for the spread of Catholicism and Methodism, the two principal forms of Christianity in Singapore, has been the involvement of these religions in education. For instance, according to my calculation about 18 per cent of the secondary students in Singapore are in Christian-sponsored schools. Many converts apparently became Christians because of their experience in Christian-sponsored schools. This means that the growth of Christianity in Singapore has not been a group event.

One of the characteristics of Singapore Christianity is the degree to which it is subdivided along communalistic and linguistic lines. About one-third of the Christians are Protestants. Nyce (1970: 102) claims there are 189 Protestant congregations; he categorized them by language usage

---

[1]It seems to us that only because this is true can Islam be considered by the modern Malay 'as an inherent part of his cultural heritage and as a distinctive feature of his race ...' (Rauf, 1964: 101).

as follows: 100 churches use English, 42 use Mandarin, 10 — Cantonese, 9 — Hokkien, 4 — Teochew, 2 — Foochow, 2 — Hakka, 8 — Tamil, 1 — Malayalam, 5 — Malay, 2 — Punjabi, 3 — others. This linguistic diversity of Christian churches expresses the absence of clear identity between Christianity (or any of its branches) and any of the local ethnic groups.[1] There seems to be little basis for any *de facto* identity between Christianity and Singapore.

The situation is quite different when we consider the Philippines. According to the 1960 census, 83.8 per cent of the population is Roman Catholic, so we will restrict our comments to a discussion of Philippine Catholicism.

The emergence of the Philippines as a social entity is connected with mass conversions to Catholicism.[2] The Catholic church was part, some would say the most important part, of the Spanish colonial government. To the peasants government at the local level meant the friars. There is a clear connexion between the history of the Philippines and the history of Philippine Catholicism.

But throughout Philippine history the attitude of the people toward the Catholic Church has been mixed. On the one hand, the people have continuously rebelled against the clergy, and especially the friars, as colonialists exploiting the masses — 'on an average of once every twenty-five years throughout the Spanish period, the Filipinos raised the standards of insurrection against the colonial government and the friars' (Gowing, 1967: 53). The birth of the Philippine Independent Church at the turn of the century, when about one-quarter of the Catholics joined it,[3] expressed the prevalent feeling that the Catholic Church was a foreign church.

On the other hand, the historic tie between the Philippine nation and Catholicism remains strong. February 17, 1872, sometimes called the birthday of the Philippine nation, marks the execution of three priests by the Spanish authorities. The priests had been tried 'on trumped-up charges of having fomented the Cavite revolt' (Gowing, 1967: 88). Catholicism seems to have been an important part of the history of the Philippine nation. Yet, at the same time, people have been continuously aware of the foreignness of this institution. This suggests a fundamental ambivalence about the identification of the Philippines and Catholicism.

[1]Lindbeck has noted the consequences of linguistic divisions for ecumenicalism. He described several church structures as follows: 'The Methodist Church ... is divided into English, Chinese, Iban and Tamil conferences possessing considerable autonomy. Anglicans have separate boards for Chinese and English language work, and have both Tamil and Chinese congregations. Presbyterians are from this point of view more united because, with the exception of a few historically expatriate congregations which are now in the process of joining the larger body, they are all ethnically Chinese...' (Lindbeck, 1967: 76).

[2]On the history of Christianity in the Philippines see Gowing, 1967.

[3]In 1960 only about 5 per cent of the population belonged to the Philippine Independent Church.

Our Indonesian Christians are mainly members of the Batak Protestant Christian Church. This is truly an ethnic church. The members of this Church are mostly Toba Bataks;[1] there are other Batak churches for Karo Bataks and for Simalungun Bataks. 'In a variety of ways the Batak Church has developed a life and style of its own. It is an ethnic church in which the Batak language, Batak *adat* (custom and law) and Batak identity play a strong role' (Cooley, 1968: 68). The Toba Bataks converted *en masse* to Christianity at about the same time they entered into modernization, i.e. had prolonged contact with processes of urbanization and commercialization. Becoming modern and becoming Christian are closely connected in the history of the Toba Batak people. In fact, of all the religious groups studied the closest connexion between the social history of a people and the history of a religious group seems to exist between the Toba Batak people and the Batak Protestant Christian Church.

Our second indicator of degree of *de facto* identity is indigenization. It is our impression that Islam is locally controlled by local people. In other words Islam is structurally indigenous. On the other hand Christianity still retains the image of a foreign religion. Among the forms of Christianity studied perhaps the Batak Church is the most indigenized. From the very beginning of this church emphasis was given to the training of local religious leaders. At present the Batak Church is an independent church, although affiliated with the Lutheran World Federation. The Church does receive funds from Lutheran organizations, and there are some foreign teachers at the Theology Faculty of Nommensen University, which is controlled by the Batak Church. Overall, however, this Church compared to other Christian churches is indigenized.

Perhaps at the opposite pole from Islam is the Philippine Catholic Church. This Church has long been the battleground for power struggles between local religious and foreign religious. Deats (1967: 52) reports that in 'November, 1957, six Filipino priests sent a memorial to the Vatican urging recognition of Filipino leadership in the Roman Catholic Church in the islands'. In 1965, there were 2,240 priests in the religious orders, all but 349 being foreigners. In addition to these, however, there were 1,935 secular priests, almost all of whom are Filipino. Overall, in 1965 almost half the priests were foreigners (Gowing, 1967: 182).

We were able to test our impressions concerning indigenization with data collected in the present project. The students were asked: 'Were you ever instructed by a religious teacher who came from a country different than your own?' If they answered 'Yes', the students were asked — 'For how many years were you instructed by this 'foreign' teacher or teachers?'

[1]The abortive coup of 1965 seems to have caused a considerable shift in religious affiliations. For instance, Pedersen (1970: 190) reported — 'One HKBP [Batak Protestant Christian Church] congregation in Medan has baptized over a thousand Javanese in the last year.' Pedersen, also, reported that many Karo Bataks have become Christian since 1965 (p.189).

TABLE 17

INDICATOR OF INDIGENIZATION OF RELIGIOUS ORGANIZATIONS:
(Per cent of Respondents Instructed by a Foreign Religious Teacher and Number of Years of such Instruction)

Religion	Subsample	Per cent Received such Instruction		Number of Years of such Instruction[1]	
		No	Yes	0 – 2 Years	3 or More
Islam	Nommensen (N=28)[2]	93	7[3]		
	Sriwidjaya (N=107)	88	12	90	10
	Singapore (79)	76	24	79	21
Catholicism	Singapore (92)	12	88	44	56
	Nanyang (34)	62	38	85	16
	Philippines (245)	43	57	50	50
Protestantism	Singapore (91)	35	65	85	16
	Nanyang (38)	68	32	92	9
	Philippines (42)	43	57	50	50
	Nommensen (132)	65	35	80	20

[1]Percentages based on number of people who said they were instructed by foreign teachers and who answered the question about how many years they received such instruction.

[2]The number in parenthesis is the number of cases on which the percentages are based.

[3]The two people who replied 'Yes' did not give the number of years.

The results are shown in Table 17. Clearly Islam is indigenized. As expected, the Batak Church compared with other Christian groups is fairly well indigenized. But so are the Chinese-speaking Christians at Nanyang University. This semi-private University attracts the Chinese-speaking who would attend Chinese-language churches. Since few foreigners speak Chinese, it is not surprising that these people are relatively isolated from foreign influences. What is more surprising is that Singapore Christians, and especially Catholics, have had more contact with foreign teachers than Filipino Christians. This does not change the fact, however, that the Philippine Catholic Church's lack of indigenization is a public scandal for many Filipinos. The Philippine Catholic Church has received a worse 'press' than the Singapore Catholic Church.

VI

Neither Islam nor Christianity could be considered a symbol of Singapore. The Philippine Catholic Church seems to have been too rent by local-foreign struggles within its own structure to serve as a symbol of the Philippines. The only meaningful symbolic tie seems to have been between Islam and Indonesia. (For a discussion of this relation see Van den Mehden, 1963.) In the beginning of the nationalist movement in Indonesia Islam served as a symbol for the locals just as Christianity symbolized the colonialists. As Benda (1958: 15) has pointed out the *ulama* had long served as a focal point for rural discontent. It was understandable that when nationalism first arose, it would at least initially involve the Muslim teachers and, through them, Islam. It would seem reasonable that this symbolic tie between Islam and Indonesia would still linger on, especially on Sumatra, one of the centres of devotion to Islam.

VII

To what extent do the religions studied tie being religious to being a good citizen? In statements made by Christian officials concerning nationalism, the Philippine Catholics and the Indonesian Protestants are ambivalent. They see the need for loyalty, but also support a critical attitude toward the state. The position of the Indonesian Council of Churches seems applicable to the Batak Church, a member of the Council. Writes Pedersen (1970: 161) about the HKBP (Batak Church) — 'Government authority is accepted by Batak Christians... [But] The ultimate loyalty [is] ... religious rather than political .... The HKBP Ephorus [leader] affirms ... that 'we do not believe that the voice of the nation is the voice of God'. Statements most clearly suggesting role-linkage are those made by the Singapore Catholic Archbishop.

Statements made by Christian youth groups in Singapore about nationalism are more critical than the Singapore Archbishop's statements. At the same time it must be remembered that these Singapore student groups speak for very few students.

Regarding Islam it is difficult to say to what extent we can speak of linkages between being a Muslim and dedication to the state. In many Muslim countries state and religion are identical,[1] so that we might suspect that Muslim teachers would stress sacrificing for the national government.

[1]The fourth chairman of the Muslim party *Nahdlatul Ulama* was quoted as saying: 'Religion can never be separated from national problems and no doubt all missionaries, mubalighs (Muslim preachers), as well as religious teachers, should be of Indonesian nationality.' *Review of Indonesian and Malayan Affairs*, 1 (December, 1967), 27.

On the other hand, at least the Muslim political parties in Indonesia have been quite critical of the central government. It is difficult to know what is happening at the 'grass roots' level of Islam.

It seems as if Singapore Catholicism is most linked with the government, while Christianity in the Philippines and Indonesia maintains a position of balancing role-linkage and role-conflict. It is difficult to compare Islam on this point.

To summarize: we have tried to describe the extent to which the following conditions exist in the countries studied: *de facto* identity (overlapping social and religious history, and indigenization), symbolic identity, and role-linkage. Trying to combine these different conditions, the existence of which makes our basic hypothesis inappropriate, it seems clear that Islam in the region is most likely to be seen in association with the national government rather than as distinct from it. Islam is involved in the social histories of local groups, is indigenous, and at least in Indonesia, was recently a symbol of the nation. Close to Islam is the Batak Church, but it is less indigeneous and seems more officially critical of the government. At the opposite pole from Islam would seem to be Singapore Christianity, except that at least for the Catholic segment of it, it is very co-operative with the national government.

To test our historical analysis we predict that our basic hypothesis will be most clearly supported among Singapore Christians, and least supported among Indonesian Muslims, with the other groups falling in-between.

It must be kept in mind that our respondents are University students. The atmosphere on university campuses will affect our results. The University of Philippines' campus is politically alive and critical. On the other hand recent events at Nanyang and the University of Singapore suggest suppression at Nanyang and apathy at Singapore.

Reports about Indonesian students seem inconsistent. Sommer (n.d: 6) has written about Indonesia — 'In no other country among the six (the Philippines, Indonesia, Malaysia, Pakistan, Thailand, India) visited does there appear such a widespread and apparently genuine interest in engaging youth in the national mission.' On the other hand, an American who has lived two years with Indonesian students recently described them as follows — 'For a while, despite their confusion, students felt that they had helped to change history (by changing governments) and that things were going to get better. This sense of confidence has since given way to cynicism as educational costs skyrocket and students find that they do not have the power to end corruption' (Schiller, n.d.: 4).

It seems clear that Filipino and Indonesian students are politically involved, while Singapore students are not. What the absence of involvement in Singapore is due to is not clear, but it is possible that the very absence of political participation will dampen students' willingness to sacrifice for the government. The relatively positive reception student activity receives from the Indonesian government might increase their willingness to sacrifice.

VIII

TABLE 18

RELIGIOUS IDENTITY SCORE AND WILLINGNESS TO SACRIFICE FOR THE GOVERNMENT BY RELIGION: MALES ONLY (IN PER CENT)

Religion	Religious Identity Score	Sacrifice for Government Score					
		2 (High)	3	4	5	6 (Low)	N[1]
Islam	(High) 3	26	32	42	–	–	(19)
	4–6	2	21	50	17	10	(42)
	7	18	18	40	16	8	(50)
	(Low) 8–9	16	3	39	16	26	(31)
Catholic	(High) 3						(6)
	4–6	4	–	43	14	39	(28)
	7	–	18	46	18	18	(22)
	(Low) 8–9	11	11	32	24	22	(54)
Protestant	(High) 3	12	18	47	12	12	(17)
	4–6	13	16	31	22	19	(32)
	7	16	26	32	11	16	(38)
	(Low) 8–9	9	16	45	19	11	(64)
No Religion		8	15	24	18	35	(159)

[1]Number in parenthesis is basis for percentages in each row.

Tables 18 and 19 show the relationship between degree of religious identity with Islam, Catholicism, and Protestantism and willingness to sacrifice for the national government for males and females separately. We predicted an inverse relationship between degree of identity and willingness to sacrifice.

No consistent pattern appears in these tables. For the male Muslim subsample there appears to be a positive relationship between religious and national identity. The higher the identity score the higher the percentage

TABLE 19

RELIGIOUS IDENTITY SCORE AND WILLINGNESS TO SACRIFICE FOR THE
GOVERNMENT BY RELIGION: FEMALES ONLY (IN PER CENT)

Religion	Religious Identity Score		Sacrifice for Government Score 2 3 4 5 6 (High) (Low)					N[1]
Islam	(High)	3	11	44	44	–	–	(9)
		4–6	9	–	9	46	36	(11)
		7	7	11	30	22	30	(27)
	(Low)	8–9	–	15	23	23	39	(13)
Catholic	(High)	3	4	9	30	39	17	(23)
		4–6	3	11	32	35	19	(74)
		7	4	3	41	19	33	(69)
	(Low)	8–9	2	8	20	31	39	(64)
Protestant	(High)	3	10	29	33	10	19	(21)
		4–6	–	3	23	33	41	(39)
		7	4	11	33	26	26	(27)
	(Low)	8–9	4	23	23	27	23	(26)
No Religion			9	11	34	16	30	(159)

[1]Number in parenthesis is basis for percentages in each row.

of sacrificers. No consistent pattern appears in the female Muslim subsample; however, it is true that the females highest on religious identity are
also high on willingness to sacrifice. But the subsample sizes for the female
Muslims are too small to justify discussion of this sample.

Among the Catholic males no trend appears even when we compare
them with the respondents lacking any religion. Among the Catholic
females, as religious identity decreases there is a shift from middle-scores
to low scores on the sacrifice scale. Again, this finding suggests a positive
relation between religious and national identity.

Among the Protestants no clear pattern emerges.

The absence of consistency in the data suggests the need for further
'controls' in the analysis.

IX

Significant ethnic subdivisions readily become apparent in the Malay
archipelago. First, there is the division between Chinese and the non-

TABLE 20

RELIGIOUS IDENTITY SCORE AND WILLINGNESS TO SACRIFICE FOR THE GOVERNMENT BY RELIGION, CITIZENSHIP AND ETHNICITY

Citizenship	Ethnicity	Religious Identity Score	Sacrifice For Government Score					
			2 High	3	4	5	6 Low	
ISLAM Indonesian	Non-Chinese, Non-Javanese Sumatrans[1]	3 4–6 7 8–9	24 3 13 20	29 14 21 30	48 59 53 40	– 17 11 –	– 7 3 10	(21) (29) (38) (10)
Singaporean	Malays[2]	3 4–6 7 8–9	– – 6	17 6 –	17 13 22	33 38 28	33 44 44	(1) (12) (16) (18)
CATHOLIC Filipino	Non-Chinese	3 4–6 7 8–9	9 2 2 6	9 6 2 10	26 43 47 33	35 27 20 26	22 22 29 26	(23) (49) (49) (51)
Singaporean	Chinese	3 4–6 7 8–9	– 3 6 4	7 6 7	29 47 4	32 24 41	29 18 44	(2) (31) (17) (27)
PROTESTANT Indonesian	Non-Chinese Batak Speaking[3]	3 4–6 7 8–9	25 10 12	19 28 21	50 38 46	– 14 18	6 10 3	(5) (16) (29) (33)
Singaporean	Chinese	3 4–6 7 8–9	6 – – –	35 3 8 15	35 17 23 26	6 35 23 26	18 45 46 33	(17) (29) (13) (27)
NO RELIGION Filipino Singaporean Indonesian	Non-Chinese Chinese		7 8	7 13	47 27	7 18	33 34	(15) (215) (4)

[1]Non-Chinese means did not answer a question marked 'Chinese Only'. If the respondent's mother or father spoke Javanese, Sundanese or Buginese the respondent was excluded. Because of the coding procedure used it is possible that the subsample used contains a few respondents whose parents speak more than two Indonesian languages (other than Indonesian itself), possibly including Javanese, Sundanese or Buginese.

[2]'Malay' means both parents speak Malay but not any Indian or Pakistani languages and respondent is not 'Chinese'.

[3]This subsample of members of the Batak Church and people who either called themselves 'Lutherans' or 'Christians' or who did not respond to the question about specific denomination but whose parents speak Batak and no other Indonesian language (except Indonesian).

Chinese. Second, there is the distinction between the Javanese and the outer-islanders in Indonesia. Of course, even these divisions are gross. Among the Chinese there are what we call in Singapore 'the English-stream Chinese' and 'the Chinese-stream Chinese'. A similar division of the Chinese is made in every country of the region, the two categories referring to the less traditional and the more traditional Chinese. Similarly, among the Indonesian outer-islanders we can distinguish the Sumatrans, and among them the Bataks, the Minangkabau, etc. For our present analysis, however, we shall use the gross dichotomies: Chinese — Non-Chinese, Javanese — Sumatran.

Table 20 contains the relevant data.

What can be said about our hypothesis that there would be a negative relationship between degree of religious identity and willingness to sacrifice for the government? The data suggest some interesting tendencies here and there, but our conclusion must be that there is no significant support for the hypothesis.

What of our suggestion that Indonesian Muslims would be most likely to associate religion and state, and that, therefore, for this subsample there might be a positive relation between religious and national identity? Indonesian Muslims clearly are high on willingness to sacrifice compared to Filipino or Singaporean subsamples, but so are Indonesian Protestants. It is not that Indonesian Muslims are willing to sacrifice but that simply Indonesians are willing to sacrifice.

The differences in willingness to sacrifice are associated not with degree of religious identity but with citizenship. Indonesians are willing to sacrifice. Singaporeans, whether they are Malay Muslims or Chinese Christians seem unwilling to sacrifice (although the Muslims are somewhat more reluctant than the Christians). The Filipino Catholics are slightly more willing to sacrifice than the Singapore Catholics. The data give little reason for believing that a preference for religious communalism affects the willingness to sacrifice for the government.

Comparing the Singapore Christians, whether Catholic or Protestant, with Singaporeans having no religious affiliation suggests that the former might be less willing to sacrifice than the latter. A more refined analysis of the Singaporean sample was done, controlling for University and sex (see Table 21). No consistent difference between Christians and those without a religion appears. The University of Singapore students, and especially the females, seem quite reluctant to sacrifice, but a discussion of this fact is beyond the scope of the present paper. Among the males those without a religion are more polarized than the Christians, i.e. fewer have a score of '4'. But the data in Table 21 do not suggest that having a religious identity leads to a lack of willingness to sacrifice for the government.

TABLE 21

COMPARISON OF CHRISTIANS AND PEOPLE WITH NO RELIGION
ON WILLINGNESS TO SACRIFICE FOR THE GOVERNMENT BY
SEX AND UNIVERSITY: CHINESE SINGAPOREANS ONLY

University	Sex	Religion	Sacrifice For Government Score					
			2 (High)	3	4	5	6 (Low)	N
Singapore	Male	Christian	–	5	31	23	41	(39)
		No Religion	7	7	17	26	43	(54)
	Female	Christian	–	6	18	34	41	(99)
		No Religion	5	9	26	21	40	(58)
Nanyang	Male	Christian	–	22	36	7	36	(14)
		No Religion	12	18	18	18	35	(40)
	Female	Christian	11	24	39	24	3	(38)
		No Religion	11	18	44	8	19	(63)

X

The evidence strongly suggests abandoning the scarcity hypothesis. Of
course, methodological objections can and should be raised regarding the
present study. Some might argue that our measures were inadequate, that
preference for religious communalism is not the same as intensity of religious identity or that even in new nations the attitude toward the national
government is not to be considered indicative of national identity. Others
would argue that we have not controlled for personal religiosity measured
in terms of religious conviction, devotionalism or moralness, nor have we
yet considered the effects of social class. Perhaps the most telling criticism
would be that we have concentrated on the wrong form of communalism,

that in the archipelago it is ethnic communalism that is important.[1] All of these objections are valid, especially the last, and we shall consider these as we continue the analysis of our data. Yet, it remains quite clear that for a variety of subsamples, differing in terms of the conditions likely to nullify the basic hypothesis, we found no support for the scarcity approach.

A final word about national identity. We have noted the homogeneity of attitude toward the government within each country regardless of religion. Indonesian students are willing to sacrifice, the others seem reluctant.[2] Why? One answer is that Indonesia does have a national identity, while the other countries do not.

Singapore is a multi-racial society in search of an identity. To many it is a Chinese society, but this is officially unacceptable. As part of the attempt to create an identity Singapore is writing new local history books. But a newspaper story reviewing the first such book, a primary three history book, was headlined 'Materialism as History' (Koh, 1970). Singaporean pragmatism or materialism, to the extent it creates an identity, might not be adequate to the task of inspiring sacrifice. (Chan and Evers, 1972.)

Recently a book was published on Philippine mythology. In fact, of course, it contained bits and pieces from the mythologies of a variety of ethnic groups, e.g. Tagalog, Igorot. The premise of this valuable book is that to understand themselves Filipinos must know their mythical history — 'these native lore give them a sense of being Filipinos' (Jocano, 1969: 6). But the author fails to explain how one identity is to emerge from his catalogue. The preface to the book contains the following statement: 'We hope to broaden, to deepen, and to sharpen our knowledge of ourselves as Filipinos and thereby perhaps mitigate the irony of having to fall back on overseas scholars for this much needed insight' (p. ix). It seems to me that this statement reveals the only Filipino identity, i.e. anti-foreignism.[3] Like 'materialism' this might be an inadequate inspiration for sacrifice.

[1]But the work of others suggest that there will not be an inverse relationship between ethnic and national identity. Liddle (1967: 425-33) stressed the importance of ethnic identity to the Sumatrans he studied; in fact, he sees a sense of ethnic self-consciousness growing because people are meeting individuals from different ethnic groups. But Liddle believes that a sense of national identity is also developing in Sumatra. Consider, as well, the comment by Maretin (n.d.: p. 41) — 'Among the Minangkabau nationality, which has an advanced sense of its own ethnic existence, the feeling of Indonesia-wide self-awareness is also highly developed'.

[2]A not very glamorous explanation of this difference between the Indonesians and others is that the former completed the questionnaire under less controlled conditions than the others. It is possible that the Indonesians consulted with each other and felt more 'public' than the others in completing the questionnaire. It is, also, possible that Indonesians are more interested in giving the answers that will please questioners and that the students thought I would be pleased by responses indicating a willingness to sacrifice.

[3]Corpuz (1965: 71) states that nationalism as a mass phenomenon is new in the Philippines: 'It was not until the early 1960's that nationalism became acceptable to the Filipino people'. He also writes: 'The Filipino national community is essentially an aggregate of local communities where... the order of values are local' (p. 6). Only Catholicism spans the country and in many ways it is foreign.

The question remains what is the Indonesian identity. The last chapter of John Legge's book on Indonesia (1964) is entitled 'Indonesia's Search for Identity'. The implication is clear enough. There is, of course, the national ideology of *Pantjasila* (which consists of five principles: monotheism, nationalism, humanism, social justice and democracy). This ideology seems quite real to Indonesians; it was mentioned several times in my presence during brief stays in Indonesia. More recently the political leadership uses the acronym NASPIKA, meant to suggest a policy based on three forces — nationalist groups, functional groups and spiritual groups. Perhaps what is most important about Indonesia is not that it has a clear identity, but that clearly it is attempting to develop an ideology that is both positive and something more than merely materialistic. What is important in other words is that Indonesia is trying to be noble in a world of common nations.

But we must also remember the more active role students have played in Indonesia. In Singapore students seem disinterested, in the Philippines angry and frustrated. The willingness to sacrifice on the part of Indonesian students might reflect their sense of participation in national politics.

12 Ideology and Radical Movements in the Philippines: A Preliminary View

F. LANDA JOCANO

I

THE study of modernization constitutes one of the major interests of contemporary social science research. No observation could be more commonplace than during the last two decades of the second half of the twentieth century when rapid and radical changes characterized anew the experiences of most nations. The phenomena of change, in fact, acquires an exaggerated proportion when one examines the reactions of many developing countries to the inroads of modernization. This is particularly true in much of Africa, Asia, and Latin America. In some countries in these areas, change is dramatized in unprecedented scientific and technological achievements. In others, it is characterized by political upheavals and social unrests. In the case of the former, economic affluence is its most visible consequence (to say least of its possible expression in military power), as in the case of Japan. With respect to the latter, new political forms, often consumated through violence and accompanied by the production of ideology, are established. Sometimes both emerge simultaneously; if they do not, one often functions as the natural stimulus for the other. In either case, the phenomena of modernization always cause deep-seated alterations in the social fabric of community or national life.

The Philippines, as one of the developing countries in South-East Asia, has its own share of this world-wide phenomena. The inroads of modernization have stimulated varied reactions among the people. In some areas of the country, assimilation of new ideas from the outside, particularly those coming from the west, has been remarkably successful. In others, however, rejection or at most mass protest against what have been initially accepted has occurred. Such protests were registered through radical movements and manifested in violent actions. It is this latter kind of reactions to modernization that we are concerned in this chapter. Most students of Philippine society have not given this phenomena much attention if only because the concept of modernization has always been defined in terms of the economic and technological aspect of change.

Historically, radical movements, directed at overthrowing or at least challenging the established authorities — religious or civil — which initiated the change or which are believed to cause the sufferings of the people in the process, have emerged one after another. The apparent and immediate reasons for their appearance are as varied as the forms they take. Some are religiously inspired; others, socially or politically motivated. At any rate, these radical movements, to my mind, represent the sum total of the peoples' reactions to incongruities that result from the disparity between the adaptive requirements of modernity and the limitations of available local resources to meet them. By radical movement is meant, in this study, conscious and collective efforts by members of an organization (or of an amorphous unit built around a prophet or charismatic leader) to challenge the constituted authority in an attempt to change the existing conditions for what they believe to be more satisfactory ones. Viewed in this way, radical movements are akin to programmes of planned or directed change. What differentiates them from the latter approach to innovation is the use of violence to achieve their goals.

Radical movements in the Philippines, insofar as documents are concerned, may be classified into two types: millenial and socio-political. This classification is arbitrary and tentative. Millenial movements were the dominant upheavals during the early Spanish and American regimes and they were mostly short-lived. The socio-political ones took place at the end of the Spanish period in 1896–8 and of the American rule in 1946, respectively. The latter movements had more realistic objectives than the former. Moreover, they enjoyed greater mass support and, apparently, possessed an organized or planned approach to armed conflicts.

The overall result of all these movements is the same: they failed to achieve their major goals. The term failure is used here advisedly to mean inability of the movement, at the height of its popularity and during the open conflict, to dislodge and to take over the functions of the authority in power to which radical actions have been directed or to introduce the radical change it sponsored. Even the two major revolts — the revolution of 1896–8 and the Huk rebellion of 1945–54 — which scored many initial successes in their struggle to overthrow the constituted state power failed to achieve their ultimate social and political goals. The pattern of failure is interesting: they suffered major setbacks when they were about to win their cause. What could have prevented them from winning? What made them lose their initial vigour? What could have possibly alienated the people, if at all, from the cause championed by the leaders or for the authorities to recapture their lost charisma?

There is no clear-cut answer to any of these questions. In fact, they lead us to ask some more. Any analysis of radical movements has to explore not only the form but also the content of the upheavals. Sometimes this is a frustrating endeavour for the beginnings and ends of most radical actions are difficult to pinpoint with precision. Dates and outbreaks of revolutions, to paraphrase Godfrey Elton (1923: 1–2), are for the conventions and conveniences of history. These are not important aspects of revolutionary change. Any radical upheaval is a by-product of a long process of social evolution, deeply rooted to the past and closely linked with future events.

The link between the past and future events is established by the ideology of the movement, formulated either before the open conflict begins or produced after the seizure of power has taken place. As used in this study, ideology refers to a set of ideas underlying patterned reactions to patterned strains of roles in society, expressed either in cultural or political philosophy. It functions as a guideline and source of justifications for radical actions. As a generic term for ideas potent in specific situations of conduct, to quote David Apter (1964: 17), ideology represents not just '*any* ideals, only political ones; not *any* values, only those specifying a given set of preferences: not *any* beliefs, only those governing particular modes of thought'. As such, it may either be candid, vague or irrational. Nevertheless, the ideas it contains must have such popular appeal as to make the upheaval seem natural.

Because it establishes the link between fundamental beliefs and actions, 'ideology helps to make more explicit the moral basis of action' (Apter, 1964: 17). That is why ideologies are central to all radical movements or to the thinking of revolutionaries. As Lenin argues: 'There can be no revolutionary action without a revolutionary theory' (quoted by E.H. Carr, 1964: 149). That is, a movement must be anchored on some set of ideas if it has to have direction, form and character or if it wants to stay in power after the upheaval. This does not mean, to paraphase Brinton, that ideas cause revolutions or that the best way to prevent revolution is to censor ideas. It merely means that ideas form part of the process and therefore needs to be seriously considered when studying revolutionary events (1958: 52).

What ideologies define the framework of each of these radical movements in the Philippines? In the past, were millienial movements strictly religious in content because they were ritualistic in form? If so, why did millenialism appear only in some areas of the Philippines and not in others when, as records show, religious oppressions were relatively similar all over the country? What was the political ideology of the revolution of 1896? Was the post-Second World War Huk movement a struggle for political ideology or was it a nationalist (reformist) fight for peasant uplift? If the Huk movement was a political struggle, what kind of political ideology did it really champion? On the whole, why have these movements fallen short of their ultimate aims? Is political ideology a necessary precondition for the success of a radical movement or could it also be one of the major causes of its failure, particularly in a peasant society like the Philippines?

For descriptive answers, let us turn to what has been recorded about these radical movements. My approach to this intriguing problem is that of an anthropologist using the tools of the historian wherein historical events are examined in the context of the social system where they occurred. Of important consideration to this analysis is the temporal dimension of the events themselves for like any social phenomena, radical movements are products of time within which they appeared and of circumstances which stimulated their emergence.

II

The early forms of radical movements in the Philippines were millenial in nature, in spite of claims to the contrary by many students of Philippine history: The term millenialism has been used by scholars rather loosely and differently. Almost all however agree that the term refers to a set of beliefs which upholds 'an apocalyptical world transformation engineered by the supernatural' (Wallace, 1956: 267); a *final* state of society in which all conflicts are resolved and all injustices removed after a preliminary period of purging and transformation (Shepperson, 1962: 44). Although the *final* state of society is often predicted, a closer examination of the goals of most movements indicates that millenialism has a transitional rather than final character. They are likewise premised on the promise of bounty or the elimination of stress and frustrations allegedly existing in the social system. Once this utopia is set, however, the movement tends to generate collective and strong adherence to the cause championed by the leader or by the prophet. It is this apocalyptical nature of millenialism which makes easier the transformation of its religious *rationale* to political propaganda as soon as the protest is dramatized in armed conflicts. As E. J. Hobsbawn argues, millenial movements in modern times are easily transformed into or absorbed by revolutionary activities of a non-religious character (1959: 59). It is here where nationalism and millenialism are difficult to untangle.

Seen in this way, it is understandable why most millenial movements in the Philippines during the early Spanish regime, as well as during the American period, have been labeled as 'embryonic nationalism', 'peasant revolts', and so on. Adherents to the movements were mostly peasants; the causes championed by the leaders were mostly emancipation from religious oppressions and social injustices by the Spanish religious and civil authorities. However, if one examines the background of the leaders, the ideology accepted as the rallying philosophy of the movements, and the goals set to be achieved by them — all point to millenialism; anchored on the premise that once the dominant authority (religious or civil), believed to be responsible for the sufferings of the people, was eliminated, the good life of the previous periods would return and the people would be liberated from their eternal bondage to poverty. Oppressions, injustices, exploitations, and other forms of difficulties in life would disappear.

The strategies to achieve these ends were varied. Some movements were launched purely on *magical* grounds; others on *rational* premises, arising as they did from frustrating conditions and not from the proddings of supernatural beings. Of course the dichotomy, adapted from Linton's theoretical approach to nativistic movements (1943: 230–40), is a superficial one in that sometimes both types of movements embodied apocalyptic and realistic aims. That is, what began as supernaturally inspired dream eventually surfaced as a social protest with realistic aims. The converse was equally true. Many social protests often turned into millenial movements as soon as open conflicts began, for always the leaders incorporated supernaturalism into their activities either to sustain the support of their followers or to maintain inner psychological strength, in the absence of any institutionalized means of defending themselves.

The magical type of millenial movements rest on the premise that should the people rise against the constituted authorities responsible for their sufferings, the spirit of the ancestors and even God Himself, would come to their aid. The assurance has been transmitted to the people through their leaders. This was the *rationale* and rallying strength of the uprisings led by Tamblot (1621–2), Bancao (1621), Tapar (1663), Lungao (1811), Apolinario de la Cruz (1840–1), and the Colorum (1923–4; 1931), to mention only a few of the well-documented ones. Among the protective powers that the believers would enjoy in their concerted efforts to overthrow the constituted authorities were: invulnerability to bullets, abundant food supply during the uprising, and resuscitation in case of death.

The rational type of millenial movements, though resembling the magical ones, are almost 'without exceptions, associated with frustrating situations and are primarily attempts to compensate for the frustrations of the society's members' (Linton 1943: 233). Sumoroy's rebellion (1640–50), Dagohoy's revolt (1744–1829), the revolt of Diego Silang (1762–63), the Palaris revolt (1762–64), to cite a few of the well-known uprisings, were protests against the oppressions and abuses of the Spanish religious and civil authorities. Elements of millenialism were incorporated into the movements only after open conflicts with the authorities began. Sumoroy, for example, claimed to have communicated with the spirits of the ancestors who told him to organize an armed protest against the Spaniards and to return to their old form of worship. The revival of the old obligations to the spirits would mean the coming of a new era of peace and plenty. That should the people rise they would be amply protected against the enemy because the gods (referring to religious statuaries) of the new religion were powerless. When the uprising materialized, the people burnt the churches, broke and 'desecrated' the holy objects inside the churches, and threw away their prayer-books — an apparent attempt to probe deeply into the power of the new religion. When nothing happened to them, Sumoroy's following and fame spread throughout the island of Samar and the neighbouring provinces.

Similarly, belief in the invulnerability of their leader against the enemy was widespread among the followers of Dagohoy, Diego Silang, and Palaris. Even the Sakdal movement, said to be ideologically socialistic in orientation, gained popularity and peasant support in its armed confrontation with the Government in 1935 because the members believed that they were impregnable to bullets of the enemy if they wore the amulets distributed by their respective leaders. It was this fusion of rational peasant demands for social and economic reforms with almost blind adherence to the belief in the protective power of the supernatural beings that muddled the real social objectives of the movement and made the authorities to dismiss the protest as nothing more than an instigation of 'crackpots' and 'fanatics'.

Sociologically, most of these movements we have just described were formed around a prophet or a charismatic leader. Often, the leaders were not of the labourer type but were village intellectuals. They were influential men — many of them were practising folk medicine. During the American period, the leaders of most millenial movements were from the educated class or from families which had maximum exposure to American influence. Whatever were the backgrounds of these prophets and leaders, an examination of their activities reveal that they were obsessed by messianic complex for so many years — a complex arising from a desire either to do good for their fellow villagers, to further themselves socially or economically, or to compensate for their disillusionment over the loss of meaningful ways of community life. Strengthened in their beliefs by some supernatural revelations, especially by promises of protection and end of sufferings thereafter, the leaders were able to organize a group of ardent followers and to bring about mass protest and open defiance of the existing social order as to require armed Government forces to contain or suppress them.

In both magical and rational millenial movements, the influence of the dominant culture enters into the strategy of the leaders. For example, Tapar, in his rebellion of 1663, claimed that not only were the spirits of the ancestors behind him but also the gods of the Spaniards. Thus, he appropriately proclaimed himself *Eternal Father* and appointed members of the movement as the *Son, the Holy Ghost* (spirit), and a woman *Maria Santisma*. Next, he appointed apostles, a pope, and several bishops. With this structure laid out, simulating the Roman Catholic religious hierarchy, the members met regularly and performed ceremonies characterized by both indigenous and Catholic rituals. When the Spanish authorities attempted to pacify the group, after conflicts broke open, the 'people refused to listen because they were accompanied by the Holy Trinity, the Blessed Virgin Mary and all the apostles, who would defend them by working the miracles'.

Similar perpetuation of the old and the acceptance of new religious concepts characterized the Lungao movement. In summer of 1811, Lungao, a *babaylan* (religious healer), dressed himself in flowing robe and declared that he was *Christ*. He represented God's second coming to earth. He went to several villages along the coast of Ilocos Norte and preached to the fishermen about his new mission. He announced to them their deliverance from earthly sufferings should they follow him. There would be no more taxes, forced labour, and other forms of duties to the Spaniards. Fired by this apocalyptic promise, they utilized Christian paraphernalia and dressed in long robes as ancient Christians did. Lungao also appointed several apostles and together they preached the gospel of redemption and new ways of life. Open and bloody conflicts resulted when the Spaniards attempted to suppress the religious activities of the group.

Notable changes took place in the structure and content of later millenial movements when the Americans occupied the Philippines in 1900. The use of the army during the pacification campaign, following the defeat of Filipino resistance movement led by Aguinaldo, influenced the peasants' perception of power and authority. In the past, the Church represented the source of power and now the army had taken over the function. The cross had been replaced by the gun; the mystical priestly attire by the impressive military uniform. It is understandable that, as reactionary groups, the latter millenial movements incorporated into their conceptual and organizational structure elements of the new source of power — the army. Thus, the Colorums of Pangasinan were organized in a military manner — from enlisted men to generals. Pedro Calosa, the leader of the group, proclaimed himself *Primero General*. Even if the military structure was strictly followed, the supporting ideology was religious. The members were rallied behind Calosa on the belief that he possessed powerful *anting-anting* (amulets) which made anyone who followed him invulnerable against the enemy. In Bisayas, Flor Intrencherado was able to organize a group of 10,000 dues-paying followers in 1927 by giving them impressive military and civil titles. He declared himself Emperor with divine powers. Living members of this movement still believe today that Intrencherado really did possess supernatural powers. They say 'he could not be hit by the American soldiers and, on several occasions, bullets simply passed through him without effect'.

III

Another set of radical movements which emerged in the Philippines towards the end of the nineteenth and the mid-twentieth centuries were socially and politically motivated, with some millenial hangovers. These were the Katipunan-initiated revolution of 1896 and the Huk uprising immediately after the Second World War.

The Katipunan revolt. The Katipunan-led revolt against the Spaniards climaxed the failures of peaceful campaigns for reforms in the religious and political structure of the Spanish administration of the archipelago. Those who were in power continued their abuses, oppressions, injustices and immoralities. Somehow, they were not checked because there were no institutionalized means of censuring their activities. The Propaganda Movement, composed mostly of Filipino intellectuals and Spanish sympathizers, was not radical in the strictest sense of the word. The members were idealists who believed in due process of the law and peaceful negotiations for reforms. They did not fight for independence; instead they advocated for 'assimilation' into the Spanish political culture by making the Philippines a province of Spain. By becoming citizens, the propagandists argued, the Filipino could have equal rights with the Spaniards in all respects of social, political, economic, and religious life in the country.

These demands however were ignored. In fact, the Spanish administrators in the Philippines became more hostile. People suspected having any connection with the Propaganda Movement, directly or indirectly (i.e. having acquaintances or friends who were members) were charged with subversion and were punished. To rally responsible people in Madrid, the leaders of the movement founded a fortnightly newspaper known as La Solidaridad. Systematically, the evils of the Spanish administrators in the islands were exposed. Some liberal-minded Spaniards took the cause of the Filipinos and in 1889 an organization known as the Hispano-Filipino association was formed. Campaigns for reforms were stepped up. But as before, their demands were likewise ignored. This disappointed the leaders some more. In their disgust, they affiliated themselves with the Masonic Lodges in Spain — hoping that through this organization they could get a hearing. They likewise organized several lodges in the Philippines in order to provide continuity of activities in these two places. As expected, nothing happened to this struggle for peaceful reforms in the Philippines.

One of the outstanding leaders of the propaganda movement was Jose Rizal. A man of many talents, he wrote two novels and numerous articles attacking the Spanish abuses in the Philippines. He exposed the conditions in the colony to the outside world. Angered, the Spanish authorities in the Philippines prohibited the circulation of his books in the islands.

Rizal, in 1892, founded the *La Liga Filipina* as an alternative movement to obtain the much needed reform. This time, the target-group was not the Spanish authorities but the Filipinos themselves. Rizal attempted to create an atmosphere of national consciousness for which there was none existing in the islands then. Among the major aims of the *La Liga Filipina* were:

(1) to unite the whole archipelago into one compact, vigorous and homogeneous body;

(2) mutual protection in every want and necessity;

(3) defence against all violence and injustices;

(4) encouragement of instruction, agriculture, and commerce; and

(5) study and application of reforms (cf. Agoncillo and Alfonso, 1967: 167; Kalaw, 1969 ed: 4).

The *La Liga Filipina* did not last long. It met its early demise when Rizal was arrested, exiled, and later executed. A few of the original members attempted to carry on the movement but since the Spaniards outlawed it, many of them became passive in their commitment to the cause. Moreover, many gave up hope for achieving what they wanted. Some argued that even the Spanish Government did not listen to the leaders in Madrid; hence, it was unlikely that they would heed those who were in Manila. Moreover, the execution of Rizal confirmed their suspicion that the Spaniards were not bent on introducing reforms. A more radical movement was needed and it was not reforms that ought to be aimed at but complete separation from Spain. Thus, the Katipunan was organized and supported.

The new organization was founded by a labourer, Andres Bonifacio. At the beginning, the Katipunan was not a revolutionary unit as its original objectives indicate. It was structurally a brotherhood, a fraternity concerned with 'the teachings of good manners, hygiene, good morals, and attacking obscurantism, religious fanaticism, and weakness of character'. The civic aim of the movement 'revolved around self-help and the defense of the poor and the oppressed'. This is understandable because Bonifacio himself was a mason and a member of the defunct *La Liga Filipina*. Moreover, the leading members of the organization were then engaged in propaganda — in crystallizing national consciousness which Rizal had insisted on as a precondition for winning a libertarian cause.

Being a secret society, many young men from the working class were attracted to Katipunan. Moreover, it was the only one existing after the demise of the *La Liga Filipina*. Its secrecy and rituals during the initiation rites added glamour and mysticism to the structure of the organization, giving it its inner strength. Soon a number of intellectuals became members; the elite however remained aloof. As the organization expanded, the leaders became apprehensive that sooner or later they would be exposed and therefore it would be necessary to prepare for this eventuality. Thus, the Katipunan armed itself and turned revolutionary. And as predicted, the organization was later betrayed, and this precipitated, what historians call, 'the reign of terror'. Hundreds of people were arrested, tortured, and jailed. There was no other recourse but to take up arms.

As the rebellion became widespread, the Spaniards threw their full force against the Katipunan. In several skirmishes which took place in Manila and suburbs, the rebels scored several initial victories. These successes however were followed by reverses when the Spaniards concentrated their military strength in Kalookan, Marikina, and Makati areas where Bonifacio and his poorly armed men were entrenched. Meanwhile, in the southern areas of Cavite, Batangas, and part of Laguna, the rebels were out-manoeuvering the Spaniards. Led by two sub-units of the Katipunan — the Magdiwang, headed by Mariano Alvarez, Bonifacio's uncle-in-law, and the Magdalo, headed by Baldomero Aguinaldo — the Cavite command was winning. Emilio Aguinaldo, a Magdalo field commander, showed military skill and in the battle of Imus scored a major victory over a big Spanish unit commanded by General Aguirre. He captured arms and ammunitions and killed hundreds of Spanish soldiers. He became a recognized hero overnight and his popularity spread when he continued to repulse Spanish attacks of the rebels' strongholds. A charisma was built overnight, supported by the rumours that he possessed a powerful amulet (*anting-anting*) which made him invulnerable to enemies' bullets.

The victories scored by the Magdalo group elevated the standard of the revolution to an equally powerful force capable of containing, if not defeating, the Spanish army. As these took place, rivalries and jealousies between the two factions developed. The Magdiwang group, having initiated the uprising in Cavite, believed that it had 'the priority right to rule over the insurgents of the province' (Agoncillo, 1956: 202). On the other hand, the Magdalo group, 'believing that most victories in the whole territory were won by their leaders, wanted to appear the stronger and, therefore, the better fit to rule' (loc. cit.). When the conflict surfaced in the open, with either faction refusing to cooperate where the other's assistance was needed, the leaders invited Bonifacio to intervene in his capacity as *supremo* of the Katipunan.

But instead of patching up the misunderstanding, Bonifacio deepened the controversy through no fault of his own. Because he was not scoring major victories in his area, the Magdalo men did not hold him in high esteem. Moreover, the fact that he was a relative of Mariano Alvarez, leader of the Magdiwang, aggravated the feeling of the Magdalo men that he was out to favour the former group. In addition, Bonifacio was a northern Tagalog, being a Tondo (Manila) resident, and most of the men of the Magdiwang-Magdalo factions were southern Tagalogs. Regional animosity, in other words, was already present in the attitudes of the two factions and to allow a northern Tagalog to intervene was tantamount to surrendering their birthright. Thus, the first meeting achieved nothing and a second was therefore scheduled. In the second meeting, plans were presented by the

Magdalo faction that a new organization ought to replace the Katipunan. They argued that the organization having been exposed ceased to be a secret society and with the beginning of an open conflict, it should be superseded by one more in keeping with the demands of the period (Agoncillo and Alfonso, 1967: 213). This was opposed by the Magdiwang group and tempers went high.

To patch up the quarrel and restore unity among the rebels, Bonifacio himself acceded to the plan of replacing the Katipunan and establishing a Revolutionary Government. In the election which followed this introduction of political ideology into the movement, Emilio Aguinaldo was elected president, in absentia, and Bonifacio was relegated to a minor position of secretary of the interior. Even this position was objected against by Daniel Tirona, a Magdalo, as not befitting Bonifacio on the ground that he was not a lawyer. This angered the *supremo* and, unable to accept this humiliating defeat and insult, he declared the proceedings of the convention (known as the Tejeros Convention, after the name of the town where it was held) null and void. Then he and his men left the hall and wrote the *Acta de Tejeros* in which they gave their reasons for not accepting the results of the convention of 22 March 1897.

Having been elected president of the Revolutionary Government, Aguinaldo attempted to bring Bonifacio back to the fold of the new movement. Bonifacio refused to acknowledge the leadership of Aguinaldo and his newly constituted government. The latter, believing that disunity within the rank and file of the rebel would be fatal to the cause of the movement, ordered the arrest of Bonifacio and, as historians have judged, had him shot.

The elimination of Bonifacio brought about several significant defeats of the revolutionaries. When Camilo de Polavieja was replaced by Primo de Rivera, both as Governor-General and Commander-in-Chief of the Spanish army, the revolutionary movement suffered tremendously. The Spaniards concentrated their efforts in Cavite and Batangas. This broke the morale of the rebels. Why were the Spaniards able to recover their lost inertia? As stated earlier, the murder of Bonifacio demoralized his men and the northern Tagalogs participated less actively in the struggle. Even if they continued the fight, their aggressiveness was not strategically important and the encounters were not carried out on a large scale. This gave the Spaniards a better tactical initiative for manoeuvres and a more effective counter-offensive force inasmuch as there was only one major front to contend with — Cavite and Batangas.

Aguinaldo, now harassed from all sides, retreated and transferred to Biac-na-Bato. Here he set up the new Government and continued the struggle against the Spaniards. Sensing that the revolutionaries were at a disadvantage and not willing to waste more of his men in the field, Primo de Rivera issued several decrees proclaiming amnesty to those who would surrender. At first, the rebels ignored his peace overtures. Later, Aguinaldo came out with a proclamation, calling the Filipinos to rise against the Spaniards. Even if the proclamation was presented as a call to arms, a careful rereading of the document shows that by this time Aguinaldo actually wanted to stop the fight. But to initiate it would be disastrous to the morale of those who were in the frontlines. Nevertheless, he realized he needed a truce to give rest to his much-harassed men and to raise more funds for the movement. Thus, he found in Primo de Rivera's overtures a chance to carry this out and still maintain the loyalty of his men.

At this point, Pedro Paterno appeared in the scene and negotiated for the truce between the two protagonists. The Spanish government promised to introduce the long-delayed reforms in the administration of the islands provided the Filipinos agreed to stop the revolution. The Spaniards likewise agreed to pay the rebels an indemnity of Peso 800,000, payable in three instalments, provided also that Aguinaldo and his companions would go into voluntary exile abroad. The agreement, known as the Truce of Biyak-na-Bato, was signed on 15 December 1897. Two days later, Aguinaldo went into voluntary exile in Hongkong. With his departure, the Katipunan-led revolution against the Spaniards ended. Another phase of the struggle would have developed for both parties failed to carry out their respective parts of the bargain. However, at this point the Spanish-American war broke out. Defeated, Spain ceded the Philippines to the United States. Filipino-American conflict followed this event. With superior arms, the Americans easily quelled the resistance. Aguinaldo was captured on 23 March 1901 and with his fall the resistance also collapsed.

The Huk movement. Another radical movement which challenged the constituted authority of the post-Second World War Philippines was the *Hukbalahap* (*Hukbong Bayan Laban sa Hapon*), later changed *Hukbo na Mapagpalaya ng Bayan* (Liberation Army), or in short, Huk. This movement was organized and led by the Communist Party of Philippines. Communism, as a political ideology, was formally introduced in the country on 26 August 1930, with the founding of the Communist Party. Of course, the propaganda work began earlier. The Party was outlawed in 1932, two years after its organization. Because it could not operate openly, the Party carried out its activities through the various groups, particularly the labour unions. During the Second World War, it likewise kept at the background and set aside its ideological propaganda machinery 'to effect a united front with all anti-Japanese elements of the population, including some big landlords' (Saulo, 1969: viii). This strategy reinforced the strength of the Party among the peasants who believed that the Huk movement was truly a nationalist movement resisting the Japanese. Of course, it is wrong to say that the members of the communist party were or are not also nationalist. They are, and, in fact, it is this nationalism that makes their commitment to communistic ideology endure the acid test of Government suppression.

Immediately after the war, the Huk disbanded into small units but was later reorganized into a unit known as the Hukbalahap Veterans' League with Casto Alejandrino as the head. The purpose of the reorganization was to set up a plan for a more acceptable proselytization. For one thing, the Party could not operate in the open because it has been outlawed. But it needs legal and parliamentary tactics to further its ends; armed struggle was too premature. Thus planned, the CPP spread out its members to different labour groups for it was strategically realized that communism — as in its European prototypes — could not grow without organized labour. It is this group of wage-earners that could easily be swayed because of their marginal, almost alienated positions in society. Most of the labourers were and still are rural migrants to the city. Once this group has been 'ideologized', it can provide a strong operational base for further ideological proselytization.

On the other hand, the elite members of the Party also played their roles. They joined the 'nationalist bourgeois elements' to form a new political force, known as the Democratic Alliance. The non-communist members were well-known progressive intellectuals and prominent businessmen. It was anticipated that through this political front, CPP could obtain legal and parliamentary force in order to balance its growing strength among the labourers. The first test of CPP's skill in mass organization was demonstrated on 2 September 1945 when it staged the big 'March on Malacanang' demonstration. This show of strength was recognized by many political leaders and it led to the coalition of the Democratic Alliance with the Nacionalista Party which supported Osmena's bid for the presidency of the Philippines in the 1946 election. Although decisively defeated in the presidential position, the Democratic Alliance candidates in central Luzon won all the seats they aspired for in Congress. In spite of its victory, the Liberal Party, headed by Manuel Roxas, did not garner sufficient seats in Congress to insure the passage of the administration's pet projects.

Knowing this and of the ideological leanings of the DA congressmen, the Roxas administration arbitrarily ousted them, including one Nationalista congressman and three senators. The grounds for suspension were fraud and terrorism at the polls. These were plainly political manoeuvres for, as the Supreme Court later judged, the 'ejection of the minority senators and congressmen had nothing to do with the alleged commission of fraud and terrorism but with the "party" issue, i.e. whether or not American citizens should be granted parity or equal rights as Filipinos in the exploitation and development of Philippine natural resources and in the operation of public utilities' (Saulo, 1969: 47–48).

The unseating of these minority legislators created general discontentment among the people. To cap all these, the parity bill was approved by the Liberal Party-controlled Congress. Troubles started to emerge both in the labour front and in the peasant area in central Luzon. The latter turned the central plain into a seething cauldron of social unrest in the rears which followed. The Roxas administration retaliated with iron-clad punitive operations, designed to smash the mass base of anti-American and anti-feudal movements (Saulo, 1969: 47–8). It was of no avail. The turmoils continued unabetted.

Changing its tactics, the administration appealed to the Democratic Alliance leaders for cooperation in pacifying the peasants. In spite of their disappointments, Luis Taruc, Mateo del Castillo, and Juan Feleo, promised to help the Government. Taruc went to Pampanga, del Castillo to Nueva Ecija, and Juan Feleo to Bulacan. On his way back from his mission, Feleo was murdered and this cut short all possible means of settling peacefully the problem in central Luzon. Taruc wrote an ultimatum to Roxas to do something about the case for the peasants were geared for more serious trouble. Roxas responded with a firm resolve to deal with the peasant problem by force. On 6 March 1948 he outlawed the Hukbalahap and the PKM and then proceeded with armed pacification campaigns in the trouble spots of central Luzon. This was cut short by his death in April of the same year.

For its part, the CPP regrouped its relatively disorganized and demoralized cadres and fought back. Taruc, as chairman of the military department of CPP and commander-in-chief of the movement, revived the war-time Huk and revitalized it into the *Hukbo Mapagpalaya ng Bayan* or HMB. The new military unit was divided into ten regional commands or Recos, the most active of which were those operating in central Luzon. Effective guerrilla warfare began. From 1948 to 1950, the Huk scored numerous victories against the Government forces. The success of these operations could be attributed to the growing mass support of the movement due to general disillusionment of many over the Liberal Party leadership. This was deepened by the victory of Elpidio Quirino over Jose P. Laurel in 1949. Mass resentment followed this 'victory' because the people felt that Laurel won but Quirino, through alleged 'terrorism' in the polls, was declared the winner. Moreover, graft and corruption in public office remained unabated in spite of promises politicians made to reform the bureaucracy.

From its base in central Luzon, the HUK expanded its activities throughout Luzon and into the Bisayan islands. Three things facilitated this: the continuous deterioration of faith of the people to the Government, growing economic discontentment, and the punitive ways the Government handled its pacification campaign. In contrast, the Huk adopted an effective policy of assisting the people through the different BUDC (Barrio United Defense Corps). As Taruc wrote about these associations:

The BUDC, or, as it was called often, the STB (*Sandatahang Tanodang Bayan*, the people's home defense guard) was one phase of our united front activity. Although, as its name implies, it had its military aspects, being coordinated closely with our army and having its own armed guards, the BUDC, in a deeper sense, brought a hitherto unknown phenomenon into the barrios: democratic government. After centuries of *caciquism* the people were given the opportunity to rule themselves ...... (1953: 117).

Thus through the BUDC

we were able to build mass reserves for the Huk. For every Huk soldier in the field there were two others in reserve in the barrios, where they engaged in production work or in civilian pursuits that otherwise aided the overall struggle (1953: 120).

On the basis of the existing condition and of the Huk guerrilla victories over the Government military force, CPP leaders tactically assumed that there existed in the country in early 1950 a revolutionary condition. Jose Lava, then general secretary of the Party, presented to the Politburo a resolution that there was indeed such a revolutionary situation as was reflected in the sagging economic condition and unpopular political leadership. There was apparent discontentment among the people. Therefore, the CPP, particularly the military department, should formulate a time-table for the seizure of power. This plan included, among others, establishment of provisional revolutionary government in Huk-controlled areas, expansion of the movement to all provinces, organization of committees for the distribution of lands, also in Huk-controlled areas, and control of factories, and the conversion of the HMB guerrilla force into a regular army.

To test the readiness of the Huk movement to carry out these plans, a 'dress rehearsal' was prepared and actually staged on 29 March and 26 August 1950. These raids were successful and they showed remarkable striking power of the Huks. Thus convinced, another bigger attack was planned for 7 November 1950, a date which coincided with the Russian revolution, and the founding of the Communist Party of the Philippines. The plan however failed to materialize. After the surprise raid on 26 August on Camp Macabulos, Tarlac, President Quirino realized the need for a strong counter-attack by the Government forces. He appointed Ramon Magsaysay — then congressman from Zambales — as Defense Secretary.

Magsaysay cleaned the army of 'deadwoods' and personally led the counter-offensive against the Huks. He was able to restore the people's faith in the military force and to equal the guerrilla tactics of the movement. But Magsaysay's success was not solely due to his reforms in the army and skilful counter-intelligence (to say nothing of the U.S. military assistance). The Huk movement itself was, at this time, riddled by internal dissension among its top officials. Following the 'successful August 26 dress rehearsal' the rift between Lava and Taruc became serious — but not so serious as to hamper the movement. Because of this factional trouble among the leaders, coordination of activities also became strained. Moreover, the Huks became too confident of their success that the leaders started to operate in the city. At this point, a disenchanted field commander Taciano

Rizal, alias Arthur, approached Magsaysay and gave him information as to the whereabouts of the top Politburo officials operating in Manila. This tip resulted to the arrests of 105 members, including their top leaders on 18 October 1950. This was a big blow to the movement; Jose Lava, the party's secretary, was also caught in this raid.

In spite of this turn of events, the CPP was still convinced that there was a revolutionary situation in the Philippines. In February 1951, a second conference of the Politburo was held. Jesus Lava succeeded his brother, Jose, as the general secretary of CPP. Taruc, because of his opposition to the Party's decision, was replaced by Casto Alejandrino as Huk *supremo*. He was however retained as a field commander. By this time Magsaysay was continuously pounding the movement, keeping close to the heels of the different guerilla units. He gave them no rest at all. In September 1952, Taruc issued an open letter to the newspapers outlining the ways of 'peaceful settlement of all outstanding problems between the government and the Huks' (Saulo, 1969: 65). He knew that his beleaguered men needed much rest and the movement required a pause in order to reconsider the organization, as well as coordination, of the different fighting units. At first, the Lava-Alejandrino group endorsed the proposal but for an unexplained reason they changed their position. They condemned the move as some kind of a 'sell out', an act contradictory to the general policy of the Party. Thus, Taruc was suspended as Huk *supremo* and his brother, Peregrino, was expelled. Peregrino's expulsion from the Party was the result of his memorandum entitled 'New Situation, New Task' which supported his brother's peace overtures.

In spite of the overruling of Lava's proposal that the CPP and its mass organization should be placed under military discipline on January 1950, the policy seemed to be unofficially accepted and enforced by the Politburo among its members. This is understandable because if a revolutionary situation, as assessed, was believed to exist, then an ideological discipline — i.e. conscious, automatic, and unquestioning attitudes — should prevail. At this point, criticism, dialectical contradictions, and debates could cause delay in decision-making. Time and speedy execution of field strategies were important in out-manoeuvering the enemy. Moreover, the Lava group believed that a peaceful overture at this time would have a demoralizing effect on the supporting peasants and workers. Thus the Secretariat adopted an anti-war policy which could mean that for as long as the Government launched a continued attack on the movement, the fight would also be continued for this would mean that the Government was at war with the peasants.

At any rate, Luis Taruc, in spite of his suspension, remained loyal to the Party. He requested for another Politburo conference — an enlarged one which would include a number of field commanders in order to assess the real situation and to thrash out the cause of the rift between his group and the Lava group. At this time, Pres. Quirino sent emissaries to Pampanga early in 1953 to negotiate for peaceful solution of the problem. Although Taruc had no role in the first meeting, he decided to participate in the second meeting in order to, to quote Saulo's account, 'obtain a truce so that he could have an opportunity to consult with the Secretariat in Southern Luzon' (p. 66). For some reasons, still unknown, the Quirino peace negotiation failed to achieve its purpose. Taruc's participation in the negotiation was well-publicized in the newspapers and this 'angered' the Secretariat for he (Taruc), as a suspended party-member, had no authority to negotiate. Consequently, Taruc was expelled in *absentia*.

The expulsion of the Taruc brothers from the Party demoralized their followers. Their men lost their fighting spirit. To cap all these, Amando del Castillo, alias Alunan or Pepito, was sent to Candaba in November 20 to take over as field commander of Reco 2, composed mostly of men from Pampanga, Tarlac, Bataan, and Zambales. It was in these provinces that Luis Taruc had an unquestioned following. By December 1953, Reco 2 became less active in their struggle for national liberation — widespread bickering and demoralization occurred. This gave Magsaysay and his men a good advantage in terms of tactical manoeuvres.

On 15 February 1954, shortly after his assumption to office as president, Magsaysay sent Col. Osmundo Mondonedo to contact Alejandrino near Mount Banahaw for a possible peaceful negotiation between the Huks and the Government. The Huk demands were not met and the negotiation failed. Alejandrino returned to the field. Because Reco 2 was no longer as active as it should have been, Reco 4 and 3 carried the burden of fighting. Reco 4 and 3 covered the provinces of Laguna, Batangas, Cavite, Quezon, Bulacan and Rizal. This caused major resentments within the ranks of the movement. After the failure of Magsaysay peace overture, Alejandrino mobilized his men. He proceeded from Mount Banahaw to Bulacan, following the shielded foothills of the Sierra Madre Mountains. Through a confidant in Alejandrino's own group, Taruc learned that the Secretariat had ordered his arrest.

A day after he learned of this, Taruc was contacted by President Magsaysay through his emissary Manuel Manahan, urging him to surrender. Placed in a dilemma — whether to wait for the arrest of his own Party or to surrender to the Government — he asked for time to consider the situation. Bitterly disillusioned with his own Party and seeing that the Government was gaining the peasants' support, he saw no other recourse but to surrender. So on 16 May 1954, he gave up.

Taruc's surrender caused general demoralization in the movement. Alunan, who at the beginning was not liked by the Huks in Pampanga, could not check the large-scale surrender of Taruc's men in Reco 2. Likewise, the men in Reco 1 also gave up without a struggle. This included top field commanders. The armed struggle ended. Casto Alejandrino regrouped the remaining cadres of Reco 3 and Reco 4 and continued the underground work. With reforms introduced in the Government, the movement lost the mass support of the farmers and labourers. Alejandrino and Lava continued the underground work but were likewise apprehended later. Alejandrino was captured in 1960 and Lava in 1964. The Huk movement today is far from suppressed. The underground work is presently carried out by Bernabe Buscayno (alias Dante), a protegee of the recently captured leader Commander Sumulong. It is too premature to judge the outcome of the new movement if only because it has just emerged as an active group and documentation of its activities is still limited to newspaper reports.

IV

The preceding discussions of radical movements in the Philippines bring out the salient features of the impact of new ideas on traditional life, and the nature of reactions it stimulated among the Filipinos. These movements, it must be held in mind, represent the various phases of Philippine experiences with social change in modernity through time — namely, the introduction of Catholicism as the national religion by the Spaniards, the adoption of republican government as the political ideology of the revolution of 1896–8, and the attempt to rework over the national political culture under the aegis of the socialist-communist controlled Huk movement from 1946–64.

Let us examine the first attempt at planned change in Filipino traditional life. Catholicism was introduced into the country when the Spaniards came in 1521 and was enforced as the national religion of the colony from 1565 to 1898. Over the centuries, Catholicism has become part of the traditional life of most Filipinos and has functioned as one of the powerful integrating elements of the social system. It has become deeply ingrained into the structure of the people's world view, and, in fact, has articulated for many people much of their contemporary social values.

Catholicism was easily accepted as the national religion during Spanish times because it was (and still is) structurally similar with the indigenous religion. The belief in the ancestral spirits was simply replaced by beliefs in saints who could also be manipulated for assistance through prayers and specific rituals. The function of the native religious leaders was taken over by the missionaries who, comparatively, performed similar, although colourful rites. Moreover, the content of the new religion complements much of that found in the old one. It dramatized the indigenous concept of the role of supernatural beings in the lives of men, the continuity between the land of the living and that of the dead, the moral implications of brotherly love and assistance, and, above all, the achievement of bounty in life through close observations of the various religious obligations. In short, the structure of the indigenous religion was viable enough to accomodate Catholicism for much of what it has to offer was already present in the former although articulated in life in less dramatic and colourful fashion.

A breakdown in religious modernity took place when the Spanish authorities — missionaries and civil — contradicted much of what the new religion preached and promised. General discontent prevailed soon after the Spaniards exacted various taxes for the support of the church and to abuse their newly acquired powers. The new religion, insofar as the natives were concerned, ceased to represent the ideals that the indigenous one, in its simplistic way, tried to achieve for them. Rather, it became a threat to whatever remained of the meaningful way of life. While the stress remained tolerable in some areas of the country, in others, it reached a point at which some alternative way must be considered. Millenialism was almost instantanous in places where there were high degree of 'stress for individual members of the society and disillusionment with a distorted cultural Gestalt' (Wallace, 1956: 279).

The movements varied in form, content, and structure. The purely religious ones were often crudely organized and they involved powerful emotions and 'irrational fantasies'. However, those which emerged from secular actions were consistent and realistic in their strategy to gain redress. In either case, the movements were organized around a prophet or a charismatic leader who was himself believed to possess supernatural powers to bring back 'the good old days' and to protect those who followed him. This belief achieved for the followers similar feelings of confidence and derived from its satisfaction of what Wallace calls 'dependency needs in the charismatic following' (Wallace, 1956: 279).

However, because these movements were isolated and poorly organized as insurgent groups, they were easily quelled. Moreover, they were not aimed at the overthrow of the government but simply the removal of the hated religious officials. As such, they did not have plans for governing society should they win — they possessed no ideology at all but many expected that some divine powers would come to resolve all the problems for them. At any rate, millennial movements, as these occurred in the Philippines, symbolized and articulated what Eisenstadt called the 'breakdown of modernization' (1964: 345–67).

The revolution of 1896 represented an entirely different type of protest against the dominant culture. The focus of the movement was on problems arising from disparity between the ideals set by the new socio-political order and the practices of those in power. The Spaniards imposed upon the indigenous social system a political structure which was, in many ways, similar to the existing ones. That is, in the traditional regimes the office of the leaders were legitimized in traditional religious terms and their respective political roles were not distinguishable from their societal role in relation to the people. The merging of the church and the state wherein the religious people were often the most powerful bureaucrats complemented much of what was structurally understood in the indigenous social system. Hence, the Spanish colonial political order was received with much tolerance and was perceived as legitimate source of social order.

However, when the political authorities fought for more secularization of their political roles — leading to the protracted quarrel between the state and the church — the legitimacy of the political symbols associated with the colonial administration, insofar as the mass base was concerned, disintegrated. This was aggravated by the abuses of civil authorities when their leadership no longer enjoyed mass support. The political elites, mostly Spaniards, were increasingly unable to give direction or meaning to the political processes or to give protection to their myths and symbols. The relations between the leaders and the followers, composed mostly of Filipinos, became more and more untenable such that by the last decade of the nineteenth century a revolutionary situation emerged in the country.

The Katipunan movement, an offshoot of a long struggle by Filipinos for peaceful reforms in the political and religious structure of the Spanish colonial policy, emerged as the rallying organization for a general uprising. The Katipunan was not a revolutionary movement at the start — rather, it was a fraternity, a brotherhood with no political ideology. It possessed, instead, a messianic character and was shot through with religious or semi-religious rituals, ranging from the initiation rites to duties of the respective members. It was this religious undertone which, in the last analysis, attracted many young labourers in Manila and appealed to the farmers in the countryside; not its socio-political platforms of which it contained very little. Thus, when open conflict began on 26 August 1896, the Katipuneros fought as segmented units without overall military coordination. Since there was no uniform strategy the Spaniards were at a loss in organizing a coordinated counter-offensive. The Katipunan was initially successful; the different units utilized effectively the guerrilla technique of annihilating the enemy.

The success of the Katipunan at the initial stage of the revolution led to feuds and struggle for power within its ranks. Although the Katipunan was acknowledged as the mother-organization, its influence over the various fighting units was only in the abstract — it did not actually possess organizational power over them. Thus when the rift between the two sub-units of the movement operating in Cavite province — the Magdalo and the Magdiwang — occurred, Bonifacio was requested by the leaders to intervene in his capacity as the *supremo* of the Katipunan. Coming from the northern side of Manila, Bonifacio's presence did not help; instead the southerners thought that he came to Cavite to extend his powers beyond the limit of his regional base. Moreover, since Bonifacio's men suffered several reverses in their area, the southern Tagalogs did not hold them in high esteem. The cleavage between the two groups became marked when it was known that Alvarez, the leader of the Magdiwang faction, was

Bonifacio's uncle-in-law. The Magdalo group suspected that the *supremo* would favour the Magdiwang.

As expected, the Magdalo group did not acknowledge Bonifacio's leadership or that of the Katipunan. They clamoured, instead, for a new organization which would truly represent the revolutionary movement. Putting the interest of the revolution over that of his own, Bonifacio acceded to the suggestion after several meetings with the leaders of the two factions. A revolutionary government, with republican system of political structure, was set up. Bonifacio was defeated in the presidential election and his role in the revolution was relegated to a minor position of the secretary of the interior. Emilio Aguinaldo, then a minor field commander of the Magdalo faction, was elected president. Capitalizing on their initial victory in the election, Daniel Tirona, a Magdalo member, questioned the propriety of Bonifacio's occupying the secretaryship of the interior because he was not a lawyer. This was uncalled for because there was a previous agreement that everyone should abide by the decision of the majority. Angered, Bonifacio nullified the convention and left.

Operating under the concept of centralized government, Aguinaldo attempted to bring Bonifacio back to the fold of the revolution. When the latter refused to acknowledge his authority, Aguinaldo had him arrested, charged with sedition and shot. This changed the posture of the revolution. The northern Tagalogs who were loyal to Bonifacio did not participate in the struggle as enthusiastically as they did before. The burden of the revolution fell on the shoulders of the southerners. This rift enabled the Spaniards to regroup their forces and to concentrate on Aguinaldo's position. The revolution was smashed and Aguinaldo was persuaded to agree to a truce. He was likewise made to agree to go into voluntary exile abroad. With his departure, the revolution collapsed.

In sum, it is sociologically apparent that the revolution failed because a political ideology, in the form of centralized government, has introduced into the movement rather late and at the height of the uprising. As such, it was not able to provide effective leadership that could instill among those involved in the struggle identity and solidarity to the cause. Instead, it created confusion, dissensions, and factional rivalries among the existing combat units of the military force based on regional and personal loyalties of the troops. This was also true among the political leaders who managed the machinery of the revolutionary government. In short, the social structure of mass base of the movement was not prepared to accommodate the doctrinal position of the central government. Many of the revolutionary leaders did not understand the mechanics of government nor the workings of political ideologies; the people were likewise ignorant of the terms in which the leaders couched their appeals.

The aphorism that history often repeats itself applies appropriately to the experience of radical movements in the Philippines. The weakness of the revolutionary government in exacting unity among the members of the movement likewise characterized the Huk organization, not withstanding the long politization among the labourers and farmers prior to the uprising. The Huk movement was anchored on communistic ideology, although many of its top leaders claimed to be socialists, not communists. It would be safe to assume that as an ideology, communism has transcendental features which are incompatible with the social system which is largely particularistic in orientation, such as in the Philippines. For a political system to be functional, David Apter reminds us, the members of the political community should be made to feel that they are products of lives lived before theirs within the context of the nation. This feeling has to be translated into family and kinship commitment as secured with the state. However, loyalty to the state has to take precedence over that of the family (1965:269). This is the problem political ideologies like communism have to contend with in a society like the Philippines where loyalty to the family, as defined by the kinship norm, takes precedence over and above all other types of loyalties. Students of Philippine politics are sometimes appalled by the manner in which politicians shift their party affiliation when the party no longer serves their familial or regional interests. But they have only to inquire deeper into the social system to understand this phenomenon.

Filipino social system is built around a bilaterally structured kinship organization. This means that relationship with kinsmen of the father and the mother is reckoned equally with no marked distinction of either sides, as in unilineal societies. There are no clans, moieties or lineage organizations. The individual may place higher associational preferences or greater affective ties with most kinsmen from either parental side. This is not an organizational principle, however, but a matter of individual or family choice. Ego and his siblings remain to function as the link to two unrelated or distantly related groups in spite of personal preference.

This symmetrical recognition of kinship ideally brings about the equal distribution of rights, obligations, privileges, and statuses to a great number of kinsmen. One of the effects on behaviour of this demand for dual kinship loyalties is the instability of affective ties in the network of group relations. When conflicts occur between these two groups of relatives, an individual finds himself in a difficult situation. Siding with one makes him lose the potential assistance of the other; taking no sides, he loses both. Thus, a compromise is often resorted to, with the individual concerned acting as the arbiter of the case.

This basic orientation of the traditional social system contradicts the cohesive requirements of political ideologies like communism, socialism, or totalitarianism. One of the basic characteristic features of these ideologies, to paraphase Hannah Arendt, is their demand for total, unrestricted, unconditional and unalterable loyalty of the individual member (1968, ed: 21). This is quite difficult to achieve in Philippine social system where individual loyalties are equally divided into two major kinship groups —

that of the father and of the mother. Moreover it is the family which makes this demand for unalterable loyalty of its respective members. Loyalty to the family is upheld as one of the powerful forces of Filipino value system. This led one observer of Philippine society to comment, in fact, that Filipino society is an anarchy of families (Fox, 1954).

Reinforcing this strong demand for unrestricted kinship loyalty is regional affiliation. Regionalism is very strong in the Philippines. The ethno-linguistic boundaries of relationship, along regional lines, are clearly defined as part of the general value-orientation. In fact, the present political parties in the country reflects this character of society. Leadership is likewise defined in terms of its regional base. This encourages factionalism and in turn affects institutional loyalties. Seen in this way, it is understandable why loyalties are primarily attached to individual leaders and not to the principle an individual adheres to or represented by the office a leader occupies, even if ideally it is accepted that this is so.

If communism as an ideology rests on 'total, unrestricted, unconditional and unalterable loyalty of the individual member', then the fragmenting, highly flexible base structure of the kinship system in the Philippines cannot at this moment, provide a favourable structural climate for serious politization. If one reviews the organizational structure of the Huk movement, one finds that leadership revolves around kinship and regional affiliations. The politburo elite centres around the Lava and Taruc brothers. The Lavas were from Bulacan while the Tarucs were from Pampanga. The secretaryship of the Communist Party of the Philippines was assumed, successively, by the Lava brothers while the military command revolved around the Tarucs. Their followers were respectively aligned along a similar base. Thus, when the Lavas and the Tarucs parted ways at the height of the Huk struggle, factional cleavage within the ranks of the movement also developed. This in turn defined the boundaries of loyalties along kinship ties and regional affiliations. The ideological requirements of communism, as the political guidelines of the Huk movement, for unconditional, unrestricted loyalty of the individual members to the party principle did not find support from the peasants. In fact, such requirements were interpreted as impingements on the individual's responsibility and organizational behaviour. It did not allow for flexibility of loyalties and therefore it had nothing to offer; instead, it dispelled its own myths of protecting the peasants when it applied coercion and suppression of those who disagreed with its precepts — the very coercive measures the government 'run by the oligarchs and the bourgeois' used in insuring peasant support.

In short, even if political ideology is necessary in stipulating the moral or social superiority of new ideas or new ways of life in the process of modernization, it does not seem to function as an important precondition for the success of radical movements as the cases from the Philippines described above indicate. One has yet to consider the nature of the social structure and of the value system which constitute the central framework of traditional society.

Bibliography

ABDULLAH BIN ABDUL KADIR, Munshi, *Kesah Pelayaran Abdullah*. (Singapore, Malaya Publishing House, 1961.)
—— *Hikayat Abdullah*. (Singapore, Malaya Publishing House, 1949.)
ADRIANI, N., *The Effect of Western Rule on Animistic Heathenism*, in *Verzamelde Geschriften*, III (Haarlem, De Erven F. Bohn, 1932).
AGONCILLO, TEODORO, *The Revolt of the Masses*. (Quezon City, University of the Philippines Press, 1956.)
—— *Malolos: The Crises of the Republic*. (Quezon City, University of the Philippines, 1960.)
—— AND ALFONSO, OSCAR M., *A Short History of the Filipino People*. (Quezon City, University of the Philippines, 1967.)
AGPALO, REMIGIO E., 'Pandanggo Sa Ilaw: The Politics of Occidental Mindoro', *Philippine Social Sciences and Humanities Review*, XXVII (December 1963), pp. 445–88.
—— Pandanggo-Sa-Ilaw: The Politics of Occidental Mindoro', *Philippine Journal of Public Administration*, 8 (April 1964), pp. 83–111.
—— *The Political Elite and the People: A Study of Politics in Occidental Mindoro*. (Manila, College of Administration, University of the Philippines, 1972.)
AKIN RABIBHADANA, *The Organization of Thai Society in the Early Bangkok Period, 1782–1873*. (Ithaca, N.Y., 1969, Cornell University S.E. Asia Program, Data Paper No. 74.)
ALATAS, SYED HUSAIN, *Sociology of Corruption*. (Singapore, Donald Moore Press, 1968.)
ALMOND, GABRIEL A. and G. BINGHAM POWELL, JR., *Comparative Politics: A Developmental Approach*. (Boston, Little, Brown and Company, 1966.)
AMINUDDIN BIN BAKI,'The Institution of Debt Slavery in Perak', *Peninjau Sejarah*, I, I–II (1966).
ANDERSON, GERALD H., ED., *Christ and the Crisis in Southeast Asia*. (New York, Friendship Press, 1968.)
APTER, DAVID E., *The Politics of Modernization*. (Chicago, University of Chicago Press, 1965.)
ARENDT, HANNAH, *On Revolution*. (New York, The Viking Press, 1965.)
—— *The Origins of Totalitarianism*. (New York, Harcourt, Brace & World, Inc., 1968.)
BAILEY, F. G., *Caste and the Economic Frontier: A Village in Highland Orissa*. (Manchester University Press, 1957.)
BANFIELD, EDWARD C., *The Moral Basis of a Backward Society*. (New York, Free Press, 1958.)

BENDA, HARRY J., 'Political Elites in Colonial Southeast Asia: An Historical Analysis', *Comparative Studies in Society and History* (April 1965). Yale University S.E. Asia Studies, Reprint Series No. 10.

―――― *The Crescent and the Rising Sun: Indonesian Islam under the Japanese Occupation, 1942–45.* (The Hague, W. van Hoeve, 1965.)

BILL, JAMES A., 'Modernization and Reform From Above: The Case of Iran', *Journal of Politics*, 32 (February 1970), pp. 19–40.

BLACK, C. E., *The Dynamics of Modernization: A Study in Comparative History.* (New York, Harper and Row, 1966.)

BLAIR, EMMA and ROBERTSON, JAMES, *The Philippine Islands.* 55 vols. Microprint Copy. (Cleveland, Ohio, A. H. Clark, 1903.)

BREMAN, J. C., 'Meester en Knecht: Een onderzoek naar de veranderingen in de betrekkingen tussen landheren en landarbeiders in Zuid-Gujerat, India.' Amsterdam, *Antropologisch-Sociologisch Centrum, Afdeling Zuid- en Zuidoost-Azië*, Universiteit van Amsterdam, Publikatie No.15, 1970.

BRINTON, CRANE C., *The Anatomy of Revolution.* (New York, Vintage Books, 1965.)

CARR, E. H., *Studies in Revolution.* (New York, Grosset & Dunlap, 1964.)

CARR-SAUNDERS, A. M. and P. A. WILSON, *The Professions.* (Oxford, Clarendon Press, 1933.)

CASTILLO, Federico, 'Report on the Last Election (1953) and the Progress and Problems of the Province of Occidental Mindoro', November 24, 1953. (A Report in Typescript Submitted to President Ramon Magsaysay in 1953.)

CHAN HENG CHEE and EVERS, HANS-DIETER, 'National Identity and Nation Building in Southeast Asia', *Working Paper No. 6*, Dept. of Sociology, University of Singapore, 1972.

CHARLES, J. ERASMUS, 'Community Development and the Encogido Syndrome'. *Human Organization*, 27, 1 (1968), pp. 65–74.

CLEMENTS, R. V., *Managers: A Study of their Careers in Industry.* (London, G. Allen & Unwin, 1958.)

CLIFTON, R. WHARTON JR., 'The Green Revolution: Cornucopia or Pandora's Box?', *Foreign Affairs*, 47 (1969).

COOLEY, FRANK L., *Indonesia: Church and Society.* (New York, Friendship Press, 1968.)

CORPUZ, ONOFRE D., *The Philippines.* (Englewood Cliffs, New Jersey, Prentice-Hall, 1965.)

COUGHLIN, RICHARD, J., 1960 *Double Identity: The Chinese in Modern Thailand.* (Hong Kong, Hong Kong University Press, 1960.)

CROSLAND, A., *A Social Democratic Britain.* (London, Fabian Society, 1971.)

DAHRENDORF, RALPH, *Class and Class Conflict in Industrial Society.* (Stanford, Calif., Standord University Press, 1959.)

DEATS, RICHARD L., *Nationality and Christianity in the Philippines.* (Dallas, Southern Methodist University Press, 1967.)

DOOB, LEONARD W., *Patriotism and Nationalism: their Psychological Foundations.* (New Haven, Yale University Press, 1964.)

DUBE, S. C., *India's Changing Villages: Human Factors in Community Development.* (London, Routledge and K. Paul, 1958.)

EISENSTADT, S. N., *Modernization: Growth and Diversity.* (Bloomington, Department of Government, Indiana University, 1963.)

—— 'Breakdowns of Modernization', *Economic Development and Cultural Change*, 12 (1964), pp. 345-67.

—— *Modernization: Protest and Change.* (Englewood Cliffs, N. J., Prentice-Hall, 1966.)

ELDER, JOSEPH W., 'National Loyalties in a Newly Independent Nation', in DAVID APTER, ed., *Ideology and Discontent.* (New York, Free Press, 1964) pp. 77-92.

ELTON, GODFREY, *The Revolutionary Idea in France, 1789-1871.* (New York, Longmans, Green & Co., Inc., 1923.)

ERIKSON, ERIK H., 'Identity, Psychosocial', in David L. Sills, ed., *International Encyclopedia of the Social Sciences.* (New York, The MacMillan Company and The Free Press, 1968), pp. 61-5.

EVERS, HANS-DIETER, 'Soziale und regionale Differenzierung als Problem der Entwicklungs-politik, dargestellt am Beispiel Malayas', in G. K. Kindermann, ed., *Kulturen im Umbruch.* (Freiburg, Verlag Rombach, 1962), pp. 279-308.

—— *Kulturwandel in Ceylon, eine Untersuchung uber die Enstehung einer Industrie Unternehmerschicht (Social Change in Ceylon: a Study on the Rise of a Class of Industrial Entrepreneurs)* (Baden-Baden, Lutzeyer Verlag, 1964.)

—— 'The Formation of a Social Class Structure: Urbanization, Bureaucratision and Social Mobility in Thailand', *American Sociological Review* 31, 4, (1966), pp. 480-8.

—— ed., *Loosely Structured Social Systems: Thailand in Comparative Perspective.* (New Haven, Yale University Southeast Asia Studies, 1969.)

—— AND SILCOCK, T. H., 'Elites and Selection' in T. H. Silcock, ed., *Thailand, Social and Economic Studies in Development.* (Canberra: Australian National University Press and Durham, N.C.: Duke University Press, 1967), pp. 84-104.

FAIRBANK, J. K., REISCHAUER, E. O., and CRAIG, A. M., *East Asia, the Modern Transformation,* (Boston, Houghton Mifflin 1965.)

FELL, H., *Population Census of the Federation of Malaya* (report no. 14), Department of Statistics, Kuala Lumpur, 1960.

FIRTH, RAYMOND, *Elements of Social Organization.* (Boston, Beacon Press, 1964.)

FORSTER, M. GEORGE, 'Peasant Society and the Image of the Limited Good'. *The American Anthropologist,* 67, Part 1 (April 1965). pp. 293-315.

FRANK, A. G., *Capitalism and Underdevelopment in Latin America; Historical Studies of Chile and Brazil.* (New York, Monthly Review Press, 1967.)

FREY, FEDERICK W., *The Turkish Political Elite.* (Cambridge, Mass., The M.I.T. Press, 1965.)

FURNIVALL, J. S., *Netherlands India, a Study of Plural Economy.* (Cambridge University Press, 1939.)

GAVI, PHILIPPE, *Konter-Revolution in Indonesien.* (Frankfurt, Europaische Verlagsanstalt, 1968.)

GEERTZ, CLIFFORD, 'Ideology as a Cultural System' in DAVID APTER, ed., *Ideology and Discontent.* (New York: The Free Press of Glencoe, 1964), pp. 47-76.

—— *The Social History of an Indonesian Town.* (Cambridge, Mass.: M.I.T. Press, 1965.)

GEERTZ, HILDRED, *Indonesian Cultures and Communities.* (New Haven, HRAF Press, 1963.)

GERSCHENKRON, A., *Economic Backwardness in Historical Perspective: a Book of Essays*. (Cambridge, Belknap Press of Harvard University Press, 1962.)

GERSTL, J.E., and HUTTON, S.P., *Engineers: the Anatomy of a Profession, a Study of Mechanical Engineers in Britain*. (London, Tavistock Publications, 1966.)

GOULD, JULIUS and KOLB, WILLIAM L., 'Assimilation', in *A Dictionary of the Social Sciences*. (London, Tavistock Publications, 1964.)

GOUROU, PIERRE, *Les Pays Tropicaux, Principes d'une G'eographie Humaine et Economique*. (Paris: Presses Universitaires de France. 4th rev. ed., 1966.)

GOWING, PETER G., *Islands Under the Cross: the Story of the Church in the Philippines*. (Manila, National Council of Churches in the Philippines, 1967.)

GULLICK, J. M., *Indigenous Political Systems of Western Malaya*. (London, University of London, Athlone Press, 1958.)

GUNAWAN, BASUKI and VAN DEN MUIJZENBERG, O. D., 'Verzuilingstendenties en sociale stratificatie in Indonesie', *Sociologische Gids*, 14 (1967).

HALL, J. W., *Changing Conceptions of the Modernization of Japan*. (Princeton University Press, 1965.)

HANKS, LUCIEN M., 'Merit and Power in the Thai Social Order', *American Anthropologist* LXIV (1962), pp. 1247–61.

HINDLEY, DONALD, 'Alirans and the Fall of the Old Order', *Indonesia* 9, (1970), pp. 23–66.

HOLMES, R.A., 'Burmese Domestic Policy: The Politics of Burmanization', *Asian Survey* VII, 3 (1967), pp. 188–97.

HOBSBAWM, E.J., *Primitive Rebels: Studies in Archaic Forms of Social Movement in the 19th and 20th Centuries*. (Manchester University Press, 1959.)

HUIZER, GERRIT J., 'Peasant Unrest in Latin America: its Origins, Forms of Expression, and Potential'. (Doct. diss. University of Amsterdam, 1970.)

HUNTINGTON, SAMUEL P., 'Political Development and Political Decay', *World Politics*, 17 (April, 1965), pp. 386–430.

—— *Political Order in Changing Societies*. (New Haven: Yale University Press, 1968.)

HUSIN ALI, S., *Social Stratification in Kampong Bagan*. (Singapore, Monographs of the Malaysian Branch, Royal Asiatic Society, 1964.)

INGLIS, JUDY, 'Cargo-Cults: The Problem of Explanation', *Oceania*, XXVII (1957), 149–263.

JANSEN, M. B., *Changing Attitudes toward Modernization*. (Princeton University Press, 1965).

JOCANO, F. LANDA, *Outline of Philippine Mythology*. (Manila, Centro Escolar University Research and Development Center, 1969.)

JACOBS, NORMAN, *Modernization without Development: Thailand as an Asian Case Study*. (New York, Praeger, 1971.)

JOHNSON, CHALMERS A., *Revolutionary Change*. (Boston, Little Brown & Co., 1966.)

KAHAR BADOR, A., 'Traditional and Modern Leadership in Malay Society'. (Unpublished Ph.D. thesis, London School of Economics and Political Science, University of London, 1967.)

—— *Political Authority and Leadership in Malay Society in Perak, Malaysia*. (Tokyo: Institute of Developing Economics, V.R.F. Series No. 5, 1970.)

KALAW, TEODORO, *The Philippine Revolution*. (Rizal, Jorge Vargas Filipiana Foundation, 1969.)

KERR, C., et al., *Industrialism and Industrial Man; the Problems of Labor and Management in Economic Growth.* (Cambridge, Harvard University Press, 1960.)

KOH, DIANE, 'Prejudice in a Primary 3 Textbook.' *The Singapore Herald* (9 November 1970) p. 2.

KUWAKI, AYAO, 'Development of the Study of Science in Japan', in INAZO NITOBE, *Western Influence in Modern Japan.* (Chicago, University of Chicago Press, 1931.)

KUZNETS, S., *Modern Economic Growth: Rate, Structure and Spread.* (New Haven, Yale University Press, 1966.)

LANDICHO, MACARIO Z., *The Mindoro Yearbook.* (Manila, Yearbook Publishers, 1952.)

LASSWELL, HAROLD D. and KAPLAN, ABRAHAM, *Power and Society.* (New Haven, Yale University Press, 1950.)

LEGGE, J.D., *Indonesia.* (Englewood Cliffs. New Jersey, Prentice-Hall, 1964.)

LEIDEN, CARL and SCHMITT, KARL M., *The Politics of Violence: Revolution in the Modern World.* (Englewood Cliffs, N.J.: Prentice-Hall Inc., 1968.)

LISSAK, MOSHE, 'The Class Structure of Burma: Continuity and Change', *Journal of Southeast Asian Studies I,* 1 (March 1970), pp. 60–73.

LIDDLE, R. WILLIAM, 'Politics in Simalungun: A Study in Political Integration'. (Doctoral Dissertation, Yale University, 1967.)

LINDBECK, GEORGE A., 'The Present Ecumenical and Church Situation in West Malaysia and Singapore'. *The South-East Asia Journal of Theology,* 11 (1969), pp. 72–80.

LINTON, RALPH, '1943 'Nativistic Movements'. *American Anthropologist,* 45 (1943), pp. 230–40.

MAC ALISTER, JOHN T. AND MUS, PAUL, *The Vietnamese and Their Revolution.* (New York, Harper and Row, 1970.)

MACDOUGALL, JOHN, 'The Genuine Singapore Revolution', Part II, *Prospect,* 1, 16 (1970), pp. 2–7.

MAJUL, CESAR ADIB, *The Political and Constitutional Ideas of the Philippine Revolution.* (Quezon City, University of the Philippines Press, 1967.)

MAKOTO, ASŌ, 'Kindai Nihon ni okeru eriito-kosei no hensen', *Kyoiku shakai-gaku Kenkyu,* 1960.

MARETIN, IU V., 'Adat, Islam and the Political Struggle Among the Minangkabau of Western Sumatra in the First Half of the Twentieth Century', *Soviet Anthropology and Archeology,* 4 (n.d.), pp. 29–45.

MATOSSIAN, MARY, 'Ideologies of Delayed Industrialization: Some Tensions and Ambiguities', *Economic Development and Cultural Change,* 6 (April 1958), pp. 217–28.

MIDDLEBROOKE, S. M., 'Yap Ah Loy', *Journal Malayan Branch Royal Asiatic Society,* XXIV, (1951), pp.3–100.

MOKHZANI, B. A. R., 'The Study of Social Stratification and Social Mobility in Malaya', *East Asian Cultural Studies* IV (1965), pp. 138–62.

MOORE, BARRINGTON, *The Social Origins of Dictatorship and Democracy, Lord and Peasant in the Making of the Modern World.* (Boston, Beacon Press, 1966.)

MORTIMER, REX, 'Class, Social Cleavage and Indonesian Communism', *Indonesia* 8: (1969), pp. 1–20.

MULDER, J. A. N., 'Aliran Kebatinan as an Expression of the Javanese World-view', *Journal of Southeast Asian Studies* 1, 2 (1970), pp. 105–14.

MYRDAL, GUNNAR, *The Challenge of World Poverty: A World Anti-Poverty Program in Outline*. (London, Lane, 1970.)

NETTL, J. P. and ROBERTSON, ROLAND, *International Systems and the Modernization of Societies: the Formation of National Goals and Attitudes*. (New York, Basic Books, 1968.)

NICHOLSEN, CLARA KIBBY, 'The Introduction of Islam into Sumatra and Java: A Study in Cultural Change.' Doctoral Dissertation, Syracuse University, 1965.

NIEBURG, H. L., *Political Violence: the Behavioural Process*. (New York, St. Martin's Press, 1969.)

NISBET, R. A., *Social Change and History: Aspects of the Western Theory of Development*. (New York, Oxford University Press, 1969.)

NOLLEDO, JOSE N., *The Constitution of the Philippines Annotated*. (Manila, National Book Store, 1966.)

NYCE, RAY, *The Kingdom and The Country* (mimeo) Singapore, 1970.

OCAMPO, ROMEO B., 'The Formal Structure and Functions of Philippine Local Governments', *Philippine Journal of Public Administration*, X (April-July 1966), pp. 127–35.

ORGANSKI, A. F. K., *The Stages of Political Development*. (New York, Knopf, 1965.)

PAREJA, INOCENCIO B., 'All About the Privileged Speech,' *Philippines Free Press* (16 March 1963a).

—— 'Congressmen and Floor Deliberations', *Philippines Free Press* (10 August 1963b).

PENDERSEN, PAUL, *Batak Blood and Protestant Soul: the Development of National Batak Churches in North Sumatra*. (Grand Rapids, William B. Eerdmans, 1970.)

PHELAN, JOHN L., *The Hispanization of the Philippines*. (Madison, University of Wisconsin Press, 1959).

PHILIPPINES, *Census of the, Islands*, 1903, Vol. II, *Population*. (Washington, United States Bureau of the Census 1905.)

PHILIPPINES, *Census of the, 1960, Agriculture, Occidental Mindoro*. (Manila, Bureau of the Census and Statistics, 1963.)

PHILIPPINES, *Census of the, 1960, Population and Housing, Occidental Mindoro*. (Manila, Bureau of the Census and Statistics 1962.)

PYE, LUCIAN W., *Aspects of Political Development*. (Boston, Little, Brown and Company, 1966.)

QUIGGIN, A. HINGSTON, *A Survey of Primitive Money*. (London, Methuen, 1949.)

RAUF, M. A., *A Brief History of Islam, With Special Reference to Malaya*. (Kuala Lumpur, Oxford University Press, 1964.)

RIZAL, JOSE, *Noli Me Tangere*, translated by Charles Derbyshire as The Social Cancer. (Manila, Philippine Education Company, 1912.)

RUSSETT, BRUCE M., et al., *World Handbook of Political and Social Indicators*. (New Haven, Yale University Press, 1964.)

RUSTOW, DANKWART A., *A World of Nations: Problems of Political Modernization*. (Washington, D.C., The Brookings Institution, 1967.)

RYAN, BRYCE, 'Social Values and Social Change in Ceylon', in W. J. CAHNMAN and ALVIN BOSKOFF, *Sociology and History*. (Glencoe, The Free Press, 1964.)

SANTILLANA, D. DE, 'Law and Society', in T. ARNOLD and A. GUILLAME, *The Legacy of Islam*. (Oxford, Clarendon Press 1931.)

SAULO, ALFREDO B., *Communism in the Philippines, An Introduction*. (Quezon City, Ateneo de Manila University, 1969.)

SCHILLER, JIM, 'Powerlessness: A Dynamic of Personal Development in the Indonesian University', (mimeo), n.d.

SCOTT, JAMES C., *Political Ideology in Malaysia: Reality and the Beliefs of an Elite*. (New Haven, Yale University Press, 1968.)

SHEPPERSON, GEORGE, 'The Comparative Study of Millenarian Movements', in Sylvia L. Thrupp, ed. *Millennial Dreams in Action; Essays in Comparative Studies; Comparative Studies in Society and History Supplement II*. (The Hague: Mouton & Co., (1962), pp. 44–52.

SHILS, EDWARD A., *Political Development in the New States*. (The Hague, Mouton and Company, 1962.)

SHINGA, FUKUSHIMA, 'The Building of a National Army', *The Developing Economies*, III (1965), special issue: *The Modernization of Japan*, 1956, pp. 520–1.

SINGER, MARSHALL R., *The Emerging Elite; A Study of Political Leadership in Ceylon*. (Cambridge, Mass., The M.I.T. Press, 1964.)

SINGH NARENDRA, 'Aid to underdeveloped countries and the scientists', *Wetenschap en Samenleving*, special issue on the green revolution, 23, 8/9, 1969.

SLATER, PHILIP E., 'On Social Regression,' *American Sociological Review*, 28 (June 1963), pp. 339–64.

SOMMER, JOHN, 'Asian Students, National Development, and the Possible Role of Outside Assistance', *Ford Foundation Report* (mimeo), n.d.

STANNER, W. E. H., On the Interpretation of Cargo-Cults, *Oceania*, XXIX (1958), pp. 1–25.

────── The Weber Thesis and Southeast Asia, *Archives de Sociologie des Religions* XV (1963), pp. 21–34.

────── Collective Representations and Economic Development, *Kajian Ekonomi Malaysia*, II (1965), pp. 104–13.

TAJFEL, HENRI, 'Aspects of National and Ethnic Loyalty', *Social Science Information*, 9 (1970), pp. 119–44.

TAMNEY, JOSEPH B., 'A Study of Involvement: Reactions to the Death of President Kennedy', *Sociologus*, 19 (1969), pp. 66–79.

TEN DAM, H., 'Desa Tjibodas', stencilled report, Bogor: 1951, stencilled report (in Indonesian).

TOMINAGA, KEN'ICHI; KOMAI, HIROSHI; OKAMOTO, HIDEO AND ISE, MICHIKO, 'The Modernization and Industrialization of the Thai Society', a Sociological Analysis, *East Asian Cultural Studies*, VIII, 1969–70, pp. 1–39 & IX pp. 1–56.

TOYNBEE, A. J., *The Present Day Experiment in Western Civilization*. (London Oxford University Press, 1962).

TROTSKY, L., *The History of the Russian Revolution*. (London, V. Gollancz, 1932.)

TURK, HERMAN, 'Interorganizational Networks in Urban Society: Initial Perspectives and Comparative Research', *American Sociological Review*, 35 (February 1970), pp. 1–19.

UNESCO, Japanese National Commission for, *The Role of Education in the Social and Economic Development of Japan*, 1966.

UTRECHT, E., 'De groene revolutie is in Indonesie nog geen succes', *Intermediair*, 6 (1970), pp.21.

VAN DER KROEF, J. M., 'Entrepreneur and Middle Class', in *Indonesia in the Modern World*. (Bandung, Masa Baru, 1956, pp. 1–62.)

VON DER MEHDEN, FRED R., *Religion and Nationalism in Southeast Asia: Burma, Indonesia, the Philippines*. (Madison, University of Wisconsin Press, 1963.)

WALLACE, ANTONY, 'Revitalization Movements', *American Anthropologist*, 58 (1956), pp. 264–81.

WAN, MIN SHUING, 'Yap Ah Loy and Hsien Szu Shih Yeh Miao', *Journal of the Malayan Historical Society*, IX, 1–2 (1965).

WANG, GANGWU, 'The Opening of Relations between China and Malacca, 1403–1405', in J. BASTIN and R. ROOLVINK, *Malayan and Indonesian Studies*. (London, Oxford University Press, 1964.)

WEBER, MAX, *The Sociology of Religion*, tr. R. Fischoff. (Boston, Beacon Press 1964.)

——— *The Religion of China*, translated and edited by H. GERTH. (Glencoe, The Free Press 1951.)

WERTHEIM, W. F., *Indonesian Society in Transition: a Study of Social Change*. (The Hague: W. van Hoeve, 1969.)

——— *East-West Parallels: Sociological Approaches to Modern Asia*. (Chicago, Quadrangle, 1965.)

——— 'From Aliran Towards Class Struggle in the Countryside of Java'. *Pacific Viewpoint* 10, 2 (1969), pp. 1–17.

WHITE, L., *Technology and Social Change*. (London, Oxford University Press 1962.)

WORSLEY, PETER, *The Third World*. (Chicago, University of Chicago Press, 1964.)

YANAGA, CHOTOSHI, *Japan since Perry*. (New York, McGraw Hill, 1949.)

——— AND WARD, R. E., eds., *Political Modernization in Japan and Turkey*. (New Jersey, Princeton University Press, 1964.)

——— *The Origin of Modern Capitalism and Eastern Asia*, 1958.

YASUNAKA, AKIO, 'Basic Data on Indonesian Political Leaders', *Indonesia*, 10 (1970), pp. 107–42.

YOUNG, FRANK W., 'Reactive Subsystems', *American Sociological Review*, 35 (April 1970), pp. 297–307.

Notes on Contributors

Hans-Dieter Evers, Dr. phil. (Freiburg), is Professor of Sociology and Head of the Sociology Department at the University of Singapore. He was previously Associate Professor of Sociology and Director of Graduate Southeast Asia Studies at Yale University. During 1970 he was a Visiting Research Fellow of the Institute of Southeast Asian Studies, Singapore. He also taught at Monash University, Melbourne and at the University of Mannheim, Germany. Among his publications are *Kulturwandel in Ceylon* (Lutzeyer 1964), *Monks, Priests and Peasants; A Study of Buddhism and Social Structure in Central Ceylon* (Brill 1972), *Loosely Structured Social Systems: Thailand in Comparative Perspective* (Yale 1969) and *Case Studies in Social Power* (Brill 1969).

S.N. Eisenstadt, Ph.D. (Hebrew U.) is Professor of Sociology at the Hebrew University in Jerusalem. He was a visiting Professor at the University of Oslo, University of Chicago, Harvard University, M.I.T., and the University of Michigan. In 1964 he received the McIver Award of the American Sociological Association. Among his publications are *From Generation to Generation* (Free Press 1956), *The Political Systems of Empires* (Free Press 1963), *Modernization, Protest and Change* (Prentice-Hall 1966). *Political Sociology of Modernization* (Misuzu Shobo Publishing Co. 1968), *Israeli Society* (Weidenfeld & Nicholson, London, 1968), *Political Sociology* (Basic Books, 1971) (editor) and *Social Differentiation and Stratification* (Scott, Foresman, 1972).

Mohd. A. Nawawi, Ph.D. (Princeton) is a visiting professor in Political Science at Silliman University, Philippines. He has formerly taught at the University of Singapore, Wellesley College and Princeton University. His present research is focused on problems of political modernization and political development in Indonesia, the Philippines and Malaysia.

Remigio E. Agpalo, Ph.D. (Indiana) is Manuel Roxas Professor of Political Science in the University of the Philippines. He also served as Chairman of the Department of Political Science in 1963–1966. In 1966-7 he was a Senior Specialist at the East-West Center, and Visiting Associate Professor of Political Science at the University of Hawaii. He also taught at the University of South Florida. Among his publications are *The Political*

Process and the Nationalization of the Retail Trade in the Philippines (Quezon City 1962) and *The Political Elite and the People* (U.P. College of Public Administration 1972).

R.P. Dore, B.A. (London) is a Fellow of the Institute of Development Studies, University of Sussex. He was previously Professor of Sociology at the London School of Economics and Professor of Asian Studies at the University of British Columbia. He is the author of *City Life in Japan* (University of California Press 1958), *Land Reform in Japan* (1958), *Education in Tokugawa Japan* (1963) and editor of *Aspects of Social Change in Modern Japan* (Princeton University Press, 1967).

Goh Keng Swee, Ph.D. (London) is Minister of Defence of the Republic of Singapore. He formerly served as Minister of Finance and as a civil servant. Economist by training, he has published *Urban Income and Housing* (Singapore Government Printing Office, 1956) and *Economics of Modernization* (Donald Moore, 1972).

W.F. Wertheim, Dr. jur. (Leiden) was until 1972 Professor of Asian Sociology in the University of Amsterdam. He was formerly a Professor at the Law School in Batavia (Djakarta). Among his publications are *Indonesian Society in Transition* (Van Hoeve, 2nd ed. 1959), *East West Parallels: Sociological Approaches to Modern Asia* (Van Hoeve 1964), and *Evolution and Revolution* (Penguin, 1973).

A. Kahar Bador, Ph.D. (London) is Lecturer in Social Anthropology and Dean of the Faculty of Arts, University of Malaya, Kuala Lumpur. He served also as a research fellow of the London-Cornell Research Project in Chinese and Southeast Asian Societies and the Institute of Developing Economics in Tokyo.

Syed Hussein Alatas, Dr. (Amsterdam) is Professor of Malay Studies in the University of Singapore. He was formerly a Senior Research Officer and Head of the Research Section, Dewan Bahasa, Kuala Lumpur and a Lecturer in Malay Studies at the University of Malaya, Kuala Lumpur. Among his publications are *The Sociology of Corruption* (Donald Moore 1968) and *Of Thomas Stamford Raffles: Reformer or Intriguer* (Angus and Robertson 1971).

William R. Roff, Ph.D. (ANU) is Associate Professor of History, Columbia University and a member of the Southern Asian Institute there. He formerly taught at Monash University, Melbourne, and at the University of Malaya in Kuala Lumpur. Among his publications are *The Origins of Malay Nationalism* (Yale 1967), *Sejarah Surat Surat Khabar Melayu* (Penang 1967) and a forthcoming edited volume *Kelantan: Religion, Society and Politics in a Malay State*.

Joseph B. Tamney, Ph.D. (Cornell) is Associate Professor of Sociology at Ball State University, Muncie, Indiana. He was previously Chairman of the Department of Sociology at Marquette University and from 1968 to 1971, a lecturer in Sociology at the University of Singapore.

F. Landa Jocano, Ph.D. (Chicago) is Professor of Anthropology and Chairman, Dept. of Anthropology, University of the Philippines. He is author of *Growing Up in a Philippine Barrio* (Holt, Rinehadt and Winston, 1969), *The Sulod Society* (U. of the Philippines Press, 1968) and *Filipino Cultural Heritage* (Philippine Women's University, 1965).

Index

ABDULLAH BIN ABDUL KADIR, MUNSHI, 166–7, 168.
Abeleda, Felipe, 44–5, 49, 52, 58: Abeleda family, 41, 49–52.
Abra de Ilog, Philippines, 40, 42, 49, 54.
Adat (customary law), 30, 31, 32, 189.
Administrative systems: traditional, 29, 31; Dutch colonial, 31–4; modernized, 39, 153; separated from politics, 39; colonial governments' recruitment to, 76, 83–4.
Afghanistan, 54.
Africa, xiv, 12; 15, 71, 97, 199.
Agpalo, Remigio E., 40, 46, 59.
Agrarian reforms, xiv, 100.
Agriculture: agricultural services, 34, 84; in Philippines, 36; subsistence type of, 39, 84, 85; loses importance, 39; equipment for, 44; population engaged in, 55, 119, 120, 156; traditional importance of, 57; new businessmen and, 58; modernized, 68; industry recruits from, 79; Europe's demand for colonies' products of, 83–4; improved methods of, 101–2, 105–6; in Malay traditional society, 139; as occupation for Malays, 158–9, 161.
Aguinaldo, Emilio, 205, 208, 209–210, 219.
Airports, 48, 69.
Alejandrino, Casto, 211, 214, 215–16.
Algeria, 69.
Aliran (vertical social structures in Indonesia), 110, 111, 116, 129.
Allowances: Philippines' use of public funds for, 52; in Perak, 140.
Almond, G. A. and Powell, G. B., 39.
Alvarez, Mariano, 208, 218–19.
Ancestor-worship, 163, 165, 204–5.
Anthropology, xii, 92, 132–3, 134.
Apathy towards progress, xvi, 53, 97–8, 100.
Apprenticeship in industry, 72, 73, 74–5, 76, 77.
Apter, David, 38, 109, 201, 220.

Architects, 73, 124, 125.
Argentina, 6, 19, 69.
Aristocrats: and social status in Perak, xvii, 134, 138–9, 144, 146–9, their importance reduced, 68; in 'strategic groups', 113, 120, 127, 128; in Thai civil service, 124–5.
Army: militarism in Japan, xiii, 154; and political decay, 19; in precolonial Indonesia, 31; separated from politics, 39; in military regimes, 89; and struggle for political power, 113, 130; in Thailand, 124; modernization of, 153, 155; Malays in, 158 (*see also* Military officers).
Asia: pattern of modernization in, xiv, 12, 15, 119; political patronage in, 36; economic development in, 81–93; origin of modernization in, 82, 90; produces raw materials, 83, 84–5, 86–7, 106; partial failure of industrialization in, 87–90, 91; peasants and change in, 97.
Asnawi, Governor, 34.
Australia, 11, 34.
Autonomy: of groups in nation-states, 12, 15; in patrimonial systems, 15; departmental, 39; local, 53, 59; national, 68.

BALANCE OF PAYMENTS, 87, 88–9.
Bancao, Chief, 203.
Banks: rural, 55, 58, 97–8; investment banks, 69; and industrialization of Japan, 78; invention of banking system, 156.
Barahan, Philippines, 43, 54.
Barrios, in Philippines, 43, 44, 55, 56, 57–8, 59, 61, 212–13.
Batak people, Sumatra, 179, 188, 193–5; Batak Protestant Christian Church, 179, 188, 189, 190, 191, 194–5.
Batangas Province, Philippines, 36, 49, 208, 209, 215.
Benda, Harry J., 109, 190.
Bengal, Permanent Land Settlement

cities, 84; renaissance of, 123; Malay traditional, 137; Western, 156; and economics, 161; Chinese, 163; bi-cultural people, 178; assimilation brought about by sharing of, 185; ideology and, 201.
'Culture System' in Netherlands Indies, 84.

DA GAMA VASCO, 82.
Dagohoy, Francisco, 203–4.
Dahrendorf, Ralf, 114, 117.
Damrong, Prince, 119.
Dato, title, 138, 149.
Daud, ex-Pasirah of Sekaju, 30, 32.
Debt servicing, 87.
de la Cruz, Apolonario, 203.
de la Cruz Palaris, Juan, 203–4.
del Castillo, Amando, 215.
del Castillo, Mateo, 212.
del Pilar, Marcelo H., 59.
Demang (Indonesian official), 32.
Democracy: in Philippines, 58, 59–60, 61–2; government finances in, 89; parliamentary, 93, 115, 120, 122, 124, 142–3, 145–6, 147, 154, 155; modernization confused with Western, 154; in Indonesia, 198.
Democratic Alliance, Philippines, 211–12.
Depati (Indonesian chief), 32–3.
de Schweinitz, Karl, 20.
Development: contrasted with modernization, xii, 39; 'convergence' theory of, xii–xiii, xv, 66–7; how measured, xv; 'late', xv, 67–82; criticism of theories of, xvi, 3; different aspects of, 10, 152; unilineal theory of, 65–6; law of combined, 66; its leading section in Asia, 86, 90; stability needed for, 90; difference between political and economic development, 91.
Dictatorship, xiii, 71, 105 (*see also* Totalitarianism).
Differentiation: of political structure, xiv, 15, 17, 39, 67; of specialization 4; social, 112–13, 115.
District Officers, Perak, 143.
Djakarta, Java, 26.
Doctors: in Indonesian rural areas, 22, 23; in Occidental Mindoro, 54; patient/doctor ratio, 65; adopt Western standards, 113; traditional, 120; Ayurvedic, 120, 127; number of, 122–3, 126; in Thailand 124; in Perak, 139, 142.
Domocmat, Salvador, 43–4.
Durkheim, Emile, 4, 109.
Dutch in Indonesia, 29, 31–4, 35, 84, 97–8, 111, 126.
Dynamism in modernization, 4, 38, 97–8.

ECONOMIC DEVELOPMENT: and political, oppression xiii–xiv; for New Nations in Asia, xvi, 86–7, 91–3; failure of, 6; modernization and, 15, 81–2, 153; in Occidental Mindoro, 38–9, 55–6; unilineal theory of, 65–6; how effected, 90; in cities, 130; religion and, 157; in China, 166; in Kelantan, 174.
Economics: development seen from point of view of, xii, xiii–xiv, xv–xvi, 81–2, 153, 200, economic variables, 81–2, 90.
Education: and development, xii, 80, 92–3; government efficiency measured by provision of, 21, 22–3 in pre-colonial Indonesia, 31; Dutch and, 34; in Occidental Mindoro, 47–8, 56, 60; and industrial jobs, 71–6; examinations and, 73, 76; purpose of, 75–6; needed for entry into government service, 84, 139, 144; in Thailand, 124; struggle for higher, 127; of People's Representatives, 147; modernization and, 153; in Kelantan, 174.
Efficiency: of government, 4, 19, 20–8; of investment, 69; in industry, 88, 92; of peasants, 91.
Egypt, 54, 103.
Eisenstadt, S. N., xii–xiv, xvi, xvii, xviii, 38, 154, 217.
Elections: a part of modernization, 17; of chiefs, 32; of officials, 37, 59; are Filipino masses' main part in politics, 48, 56–7, 60; of Governors in Philippines, 53; in Philippines, 53, 55; to barrio councils, 59; their influence on government policy, 89; in New Nations, 93; in Perak, 138, 147.
Elites: and progress, xii, xiv, xvi, 97, 104, 105; counter-elites, xiv, 37, 40–1, 46; traditional, xiv, 4, 113; international, xvii; businessmen in, xvii; in England, 6; conflict between, 12, 13–14; structural differentiation of, 15–16, 17; political, in Occidental Mindoro, 36, 37, 40–1, 44, 46–53, 56, 58, 60–1; ruling power elite, 37, 48, 52, 93; cultural, 59; dynastic, 66; local, 85; in Burma, 110; and Katipunan Movement, 207, 218.
Employment, 68, 71, 80; unemploy-

sponsored, 186.

Science: and modernization, xvi, xvii, 38, 39, 90, 154–5, 157, 164, 167, 118; in Tokugawa Shogunate, 156; religion and, 161.

Secularization, an agent in modernization, 4, 9, 37, 39, 155, 218.

Self-respect in New Nations, 68–9, 86–7.

Shils, E.A., 38.

Siam, 172 (see also Thailand).

Sicily, 100, 156.

Sihanouk, Prince Norodom, 105, 120, 125–6.

Silang, Diego, 203–4.

Singapore, 81; religion and national 'identity' in, xviii, 185–7, 189–92, 194–6; rural and urban population of, 112, 118, 119; spirit-medium centres in, 113; professional men in, 122, 124; doctors in, 123; Chinese in, 162, 186–7, 194–5, 200, colonial regime in, 164, 166; Islam in, 185, 190, 194; Malays in, 186, 194; Christianity in, 186–7, 189–90, 191; Roman Catholics in, 190–1, 194, 196; students in, 191–2, 198; Protestants in, 195–6.

Slaves and slavery, 30, 31, 83, 167–8.

Social development, xi, xii, xiii, xiv, xvi, xvii, 38, 55, 131, 153; unilineal theory of, 65–6.

Socialism, 61, 109, 204; used as a synonym for communism, 66; allied with communism, 211, 216.

Social mobilization, 5, 38, 48.

Social security, 77.

Social structure, 12, 110, 112, 116–17, 220–21, 222; stratification, xvi, xvii, 14, 125, 133–8, 140–6, 150. (see also Class).

Socio-demography, 5, 6, 38, 54, 56.

Socio-economic strata, 52, 59, 110.

Sociology (social science): and study of modernization, xii, 4, 81–2, 91–2, 102, 109, 110; and economic development, xvi; and resistance to change, 98; and revolution, 204.

Socio-political institutions: traditional, xiii, xiv, 3; modernization and, 9, 16, 17; Western nation-states, 11–12; infrastructures of, 47; and officials' affiliations, 49–51; strain of economic development on new, 91; Malayan Sultanates, 142.

Socio-political movements in Philippines, xviii, 51, 59, 200, 203–4, 206–16, 217, 218–19.

Spain: rural population of, 119; Arabic influence in, 156; and Philippines, 187, 200, 202–10, 216–18, 219.

Specialization in political system, 4, 5, 39.

Spirit-worship, 113, 162, 203, 204, 216.

Sriwidjaja Kingdom, Sumatra, 28, 186.

Sriwidjaja University, Sumatra, 180, 182–3, 189.

Stability, 14, 19, 91.

Standard of living, 73, 98, 130, 148, 155.

State: and Society, 11, 12, 14–15, 46; and Church, 60, 182, 185, 190, 217, 218; loyalty to, 220 (see also National 'identity').

State Executive Council, Perak, 147, 148.

State Legislative Assembly, Perak, 138, 140, 142, 145–7.

Status: status-honour in Perak, xvii, 134–5, 136–7, 139, 141, 145, 148–9; in Occidental Mindoro, 41, 47; education and, 75, 76; earned, 155; among Chinese, 163, 164–5.

'Strategic groups' in society, xvii, 114–17, 119, 122, 124, 125, 126, 127, 128–9; traditional, 120; in Thailand, 121.

Stratification system in society, xvi, xvii, 14, 124, 132–7, 139–45, 149.

Structural approach to study of modernization, 5, 6; structural differentiation, 15–16, 39, 67.

Structural functionalism, xi; structural specialization, 5.

Students: and education, 76; excluded from patronage systems, 117; and cultural revolution, 127; in 'strategic groups', 129; and politics, 191–2, 198; and national 'identity', 195, 197–8.

Subsidies: for governments, 24–6, 48; for students, 73.

Subsistence crops, 39, 84, 139, 165.

Subsistence economy, 84–5, 89, 104, 139.

Sudan, xiii, 154.

Suffrage, 9, 13, 59, 68; universal, 8.

Sugar and sugar-cane, 83, 84.

Soekarno, President Achmed, 29, 105, 122.

Sulawesi, South: development in, xiv; traditional government and political units in, 21–31, 34–5; Dutch administration in, 32–4; political development in, 35.